A CULTURAL HISTORY OF PEACE

VOLUME 5

A Cultural History of Peace
General Editor: Ronald Edsforth

Volume 1
A Cultural History of Peace in Antiquity
Edited by Sheila L. Ager

Volume 2
A Cultural History of Peace in the Medieval Age
Edited by Walter Simons

Volume 3
A Cultural History of Peace in the Renaissance
Edited by Isabella Lazzarini

Volume 4
A Cultural History of Peace in the Age of Enlightenment
Edited by Stella Ghervas and David Armitage

Volume 5
A Cultural History of Peace in the Age of Empire
Edited by Ingrid Sharp

Volume 6
A Cultural History of Peace in the Modern Age
Edited by Ronald Edsforth

A CULTURAL HISTORY OF PEACE

IN THE AGE OF EMPIRE

Edited by Ingrid Sharp

BLOOMSBURY ACADEMIC
LONDON • NEW YORK • OXFORD • NEW DELHI • SYDNEY

BLOOMSBURY ACADEMIC
Bloomsbury Publishing Plc
50 Bedford Square, London, WC1B 3DP, UK
1385 Broadway, New York, NY 10018, USA
29 Earlsfort Terrace, Dublin 2, Ireland

BLOOMSBURY, BLOOMSBURY ACADEMIC and the Diana logo are trademarks of
Bloomsbury Publishing Plc

First published in Great Britain 2020
This edition published in Great Britain, 2024

Copyright © Bloomsbury Publishing, 2020

Ingrid Sharp has asserted her right under the Copyright, Designs and Patents Act, 1988,
to be identified as Editor of this work.

Cover image © World History Archive / Alamy Stock Photo

All rights reserved. No part of this publication may be reproduced or transmitted
in any form or by any means, electronic or mechanical, including photocopying,
recording, or any information storage or retrieval system, without prior permission
in writing from the publishers.

Bloomsbury Publishing Plc does not have any control over, or responsibility for, any
third-party websites referred to or in this book. All internet addresses given in this
book were correct at the time of going to press. The author and publisher regret
any inconvenience caused if addresses have changed or sites have ceased to
exist, but can accept no responsibility for any such changes.

A catalogue record for this book is available from the British Library.

A catalog record for this book is available from the Library of Congress.

ISBN: HB: 978-1-4742-3827-4
       PB: 978-1-3503-8591-7
       Set: 978-1-3503-8603-7

Series: The Cultural Histories Series

Typeset by RefineCatch Limited, Bungay, Suffolk
Printed and bound in Great Britain

To find out more about our authors and books visit www.bloomsbury.com
and sign up for our newsletters.

CONTENTS

List of Illustrations		vi
General Editor's Preface		ix
	Introduction: Toward a Culture of Peace *Ingrid Sharp*	1
1	Definitions of Peace *Stella Ghervas*	23
2	Human Nature, Peace, and War: Jane Addams and Evolutionary Psychology *Ingrid Sharp*	43
3	Peace, War, and Gender: The Evolution of Women's Voices *Sandi E. Cooper*	57
4	Peace, Pacifism, and Religion *Clive Barrett*	73
5	Representations of Peace: Bertha von Suttner, Activist and Visionary on Dreams, Peace, and Justice *Laurie R. Cohen*	93
6	Peace Movements *Martin Ceadel*	111
7	Peace, Security, and Deterrence: "The greatest work of civilization": The Hague Conferences of 1899, 1907, and 1915 *Maartje Abbenhuis*	129
8	Peace as Integration: Tolstoy on Peace and the End of History *Jeff Love*	143
Notes		161
Bibliography		169
Contributors		191
Index		193

ILLUSTRATIONS

INTRODUCTION

0.1	Queen Victoria and Prince Albert inaugurating the 1851 Exhibition, Crystal Palace, 1851.	2
0.2	The Vienna Congress, 1815.	5
0.3	"Convention for the Amelioration of the Conditions of the Wounded in Armies in the Field," Geneva, 1864.	6
0.4	Florence Nightingale (1820–1910), "The Lady with the Lamp."	7
0.5	French writer Victor Hugo (1802–85), addressing the Paris Peace Congress in 1849.	9
0.6	The delivery of the Great Chartists' Petition to Parliament in 1842.	11
0.7	American peace delegates heading for the Women's International Congress at The Hague in 1915.	16
0.8	Women's International Congress, Zurich, 1919.	17
0.9	Keir Hardie speaking at a peace rally in August 1914.	18
0.10	US President Woodrow Wilson presenting the dove of peace with an olive branch.	21

CHAPTER 1

1.1	Participants at the Congress of Vienna in 1814–15, Vienna, by Jean-Baptiste Isabey.	26
1.2	The Triumph of the Tsar or Peace, by Louis Léopold Boilly, 1814.	27
1.3	France bringing peace and prosperity, November 1911.	31
1.4	Assembly of Congres de la Paix with Victor Hugo (1802–85) presiding over it, Saint-Cecile Hall, August 21, 1849, Paris. Illustration from the magazine *L'Illustration, Journal Universel*, vol. 14, no. 340, September 1, 1849.	35
1.5	The Peace Palace (The Hague, 1913): Vredespaleis, 1913, Peace Palace, seat of International Court of Justice (ICJ), Hague, South Holland, Netherlands.	38

CHAPTER 2

2.1	Jane Addams (1860–1935) in 1910.	45
2.2	Sigmund Freud (1856–1939) with his sons Ernst and Martin in 1916.	51
2.3	US psychologist William James (1842–1910).	53
2.4	Jane Addams at a press conference in 1935.	55

ILLUSTRATIONS vii

CHAPTER 3

3.1	Fredrika Bremer (1801–65).	58
3.2	Anita Augspurg (1857–1943).	63
3.3	International Women's Suffrage Alliance including Millicent Garrett Fawcett.	66
3.4	Dr. Aletta Jacobs, Dutch suffrage leader and coordinator of the Women's International Congress at The Hague, April 28–May 1, 1915.	70
3.5	Jeanette Rankin (1880–1973) in 1918.	72

CHAPTER 4

4.1	James Russell Lowell (1819–91). Engraving with handwritten poem, 1860.	75
4.2	Elihu Burritt (1810–79).	78
4.3	"Two Persuasions," *Punch*, 1878. Artist: Joseph Swain. This cartoon shows John Bright (1811–89) offering a genuine olive branch of peace, while the proffered olive branch of his opponent, Lord Beaconsfield, contains a sword.	81
4.4	Richmond Castle.	89
4.5	Conscientious objectors at Dyce Work Camp, 1916.	91

CHAPTER 5

5.1	Bertha von Suttner (1843–1914).	94
5.2	Bertha von Suttner.	96
5.3	Bertha von Suttner quoted on a protest banner in 2012.	106
5.4	Bertha von Suttner at her writing desk.	109

CHAPTER 6

6.1	Crowds outside the Great Exhibition, 1851.	117
6.2	Alfred Hermann Fried (1864–1921), co-founder of the German Peace Movement and winner of the Nobel Peace Prize in 1911.	119
6.3	Andrew Carnegie (1835–1919) at Carnegie Hall in 1907.	121
6.4	Karl Liebknecht (1871–1919) addresses a crowd on November 9, 1918.	127

CHAPTER 7

7.1	Peace Conference at The Hague, 1899.	131
7.2	This contemporary cartoon entitled "The peace oracle" presented the first Hague peace conference of 1899 as a ruse: more a conference of war and militarists than an event aimed at promoting global peace.	133
7.3	Peace envoys at The Hague, 1899.	135
7.4	This cartoon, originally printed in the German magazine *Ulk* in 1899, with the title "A new tenor in the European concert", depicted Tsar Nicholas II singing from a new song sheet.	136

7.5 This cartoon from the Dutch newspaper *De Amsterdammer* comments on the first Hague peace conference by suggesting that it would leave Death with nothing to do. 139

CHAPTER 8

8.1 Leo Tolstoy (1828–1910). 144
8.2 Tolstoy as an officer of the Imperial Russian Army in Crimea. 145
8.3 French Emperor Napoleon (1769–1821) in defeat, March 31, 1814. 149
8.4 *War and Peace* illustration, 1912 edition. 151
8.5 Field Marshal Kutuzov (1745–1813). 153
8.6 Leo Tolstoy. 160

GENERAL EDITOR'S PREFACE

RONALD EDSFORTH

When people learn that I study and teach peace history, they often look puzzled and ask me, "Does peace have a history?" *A Cultural History of Peace* is an emphatically positive response to that question. Yes, peace has a history. The original scholarly essays collected in these six volumes clearly show that peace always has been an important human concern. More precisely, these essays demonstrate that what we recognize today as peace thinking and peace imagining, peace seeking and peace making, peace keeping and peace building have long recorded histories that stretch from antiquity to the twenty-first century. All of us who have contributed to *A Cultural History of Peace* believe that present and future generations should have the opportunity to recognize and understand the importance of this peace history.

Very few universities and colleges had faculty who taught and researched peace history before the end of the Cold War. Even today, most professors who do peace history moved into it from other specializations in History or other academic disciplines. Most contributors to *A Cultural History of Peace* are professional historians, but Anthropology, Sociology, Political Science, Journalism, Art History, Religion, and Classical Studies are also represented. These fifty-six contributors work on four continents in thirteen different countries. Their participation in this project tells us that peace history has earned a global recognition in academia that not so long ago was unimaginable. Their essays build upon prior scholarship, but they also introduce new research and new interpretations. As a whole *A Cultural History of Peace* highlights our humanity, something that has been for too long overshadowed in history by the inhumanity of war and other forms of violent conflict. Pursuing answers to new and seldom asked questions, these collected essays expand our knowledge of when, how, and why people in the past pursued peace within their own societies and peaceable relations with people from other societies.

The South African novelist Nadine Gordimer wisely observes, "The past is valid only in relation to whether the present recognises it" (2007: 7). In other words, what happened in the past is not necessarily history. History is made when scholars produce meaningful answers to the questions they ask about the past. The past cannot change, but history can and does change when scholars ask new questions, and when they use previously undiscovered or ignored evidence to develop new interpretations of the past. Evidence of what people said or did, or said they did, are basic materials out of which scholars shape answers to questions like "Does peace have a history?" Of course, to answer this particular question about the past, we must have in mind some definition of peace. Like most people we probably immediately think of peace as *not war*, a classic definition that describes peace in negative terms, as an absence of the type of violent conflicts that still loom so large in popular histories and stories about the past. The American psychologist and peace activist William James succinctly summed up this common way of framing the past, simply stating, "History is a bath of blood" (1910: 1).

James's description of history still plays well in a world that during the last century experienced the massive casualties and devastation of two world wars, genocides, and numerous civil wars, as well the fears created by transnational terrorism and still-threatening nuclear arsenals. And significantly, a bath of blood framing continues to shape the priorities of most mainstream reporting of the news from around the world—"if it bleeds it leads"—when, in fact, most people today live in zones of peace where their lives are not threatened by violent political conflict. A human being's chances of dying in war have been historically low in this century, and in striking contrast to the peaks of worldwide violence reached during the global conflicts of the twentieth century (https://ourworldindata.org/war-and-peace; accessed December 5, 2018). Yet so accustomed are we with framing history *and* the present as a bath of blood, most of us have difficulty comprehending these facts. Steven Pinker recently noted this problem in the preface to *The Better Angels of Our Nature: Why Violence Has Declined*, saying "Believe it or not—and I know that most people do not—violence has declined over long stretches of time, and today we might be living in the most peaceable era in our species' existence" (2011: xvi). It is not just a coincidence that the rapid growth and globalization of peace studies has happened since the end of the Cold War. Undoubtedly, some of the questions raised in *A Cultural History of Peace* have been influenced by the extraordinary recent decline of interstate warfare and resolution of many longstanding civil wars.

A Cultural History of Peace demonstrates that for several thousand years peace has been regarded as a highly desirable social condition, perhaps most especially when the violence and cruelty of war have been in the ascendency. Describing this collection of peace history essays as a cultural history—rather than social, political, diplomatic, or international history—is appropriate because throughout history peace has emerged from the cultures of groups, societies, and nations that developed practical ways to peaceably settle serious conflicts. Here I employ the broad environmental definition of culture that psychiatrist and classics scholar Jonathan Shay uses in his brilliant book *Achilles in Vietnam*: "Our animal nature, our biological nature, is to live in relation to other people. The natural environment of humans is primarily culture, not the 'natural world' narrowly defined as other species, climate, etc." (1995: 207). Surely no human culture is ever truly homogeneous or free from conflicts that arise from serious differences between individuals and groups. Murder and warfare are the bloodiest ways that humans have dealt with those with whom they have serious differences. Bath of blood history foregrounds these activities when we peer into the past. Peace history does something very different. It reveals the long, unfinished task of making human cultures peaceable environments that encourage the expression of our most humane instincts: respect for all others who are human like us, and sympathy for those humans who are fearful and/or suffering.

In a remarkable book, *Humanity: A Moral History of the Twentieth Century*, philosopher Jonathan Glover describes respect and sympathy as "human responses" that although they are "widespread and deep-rooted" are often blocked. Frequently aggressive and cruel instincts find expression in warfare and encouragement in cultures that reserve the highest honors for warriors and their blood sacrifices. Yet clearly respect and sympathy have been absolutely necessary for the survival of our social species. Respect and sympathy are, in Glover's words, "the core of our humanity which contrasts with inhumanity." However, as Glover recognizes, "humanity is only partly an empirical claim. It remains also partly an aspiration" (1999: 24–5). *A Cultural History of Peace* presents strong evidence for the empirical claim, as well as for the aspiration. It focuses on the many people in the past who worked to establish peace within their own societies and peace with other societies by institutionalizing respect and sympathy; people who are unlikely to be highlighted as heroes in bath of blood histories.

GENERAL EDITOR'S PREFACE

As General Editor of this title in the Bloomsbury Publishers' cultural history series, I have had to follow two major guidelines. The first one required six volumes of essays that follow the same chronological order as other titles in the series. Accordingly, *A Cultural History of Peace* is presented in volumes focused on Antiquity, the Medieval Age, the Renaissance, the Enlightenment, the Age of Empire, and the Modern Era since 1920. This chronology order is Western-oriented and something of a barrier to producing a truly global history of peace. None the less, some of the essays in the first five volumes of *A Cultural History of Peace*, and all the essays in Volume 6, present peace history in a global perspective. Indeed those essays show that envisioning a more peaceful interconnected world and finding ways of realizing that vision are crucial components of the complex of historical processes we call today "globalization."

Bloomsbury's other major guideline required the eight topical essays in each volume of *A Cultural History of Peace* to concentrate on identical themes in peace history. My first task as General Editor was developing the eight major themes for these collected essays. Developing the major themes was difficult particularly because I recognized that a kind of "translation" problem arises when applying modern ideas about peace to the study of peace history in earlier eras when those ideas, or at least modern formulations of them, were absent. I only started doing peace history in 1998 after two decades of teaching and writing concentrated almost exclusively on American history. Not surprisingly, I remained focused on the modern era when preparing my first peace history courses and new research projects. That focus on the modern era was reinforced by what I learned in a peace research seminar at the University of Oslo in the summer of 2007. Thus I knew that my initial selection of themes for this collection could be criticized as present-oriented. Many hours of discussion with my colleagues in Dartmouth's History Department convinced me that this "translation" problem was not insuperable, and that after significant revision my original ideas would be viable focal points for *A Cultural History of Peace*.

These six volumes validate this conviction. Each one contains an introductory overview of the historical era written by its editor and eight thematic essays written by specialists. They develop the following themes: definitions of peace; human nature, peace, and war; peace, war, and gender; peace, pacifism, and religion; representations of peace; peace movements; peace, security, and deterrence; and peace as integration. This structure facilitates long views of key subjects in peace history. Anyone interested, for instance, in putting together a chronologically ordered history of how peace has been defined from antiquity to the modern era can achieve this goal by reading in order each of the first chapters in the six volumes of *A Cultural History of Peace*. When they do so, they will discover that the distinction between "negative" and "positive" definitions of peace that are commonly used in peace research today is useful when formulating questions about pre-modern definitions of peace. But they will also see that the modern distinction between negative peace and positive peace is a simple model that may hinder understanding the variety and richness of what people since antiquity actually meant when they spoke and wrote about peace.

How people in different times and places have understood what we usually call "human nature" has deeply influenced what they said and did about making peace and war. Human nature is, of course, a tricky term. Does it even exist? If it does, is it an endowment of fixed characteristics, or malleable and evolving? And if by human nature we mean "instinctual," does this mean "inevitable," or are instincts better understood as potential behaviors that have been repressed or expressed depending on environmental influences produced by particular cultures at particular times in the past? The essays in this collection that develop the theme "human nature, peace, and war" make clear that prevailing beliefs about human nature, whether faith-based or secular, have always played an essential role in how people understand what kinds of peace are possible in their imperfect material world.

Peace and war are among the most clearly gendered historical categories, as Chapter 3 in each volume of *A Cultural History of Peace* makes abundantly clear. It has been common all over the world for women to be regarded as "life-givers" and men as "life-takers." Of course there are deviations from this global historical pattern. The Truong sisters of Vietnam and Joan of Arc are among the most famous transgressors of the male monopoly of military power. However, women like them have been exceptional. More commonly, women have provided material and psychological support to male warriors. And perhaps most significantly, some of them have been peace thinkers and peacemakers. Indeed, the widespread idea that peace is feminine has been a source of political legitimacy for women, not just a barrier to achieving political power.

Although pacifism in Western democracies is now usually understood as a principled and often religiously inspired refusal to engage in violence, in other historical settings people who could justify certain violent actions and some wars were still considered "pacifists" whenever they opposed militarism or an ongoing war. On such occasions the deeply subversive cultural implications of nonviolence—its resistance to the idea that history must be written in blood—have been manifest. The essays herein that develop the theme "Peace, Pacifism, and Religion" enable readers to better understand the ambiguous role of religious faith in peace history. They describe religious traditions that link faith and peace, but also ancient and enduring traditions that link religion to the promotion of war.

Since antiquity countless artists, sculptors, composers, poets, playwrights, and writers have produced representations that reflected, but also shaped, understandings of peace in their cultures. Ancient symbols of peace like the olive branch and the dove that were incorporated into religious iconography have never lost their currency, even when used by secular peace activists. Many other representations of peace created during the last two millennia have also survived. Chapter 5 in each volume presents a long history of these representations of peace. These representations have often been of peace imagined because their creators could not find real peace in contemporary political cultures. The accumulated representations of peace now form a vast and priceless cultural reservoir, much of it easily accessed via the Internet. Currently, new representations of peace are being produced deposited in this cultural reservoir every day, while old ones are revived and reconfigured by peace activists around the world.

Peace and anti-war movements have always produced and deployed representations of peace, but they have not been a constant presence in the past. Chapter 6 in each volume describes collective efforts to prevent wars, or to stop them from continuing, as well as organized opposition to militarism. Throughout history peace movements have been condemned as subversive, especially when they resisted ongoing wars authorized by political authorities. And even when they have failed to achieve peace, as they have frequently done in the past, peace movements extended the contemporary cultural bases for challenging militarism and the glorification of warfare. Peace movements have in the long run produced traditions of anti-militarist thinking that in this century are mobilized by peace activists whenever interstate warfare threatens global peace.

Today most global peace activists regard the achievement of security via the threat of force as itself a problem, partly because this kind of negative peace has so frequently broken down in the past. The six essays in this collection that explore the theme "peace, security, and deterrence" none the less demonstrate the strong and enduring appeal of this approach to peace. Although the perception problem modern political scientists call "the security dilemma" has been recognized since antiquity, the political practicality and immediately recognizable results of deterrence have almost always prevailed in the face of building threats made by military rivals. Enshrined in the modern era as a form of political realism, deterrence policy shaped the nuclear arms that saw rival superpowers each deploy tens of thousands of nuclear weapons that if used would have certainly destroyed civilization. Yet today, most national governments still equate peace with security and produce deterrence policies that create military alliances and threaten adversaries with war.

The last chapter of each volume of *A Cultural History of Peace* addresses a theme that many people mistakenly identify as a modern phenomenon: peace through integration, as if it must be something resembling the European Union. These chapters show that the social order imposed by expanding empires, kingdoms, and nation-states has long been proclaimed as a form of peace, even when peace was not the reason for the warfare that preceded it. Moreover, its principal beneficiaries often have identified their empires as an expanding civilization, most famously Pax Romana and more recently Pax Americana. Yet since the medieval age another kind of peace, achieved by nonviolent agreements built upon shared characteristics of identity, has been imagined, and occasionally implemented.

Christianity's claim to be a universal church that could bring all people together in a brotherhood of Christ opened the door for identifying "humanity," a word first used during the Renaissance. Then science, especially eighteenth-century taxonomy, provided a secular path to a similar end: the recognition that all humans are in very important ways a single unique species of life. In the modern era, threats to the continued existence of this humanity in the form of global catastrophes such as nuclear warfare and climate change have contributed to an unprecedented "species consciousness" and the claim that all humans have rights that must be respected. Unprecedented communications technologies that today allow us to see and hear people from all over the world in real time have facilitated the expansion of global peace and human rights networks. Although during the five years that *A Cultural History of Peace* has been in the making, politics that divide people into hostile groups have gathered strength in many countries, the long history presented in this collection suggests the cultural foundations for peace, so long in the making, will weather the present storm, and humanity will continue to make itself a global reality.

INTRODUCTION

Toward a Culture of Peace

INGRID SHARP

The period under consideration in this volume begins with the Congress of Vienna in 1815 and ends with the founding of the League of Nations in 1920, both highly significant events in forming and reflecting contemporary ideas about peace and visions for a more peaceful world order.[1] Although the timing of these interventions was affected by immediately preceding periods of especially vicious and protracted warfare between the large armies of many nations, they should not be seen simply as a reaction to the utter devastation caused by the long drawn-out conflicts of the French revolutionary and the Napoleonic Wars at the beginning of the nineteenth century (1792–1815) and the Great War (1914–18) just over a decade into the twentieth. Both the Vienna Congress and the League of Nations reflected a desire to order relations between nations in such a way as to avoid future wars, and the ways in which this was conceived both reflect existing ideas, and shape the development of new approaches to war and peace throughout the intervening period. Histories are often given structure mainly by the wars and other violent events that occur during a given period, but this introduction will contextualize the different chapters in this volume by outlining the key events and ideas that influenced attitudes to peace. It will show the continuities in the way in which cultures of peace, despite the many setbacks and interruptions, gained ground and took shape in the course of the period covered. It will also show how industrial, scientific, and technological developments as well as changing social and political attitudes affect ideas about peace as much as they change the ways in which war is waged and the relationship between civilians and warfare.

The idea of structuring relations between nations in ways more conducive to a peaceful resolution of differences gained ground throughout the nineteenth century, with the rise and proliferation of groups committed to countering war both internationally and within the nation states. At the same time, technological, scientific, social, intellectual, and political developments had a significant effect on the ways in which war and peace were conducted and viewed. The development of transport—by rail and road, automobile, bicycle, and even by air—and communication allowed people and goods to move more freely and ideas to spread rapidly. The development of an international postal service enabled the exchange of ideas and maintenance of personal relationships through correspondence. The social order was profoundly affected by previous and continuing revolutionary demands for equality, fraternity, and liberty, and the first half of the nineteenth century in Europe and America is characterized by the demand for greater democracy as well as by urbanization and industrialization, although it is important to remember that most people spent the century in rural, agrarian contexts (Evans 2017: xxii). The spread of basic education produced more literate populations, providing a new

FIGURE 0.1: Queen Victoria and Prince Albert inaugurating the 1851 Exhibition, Crystal Palace, 1851. Credit: Photo 12/Getty Images.

readership for mass circulation newspapers. International trade was brought to popular attention through the spectacle of trade fairs in cities such as London, Paris, and Chicago from 1851 onward, which attracted large crowds including international visitors. These trade fairs showcased technological innovations and displayed national prowess through spectacular feats of engineering such as London's Crystal Palace (1851) and Paris's Eiffel Tower (1889).

Rapid change brought huge social problems, especially for the new and rapidly expanding class of urban workers who suffered in poor housing and worked long hours in terrible conditions, while technological developments and mechanization led to the destruction of the livelihoods of whole categories of workers. Contaminated food, crowded housing, and lack of sanitation led to the spread of disease, high infant mortality, and low life expectancy. It was also a period of terrible suffering caused by famines due to changes in land ownership and farming methods, often leading to mass emigration. For example, the Irish potato famine killed a million people and led to the emigration of a quarter of all survivors (Evans 2017: 127). At the same time, working-class demands were often met by savage repression and recurring revolutions. Uprisings and brutal repressions characterized especially the first half of the century, culminating in the 1848 revolutions that brought regime change across Europe. The suppression of the Paris commune in 1871 and the brutal punishment of participants showed a continued terror of subversion and a strong but ultimately unsuccessful desire to suppress all forms of socialism. The Social Democratic Party was illegal in Germany from 1875 to 1890, after which it continued to be viewed with suspicion by bourgeoisie and nobility alike. Yet despite being handicapped by a class-based franchise, it emerged as the largest and most powerful socialist party in Europe, representing some 4.5 million voters by 1914. Subversive ideas spread as revolutionaries fled repression or were exiled from their own states and gathered in large cities, forming international groups.

Despite the many genuine problems and the vast and manifest inequalities in all aspects of life, the nineteenth century can still be seen as a period of slow, grudging, and often interrupted progress toward a culture of peace, as moving in the direction of greater awareness of the interconnectedness of humanity and of individual human rights, greater democracy, and growing concern to tackle some of the most egregious social inequalities. The desire reflected in the Congress of Vienna and the Concert of Europe to restrain the Great Powers from using force in international relations was extended by a number of innovations that suggested a desire to alleviate suffering in war by regulating its conduct and agreeing rules for the treatment of prisoners of war, civilians, and wounded soldiers. Economic as well as moral arguments were developing that sought to offer scientific evidence for the folly of conducting wars, and awareness of wars increased as mass circulation newspapers reported them as they happened. Social justice concerns such as the abolition of the slave trade and child labor had gained popularity, partly as a result of literary representations such as American Harriet Beecher Stowe's *Uncle Tom's Cabin* in 1852 and Charles Kingsley's *The Water Babies* 1862–3. The socially critical novels of British authors Charles Dickens and Elizabeth Gaskell, Emile Zola and Victor Hugo in France, and Russians Leo Tolstoy and Fyodor Dostoyevski, alongside campaigning journalism, raised awareness of continuing social problems in the latter half of the nineteenth century. These concerns are reflected in changed laws and attitudes. By the time of the Berlin Congress in 1884, public support for the anti-slavery movement and the growing conviction that slavery was incompatible with a modern civilized state made it impossible for European leaders to express anything but moral revulsion. Although poverty, insanitary conditions, and overcrowding meant that diseases spread rapidly in urban centers, there were improvements in public hygiene and an increasing recognition of municipal responsibility for providing clean water supplies, uncontaminated food, and habitable housing. There were major advances in medical knowledge of how diseases are transmitted and how to prevent this, leading to greater success in combating diseases such as typhus and cholera that killed vast numbers, so that mortality rates did come down toward the end of the century, and in some regions birth rates rose for much of the period, with rising rates of infant survival. The introduction of universal education, health protection for women factory workers, and experiments in communal living such as settlement houses all gained ground as the century progressed. There was a discernible move toward more compassionate treatment of and state support for the mentally ill, the elderly, the disabled, and the destitute, even a concern for animal welfare. There were small changes in attitudes toward crime and punishment, with public executions and corporal punishment largely phased out from the mid-century onward, attempts at prison reforms, and the introduction of police forces intended to preserve public order and prevent crime. Social causes such as the campaign for the abolition of slavery, against the state regulation of prostitution, and for women's emancipation from the laws and customs that constrained them were taking hold in all developed countries. At the same time, the ideal of creating and sustaining a peaceful society was being discussed at all levels of society. A publication such as Bertha von Suttner's *Lay Down Your Arms* in 1889 had a major effect in popularizing peace ideas and bringing them to a wider public, but it did not invent the ideas: these came from the Peace Societies, which grew in size and scope after 1815, with large-scale international peace conferences held in major cities from

1849 onward. The ideal of peace gained high-profile support in the late nineteenth century with the first Hague Peace Congress in 1899, attended by heads of state and observed by prominent members of peace societies, including Bertha von Suttner. The endowment of an international prize for peace by Alfred Nobel in 1901, the second Hague Peace Congress in 1907, and the establishing of an International Court of Arbitration at The Hague in 1913 in the Peace Palace[2] suggested that war was being phased out and would soon be replaced by less violent means of resolving differences. Despite the glaring inequalities, there was widespread optimism based on a belief in progress toward a more enlightened, civilized age, which for many now included international cooperation. Peace was seen as the logical, rational direction of travel for humanity, and by the end of the nineteenth century war had become an anachronism considered virtually impossible in a cosmopolitan, urban world with civilized ideas and international trade entanglements. Even ideas that appeared to work against peace, such as social Darwinism, which suggested that life was a struggle, human beings were innately violent, and wars served an evolutionary purpose, could be used to support belief in progress toward peace. Even the invention of increasingly horrible weapons of war, it was argued, would have a deterrent effect by making future wars too costly in human lives to contemplate. It could also be argued that many of the wars that did occur in an age of swift communications, which could bring reports and even pictures from the battlefield to the reading public, served to increase revulsion at the effects of war and trigger international developments that would prevent or at least regulate future wars and prevent a return to the barbarism of the past.

THE PROGRESS OF PEACE 1815–1920

The Congress of Vienna, which began on November 1, 1814 and concluded on November 20, 1815, is seen by some as the most successful peace conference to date, as it paved the way for a far more peaceful nineteenth century in comparison with the protracted global wars of the seventeenth and eighteenth centuries that had broken British domination of North America and Spanish colonial power in Latin America (Evans 2017: 15–16). The peace it brokered between the four European Great Powers—Russia, Britain, Austria, and Prussia, all of which had suffered defeat and/or occupation by Napoleon's armies—and the defeated France avoided another major conflagration between European states until almost 100 years later in 1914. The agreement was worked out against the background of a Europe devastated after the French Revolutionary Wars (1792–1803) and the Napoleonic Wars (1803–15), which together added up to some twenty-five years of war across the whole of Europe, the Ottoman Empire, and Egypt, and involved mass armies of up to 500,000 men. The major concern of those who met at Vienna was to prevent future wars between Great Powers within Europe through cooperation in settling territorial disputes and reining in hegemonic ambitions, and intervention to suppress potentially destabilizing domestic revolutions. The signatories envisaged a system of peace maintained by regular international congresses and were prepared to cooperate in order to achieve this—indeed the commitment to mutual support was further underscored by the Holy Alliance signed in 1815 between the Tsar of Russia, the Emperor of Austria, and the Prussian king. The Congress did not of course prevent wars involving Great Powers—the Crimean War of 1853–6 involved Russia, France, and Britain, Prussia fought against Austria in 1866 and France in 1870——nor did it prevent other violent upheavals,

FIGURE 0.2: The Vienna Congress, 1815. Credit: maodesign/Getty Images.

and the rigorous repression of revolutionary uprisings and political demands was characteristic of especially the first half of the century. However, it established the principle that peace was a priority that could best be secured by collaboration, discussion, and binding treaties.

The Vienna Congress can be considered progressive in that it established the principle that international relations could be regulated by law. Its critics maintain that it was socially and politically conservative and suppressed any attempts at liberal democracy: US historian Sandi Cooper argues that "[i]n theory the Congress system was formed to keep peace; in reality, it established an interstate system to intervene against revolution" (Cooper 1991: 14). It is also criticized because it was concerned only with preserving peace between the European Great Powers, and paid scant attention to wars of colonial expansion, the use of force against smaller nations, or the use of force to control subject populations (Schulz 2015: 133). Yet the "Concert of Europe" established at Vienna held out despite continued social unrest, state repression, famines and plagues, mass movement of populations, and national struggles for independence. The revolutionary year of 1848 was a watershed throughout Europe, testing the ability of the Alliance to keep a lid on social discontent in the face of liberal pressures for democratic and social reform, and the emergence of organized urban workers as forces for change.

HUMANIZING WAR

The Congress of Vienna also reveals the beginnings of attitudes to relations between nation states as cooperative and pacific that continued to develop in the course of the century, alongside a demand for greater humanity in the conduct of war. These attitudes were expressed in the first Geneva Convention of 1864, the Hague Congresses of 1899 and 1907, the founding of the Peace Palace and the Permanent Court of Arbitration at The Hague in 1913, and culminated—as far as the period under consideration is concerned—in the ideals and hopes bound up with the founding of the League of Nations in 1920. In the aftermath of the Crimean War (1853–6) and while the American Civil War (1861–5) continued to rage, the Geneva Convention of 1864 established rules for the conduct of wars covering the treatment of wounded combatants and prisoners of war: the "Convention for the Amelioration of the Conditions of the Wounded in Armies in the Field" (Osterhammel 2014: 505). The impetus for the Geneva conference came from the harrowing sights witnessed by Swiss business traveler Henri Dunant in the aftermath of the Battle of Solferino in 1859, which he described in *A Memory of Solferino*, published in 1862. In 1863, delegates and representatives of some twenty-five nations met in Geneva at his instigation to establish new norms for the conduct of future wars. These included the neutrality of both the wounded soldiers and the volunteer medical and relief personnel, identified by the symbol of the Red Cross, after 1875 also the Red Crescent, which enabled the international relief organization to play a major humanitarian role in subsequent wars (Osterhammel 2014; 505–6).

The Crimean War was important, too, in bringing to public attention the sanitary conditions in which soldiers lived and died, many more dying of disease and infection than

FIGURE 0.3: "Convention for the Amelioration of the Conditions of the Wounded in Armies in the Field," Geneva, 1864. Credit: AFP Contributor/Getty Images.

FIGURE 0.4: Florence Nightingale (1820–1910), "The Lady with the Lamp." Credit: Bettmann/Getty Images.

as a direct result of their injuries. British volunteer nurse Florence Nightingale's (1820–1910) reports gained her widespread publicity and lasting popularity from 1854 as "the Lady with the Lamp." The image, which eclipsed that of Mary Seacole (1805–81), who set up a private hospital behind the Crimean lines, was no doubt romanticized, but Nightingale left a legacy of improved nutrition and sanitary conditions—notably sewerage and ventilation—for soldiers and of professional training for nurses (see Bostridge 1998).

Nightingale's involvement in the war was prompted by reading highly critical press reports by *Times* journalists Howard Russell and Thomas Cheney (Gittings 2012: 137–8), showing the vital role played by a press facilitated by new technologies—notably telegraphy—that allowed far-away populations to hear news of wars very quickly (Gittings 2012: 137). As outlined by Maartje Abbenhuis in Chapter 7 of this volume, The Hague Peace Conferences of 1899 and 1907 show the extent to which the peaceful resolution of international affairs had gained traction in international relations as well as in public consciousness. International relations were no longer the preserve of political elites, but were of huge interest to a growing number of politically engaged citizens. The conference of 1899, initiated by Tsar of Russia Nicolas II, was hailed by peace groups as the official recognition of their aims and the vindication of their ideals, and used as a focus for rallying supporters and publicizing their cause (Gittings 2012: 145).

PACIFISM AND MILITARISM

1815 was also significant as the first peace societies were founded in that year in North America and Britain, as outlined in Martin Caedel's Chapter 6 in this volume, and pacifism as an ideal began to take shape and develop through the interventions of thinkers, writers, and activists. These were not by any means the first articulations of an ideal of peace—Kant's essay *Perpetual Peace* had been published in 1795—but the formation of societies and groups at local, national, and international level helped shift the idea of peace from being the preserve of theologians and the intellectual elite to becoming a key motivating idea behind an increasingly popular movement by 1914. State cooperation at international level to manage conflicts without recourse to war were mirrored nationally and locally by a large number of societies, organizations, and movements that supported and worked for peace in a variety of ways. Peace historian David S. Patterson gives figures of "190 peace societies, some with thousands of members, which published twenty-three periodicals in ten languages" (Patterson 2014). As outlined here in chapters by Cooper, Caedel, and Barrett, these groups were rooted in religious, humanitarian, or social justice beliefs. They shared and publicized their commitment to peace and sought to expose the inglorious realities of war, which was neither an inevitable part of human interaction nor an expression of divine providence. The growth of democracy also played a part toward the end of the nineteenth century, when public opposition to war increasingly challenged the right of government to use war as a tool of international relations without democratic consultation.

At the same time as ideas about peace and the value of non-violent solutions to international relations were gaining ground, there was also a growth in the influence that the military exercised in civilian life. The nation most associated with rising militarism in the nineteenth century was Prussia. In 1815 still a small and relatively insignificant nation, it was none the less basking in the glory of its 1813 defeat of Napoleon in the Wars of Liberation, which had done much to raise national sentiment and to create a national identity based on military values. Military successes in 1866 and 1871 led to Prussian dominance following the unification of Germany in 1871, an event widely seen as flowing from a military predominance that should be maintained at all costs. The militarization of German civilian society was reinforced by a system of education, public discourse, and training that meant that positions of influence in Germany were inhabited by military men. Militarism led to a hierarchical way of thinking that privileged masculinity, and marginalized and derided attempts to challenge military solutions to international relations or to press the cause of women's access to citizenship and political rights. Universal male conscription in France after 1792 and Germany after 1913 fundamentally changed the relationship of civil society to questions of war and peace and linked citizenship rights and democratic participation with military service. French men, too, were liable for years of compulsory military service and their identity as free citizens of the republic was very much bound up in their willingness and ability to serve the nation. In Britain, the standing army was small and professional, with no compulsory military service. Ideas of freedom and volunteerism were key to British identity and self-understanding, and it was only with great difficulty and reluctance that conscription was introduced in 1916 in response to a crisis of recruitment in a war requiring huge numbers of mobilized men and munitions.

INTERNATIONALISM

During the period 1815 to 1920, attitudes to peace were affected by key discoveries and developments in political, intellectual, scientific, and cultural life and by the increasing mobility of people and ideas facilitated by easier travel and trade between nations (Osterhammel 2014: 469–513). Elite education included learning European languages alongside—for men—Latin and Greek, facilitating the sharing of scientific discoveries and key publications. Karl Marx, for example, spent years in Paris and Britain, wrote for the international press, and corresponded widely, including an exchange with Lincoln at the end of the Civil War and over 500 articles for the *New York Daily Tribune* during the 1850s (see Blackburn 2011). International organizations held conferences at which members could meet face to face and establish networks that were consolidated by correspondence. Women's letters in particular stressed bonds of affection and friendship (see Bosch 1990). British naturalist Charles Darwin (1809–82), whose highly influential *On the Origin of Species*, published in Britain in 1859 and America in 1860, was translated into French and German languages in 1860 and into Scandinavian and Dutch languages in the 1870s, maintained a vast international correspondence with fellow scientists that was fairly typical for the scholar of the era.

The peace movement itself was internationalized: five influential International Peace Congresses were held between 1843 and 1879, after 1867 the League for Peace and Liberty organized regular congresses, and Universal Peace Congresses were held from 1889 to 1939 (Hippler and Vec 2015: 171) and the International Peace Bureau was set up in 1891. The Peace Congress held in Paris in 1849 was of particular importance. It took place in the immediate aftermath of the 1848 revolutions and was attended by British,

FIGURE 0.5: French writer Victor Hugo (1802–85), addressing the Paris Peace Congress in 1849. Credit: Historical (Corbis Historical)/Getty Images.

American, German, Swiss, Belgian, Italian, Dutch, and Spanish delegates. It was opened by influential writer and public intellectual Victor Hugo, whose opening address became "one of the most widely cited document of European pacifism in the nineteenth century" and had full official recognition, a remarkable shift in attitude to the cause of peace (Hippler and Vec 2015: 174).

In this internationally receptive climate, some publications had a huge influence on the spread of ideas to a mass readership. As noted above, *Uncle Tom's Cabin* (1852) did much to popularize the moral position against slavery that had been gaining traction at international level since the late eighteenth century. In the 1890s, Bertha von Suttner's work *Lay Down Your Arms* achieved something similar for ideas of peace. Published in German in 1889, it was translated into English in 1892, followed quickly by many other languages. As discussed by Laurie Cohen in Chapter 5 in this volume, it was an international bestseller that prompted the formation of peace societies in Germany and Austria and probably influenced Alfred Nobel to endow an award for peace in 1901, which was awarded to Suttner in 1905. Russian author Leo Tolstoy's (1828–1910) novel *War and Peace* (1869), despite its ambiguous message about the inevitability of war discussed by Jeff Love in Chapter 8 in this volume, contained powerful descriptions of the horrors of war based on Tolstoy's own observations as a staff officer during the Crimean War (Gittings 2012: 138). Later essays and novels, in which his ideas about the moral responsibility for peace were more definitive, especially *The Kingdom of God Is Within You* of 1894, won him followers all over the world. Jean (Ivan) de Bloch's six-volume *The Future of War* was published in 1898 in Polish and Russian, and his ideas quickly spread to Britain and America (Crook 1994: 99). Bloch anticipated World War I, accurately predicting that future war would be rendered unimaginably bloody by growth in technological innovation and that it would not only kill vast numbers of combatants but would consume all the economic strength of belligerents in payment for arms and the logistics of total war. The publication of Norman Angell's *The Great Illusion* in Britain in 1909 and America in 1910 did a lot to reassure its numerous readers that war between highly developed and economically entangled nations would be so disruptive as to be almost impossible. Angell's analysis that war had become an anachronism was inspired by the move toward international arbitration and international law since 1815. In this way, with the economies and cultures of the industrialized nations apparently so interconnected, the liberal ideas of peace and social progress accepted at state level and gaining mass popularity as a moral and rational position, the threat of war appeared to recede.

SOCIALISM AND ORGANIZED LABOR MOVEMENTS

Socialist parties representing the interests of the urban poor were a major factor in industrialized nations by the end of the nineteenth century: in 1912 British Labour MP Keir Hardie was able to claim that they represented 15 million voters worldwide (Wette 2017: 33). The ideas underpinning these parties had their roots in several developments during the nineteenth century, many of which had been aimed at creating conditions for peace within nations where crass social and economic inequalities caused frequent revolutionary clashes. These include the experiments in egalitarian communes imagined by French utopian thinkers Charles Fourier (1772–1837), Étienne Cabet (1788–1856), and Comte de Saint-Simon (1760–1825), and British leader Richard Owen (1771–1858), and were expressed in Proudhon's mutualism and agrarian models (see Evans 2017: 169–77).

FIGURE 0.6: The delivery of the Great Chartists' Petition to Parliament in 1842. Credit: Mansell/Getty Images.

While some workers' parties called for the overthrow of the oppressing classes, early movements aimed to create social justice within existing structures. An example is the Chartist movement in Britain, named after the People's Charter 1838, which can be seen as the first mass popular political movement. In 1842, Chartists delivered a petition of unprecedented size signed by 3.3 million people—around a third of the population—calling for "wider political participation . . . religious and political freedom, a reduction in the hours of factory labour, home rule for Ireland" and an end to "a host of other evils too numerous to mention but all arising from class legislation" (Chase 2016). The petition, which weighed 300 kg, was paraded through the streets before being delivered to Parliament, where its huge size made it difficult to fit it through the doors.

The General German Workers' Association, Prussia's first labor organization, founded in 1864 by Ferdinand Lassalle (1825–64), and the Fabian Society (founded 1884) were forerunners of socialist parties in Europe and America (Adolf 2009: 175). In 1868, the Trades Union Congress was created in Britain to represent the interests of workers and propose non-violent ways of settling industrial disputes, for example withdrawal of labor through strikes and collective bargaining to strengthen the hand of the workforce (Adolf 2009: 175).

Late nineteenth-century socialism was not by any means a pacifist doctrine, and most theorists such as Karl Marx (1818–83), Vladimir Ilyich Lenin (1870–1924), Rosa Luxemburg (1871–1919), and the anarchist Mikhail Bakunin (1814–76) were committed to a greater or lesser degree to the use of revolutionary force to overthrow the capitalist system and take ownership of the means of production into the hands of the workers. Because of the primacy of class in what Marx called "scientific" as opposed to "utopian" socialism, workers were discouraged from making common cause with bourgeois pacifists, and there was a firm belief that peace between as well as within nations would only be possible after a fundamental economic restructuring:

> While Marx's socialist stance cannot be called peaceful, the paradigm for and analysis of social peace he put forth has been immeasurably influential, to the extent that the

history of peace and peace-making in the next century and a half cannot be understood without them.

Adolf 2009: 174

Marx saw the violence inherent in the exploitation of workers and the social inequalities that blighted and shortened their lives as well as the disproportionate burden of war on the working class, and was committed to opposing and countering both kinds of violence (Doyle 1997: 324). He also saw socialism as bringing both internal and external peace to the whole of Europe rather than in single nations, so he did not conceive of socialist states in conflict with their capitalist neighbors (Doyle 1997: 338). Socialist ideas made an important contribution to cultures of peace in the nineteenth century through their commitment to bringing about social and economic equality, improving working conditions, and through the emphasis on the international solidarity of the working class in all nations. From the outset, socialism was highly international, with state repression of activists and organizations feeding into an international movement of people and ideas: Marx's own radical ideas made his native Germany uncomfortable for him and he moved first to Paris and then to London, where he completed much of his theoretical writing.

Marx founded the Workers International Association, the first Socialist International, in 1863 (Adolf 2009: 174), on the basis of internationally shared interests of workers expressed in the rallying call of the Communist Manifesto of 1848: "Let the ruling classes tremble at a Communistic revolution. The proletarians have nothing to lose but their chains. They have a world to win. Working Men of All Countries, Unite!" (Marx and Engels: 1848).

Although later hugely influential in socialist thought, the *Manifesto* was at first largely overlooked and did not have a reliable English translation until 1888, but it attracted increasing international interest and new translations into multiple languages over the next decades.

The Second International, founded in 1889, sought to coordinate and give direction to socialists across the world, expressing opposition to war and militarism in international conferences in Stuttgart 1907, Copenhagen 1910, and Basel 1912. The International Socialist Congress at Basel in 1912 offered a very clear statement of the extent of socialist consensus on questions of war and peace. Called in response to the Balkan Wars, attended by 555 delegates from social democratic and socialist parties, and trade unions, it articulated an anti-war position based on an understanding of the cause of wars as human choices rather than divine providence, and of the prevention of war as requiring domestic social justice as well as international solidarity. Only eighteen of the delegates were women, but these represented powerful figures in socialist theory and activism, including German political leaders Clara Zetkin and Luise Zietz. The congress was conducted in the full glare of publicity and with the full support of the Swiss government—massive demonstrations for peace had been held in cities across Europe, including 250,000 in Berlin on October 20, 1912, while in Basel itself, an opening parade of 20,000 people ended in an official reception at the Basel Minster. Here, socialist banners were hoisted while bells rang out and speeches and prayers confirmed the mutual desire of church and state for peace. This did not please some observers, who objected in the strongest terms that godless socialists should have been allowed to profane the church in this way (Wette 2017: 31–5).

Despite this impressive display of strength, with impassioned speeches by Keir Hardie and French socialist leader Jean Jaurès, the conference also revealed the weakness of the socialists, who really could do little but warn governments that the tide of public opinion among workers was against war. The conference manifesto identified it as the "duty of the working classes and their parliamentary representatives . . . to exert every effort in order to prevent the outbreak of war by the means they consider most effective" (Wette 2017: 33–4), but stopped short of calling for resistance to conscription or a general strike if war were declared, and ultimately the International was powerless to override the pull of patriotism once nations were at war in 1914. According to US International Relations scholar Michael W. Doyle, "[t]hey, like many of the leaders of other parties at the beginning and during the course of the world war, also were undoubtedly guilty of national chauvinism, opportunism, and many other errors" (1997: 375). However, Doyle believes that history should not condemn them too harshly, as Lenin did in 1914, for their "direct betrayal of socialism." He argues that Marxist doctrine was compatible with defensive wars and, in any case, there was little the socialists could have done: they were simply "too weak to overwhelm the forces of right-wing militarism," although arguably a stronger anti-war showing might have given governments in Britain, France, and even Germany pause before relying on the support of their laboring classes (Doyle 1997: 375).

DARWIN AND EVOLUTIONARY PEACE BIOLOGY

Other highly influential ideas emerged during the period under consideration. Of these, different interpretations and understandings of British naturalist Charles Darwin's ideas had a particularly profound effect on arguments for and against war and in informing attitudes to racial difference in the colonial context.

Darwinism, especially in the form of social Darwinism propounded by British biologist Herbert Spencer (1820–1903), was mainly used to justify the growth of militarism and the belief in war as the legitimate way of furthering national interests. Spencer's term "the survival of the fittest" was applied to struggles between nations to suggest that war had evolutionary benefits. German biologist Ernst Haeckel's (1834–1919) hierarchy of racial types, described in *The Riddle of the Universe* (1901), was used to justify the annihilation of supposedly "weaker" races to create room for allegedly stronger, more robust races. Darwin's description of adaptation by selective breeding for desirable traits was applied to human society and underpinned eugenic ideas: Haeckel advocated leaving sick children untreated to prevent them passing on inferior traits. The elision of acquired characteristics and the effects of social milieu with genetic disposition led to crude, often gender and class-based generalizations and punitive interventions into the lives of the powerless that were often disastrous for those affected (Crook 1994: 71).

However, Darwin's ideas could also be mobilized for peace, as outlined in Australian historian Paul Crook's 1994 study *Darwinism, War and History*. Crook shows how Darwin's view of evolution could translate into ideas of progress and peace biology, in which atavistic human urges could be overcome by more peaceable instincts as humans adapted to a more interconnected global society. War enthusiasts aside, much of the justification for war rested on the belief that war was part of human nature, incapable of change, and thus simply inevitable. However, Darwin's ideas also supported strong evolutionary arguments against war, and in favor of progress toward peace. These ideas are bound up with a nineteenth-century belief in progress toward a more highly developed society populated by better educated, healthier, and hence more morally developed citizens. The argument saw war as anachronistic and no longer appropriate to modern times and cosmopolitan ways of living. It rested on a strong belief that man's aggression could be overcome and the "benefits" of war attained through other means. As discussed by Ingrid Sharp in Chapter 2 in this volume, in the US these ideas were put forward most convincingly by the psychologist William James (1842–1910) and the social reformer Jane Addams (1860–1935). Addams believed that the human instinct to nurture and protect the young and helpless was stronger than innate aggression and the urge to fight, largely attributed to masculinity. Based on her experiences among immigrant populations in Chicago, she formed the view that this tendency would win out if society was so structured as to encourage its development. Counterarguments against the evolutionary benefits of war showed that, far from ensuring the "survival of the fittest," war in fact killed and maimed the strongest and best, removing these from the national stock, leaving only the weaker and sicker to breed. This was persuasively expressed during World War I by German biologist Georg Friedrich Nikolai (1874–1964), one of very few university professors who openly opposed the war. His anti-war book *The Biology of War*, which demonstrated that war losses would make nations genetically weaker, was published in Switzerland in 1917. The same arguments were put forward by Ernst Haeckel himself, who "campaigned vigorously in the cause of pacifism, leading the German military authorities to keep [him] under close surveillance during the First World War" (Evans 2017: 684).

IMPERIALISM AND LIMITED SYMPATHIES

Internationalism and the commitment to progress, the avoidance of war, and greater humanity in the ways wars were carried out was limited to Anglophone and industrialized European nations, with a definite hierarchy of value that privileged white Western nations above non-white, however ancient the civilization. This can be seen in the disproportionate violence and coercion used by Britain against China during the Opium Wars (1842 and 1860), and the Boxer rebellion (1899–1901), and in the general acceptance of the use of force, enslavement, and intimidation in dealings with European colonies from the Belgian Congo to British India. The violence used to control colonized nations was not included in discussions of war and indeed was often referred to as "pacification," while the structural violence involved in perpetuating and deepening economic inequalities attracted little interest or concern. The Indian "mutiny" of 1857 was crushed without criticism and with little sympathy for the non-white victims or understanding of their cause, while German East Africa was subdued at a huge cost in African lives at the hands of the military or through scorched earth tactics that left 200,000 dead of hunger (Evans 2017: 656). This was nothing compared to the genocide of the Herero tribes in South-West Africa by German colonizers, who deliberately drove them into the desert to die, or worked them to death in concentration camps. On the other hand, similar tactics employed by Britain to control the civilian population during the Boer War attracted public criticism as it was seen as directed against white, Christian settlers, mainly women and children (Hochschild 2011: 33–6). Clearly, standards of "civilization" did not apply to colonies, which were ruthlessly exploited and stripped of wealth by colonizing powers who offered little or nothing in return: according to Richard Evans, "British rule in India brought disaster for the population" (2017: 667). During World War I, colonial subjects were drawn into the war in huge numbers—some 1.5 million Indians served in the British army (see Das 2007) as well as African troops serving in the French army and acting as porters (Olusoga 2014: 100–48). Again, the interests of colonial subjects were very much subordinated to those of the colonizers: the diversion of food to the British army led to widespread famine in India, while the transport of supplies by enormous numbers of African carriers left "devastation and famine" in the African villages and farmland through which they passed (Olusoga 2014: 139). According to British historian David Olusoga, the conditions of these carriers "were for the most part far worse than those endured by the soldiers, and their death toll can be measured not in thousands, or tens of thousands, but in hundreds of thousands" (2014: 139). These regions developed peace strategies of their own to oppose the use of force, sometimes meeting it with violence but also practicing various forms of non-cooperation and non-violent resistance such as that developed by Mohandas Gandhi in South Africa (Adolf 2009: 185–7). The fact remained, though, that keeping and maintaining "peace" in colonies and subject nations was often entirely compatible with the exercise of disproportionate violence, including the plundering of resources and racially based extremes of social and economic inequality.

THE WOMEN'S MOVEMENT

Successful challenges to entrenched hierarchies and discussions around social justice and the democratic rights of citizens raised women's consciousness of the discrimination they suffered in all aspects of life: unequal legal status, lack of protection within marriage, unequal access to education and employment and citizenship rights. The growth of movements dedicated to redressing some of these disadvantages was a defining feature of the latter half of the nineteenth century. This was not a new insight, and there had been important publications analyzing women's position, including *A Vindication of the Rights of Woman* (1792) by Mary Wollstonecraft (1759–97) and *On the Subjection of Women* (1869) by John Stuart Mill in Britain, *Declaration of the Rights of Women and of the Female Citizen* (1791) by Olympe de Gouges (1748–93) in France, and *On Improving the Status of Women* (1792) by Theodor von Hippel in Germany. The focus and priorities of the groups varied widely, and many were very far from claiming women's equality with men and demanding equal rights: some simply sought to make the lives of single women sustainable by allowing them access to education, training, and paid employment. Others, such as Josephine Butler's abolitionist movement, which became a Europe-wide campaign after 1875, challenged the double moral standards that demanded chastity for women while encouraging male license through state regulation of prostitution (see Jordan and Sharp 2003). Women's organizations in America and Europe increased in number and scope as the century progressed, leading to ever closer international cooperation through organizations such as the International Council of Women (ICW), founded in 1888, and the International Women's Suffrage Alliance (IWSA), founded in 1904. These organizations developed a strong sense of women's identity, which for some transcended national, racial, and class barriers, and were committed to principles of international sisterhood that saw women as naturally peace-loving. By 1899, the question of peace had become so closely associated with women that "the ICW adopted, in an extraordinary move, peace politics as a principle element of its international agenda" (Zimmermann 2015: 187) by setting up a Committee on Arbitration and Peace. The ICW remained committed to avoiding any political activities, such as campaigning for female suffrage, that might divide its international membership, so adoption of this policy was only possible as arbitration was "a question on which all women were agreed" (Zimmermann 2015: 191). The Committee, which had Bertha von Suttner as secretary, aimed at working for international understanding and the prevention of war within the "civilized world," which referred only to Europe, America, and other "developed" nations. In this way, Susan Zimmermann argues, the policy contributed to "stabilizing a world order based on ongoing violence and systematic privilege of some actors over others" (2015: 195). As outlined by Sandi Cooper's Chapter 3 in this volume, separatism on gender lines within

FIGURE 0.7: American peace delegates heading for the Women's International Congress at The Hague in 1915. Credit: Library of Congress/Getty Images.

peace groups developed throughout the nineteenth century, but it was World War I that forced the women's movement to develop concrete proposals for international cooperation and articulate their understanding of peace in ways that linked social and gender justice, human rights, and women's rights. These ideas were most fully articulated by the International Committee of Women for Permanent Peace, after 1919 the Women's International League for Peace and Freedom (WILPF), founded in 1915 at the International Women's Conference at The Hague (see Sharp 2013). This congress, hosted by Dutch feminist Dr. Aletta Jacobs (1854–1929) and chaired by American peace activist and social reformer Jane Addams, brought together over 1,000 women from belligerent and neutral nations to discuss the causes of war and conditions for a sustainable peace (see Addams et al. 1915; Wiltsher 1985).

After the congress, delegates were received by leaders of fourteen nations to discuss the possibility of mediation, which represents women's direct intervention in international politics at a time when very few women were permitted to be politically active in their own countries. The women's approach was highly political: they saw the war as proof of male unfitness to govern, so one of their key demands was for women's participation in government. Their aims went far beyond an emotional appeal to men to stop the war: they wanted to understand how wars came about and create an international order that would bring about a sustainable peace. There is evidence that these resolutions influenced US president Woodrow Wilson (in office 1913–21) in formulating his "Fourteen Points," which he put forward as the basis for a just peace in January 1918 (Wiltsher 1985: 192; Vellacott 2001: 379). Although women's groups were not formally included in the Paris peace talks, and women from defeated nations could not be present due to travel restrictions, women lobbied the politicians and wrested some important concessions from them, including the principle that women as well as men could be appointed to all offices

FIGURE 0.8: Women's International Congress, Zurich, 1919. Credit: Peace Museum, Bradford.

in the League of Nations (Rupp 1997: 210). Although they welcomed the founding of the League, they were highly critical of those elements that would, it seemed to them, perpetuate the inequalities that made wars more likely. The women of WILPF who met in Zurich in 1919 condemned the harsh terms of the Versailles Treaty, the peace treaty between Germany and the victorious powers, in the strongest terms: "[a] hundred million people of this generation in the heart of Europe are condemned to poverty, disease and despair, which must result in the spread of hatred and anarchy within each nation" (Bussey and Tims [1965] 1980: 31).

WORLD WAR I

The nature of World War I as an industrialized war, needing the efforts of entire populations as well as mass armies recruited or conscripted from all social classes, meant that governments were dependent on keeping their populations onside. This led belligerent governments to use their powers to control public opinion through the suppression of pacifist voices and the use of pro-war propaganda. The Boer War between Britain and two South African states (1899–1902), beginning only months after the first Hague Peace Congress, had attracted much criticism both in and beyond Britain, and in July 1914 there was persistent and vocal opposition to the growing talk of war that participating powers had to suppress once they had entered the conflict. In Britain, on August 2nd, huge crowds listened to speakers such as Labour politician Keir Hardie and feminist Charlotte Despard protesting against Britain's entry into the war (Hochschild 2011: 91).

In the week preceding the mobilization, a total of 750,000 people attended thirty-two peace rallies held in towns and cities across Germany, 100,000 in Berlin alone, which far outnumbered the "patriotic" demonstrations reported afterwards as expressing war enthusiasm (Hochschild 2011: 87–8). These echoed similar mass rallies in France and

FIGURE 0.9: Keir Hardie speaking at a peace rally in August 1914. Credit: Heritage Images/Getty Images.

later in London, showing how many citizens of belligerent nations wanted to find ways of preventing the war while this was still possible. This was reinforced by the internationalism and solidarity of the socialist movement right up until summer 1914. In July 1914, an emergency meeting of Europe's socialist parties in Brussels stopped short of calling for a general strike, but approved an anti-war resolution and agreed to meet in Paris, where the eloquence of Jean Jaurès might have persuaded them to back strike action, had he not been assassinated on July 31 (Wette 2017: 35). However, socialist parties did not sustain this position once their own nation was at war: even the German socialist party voted to support the war effort, with only Karl Liebknecht opposing (Wette 2017: 66–8). This looks like the collapse of socialist pacifism and internationalism, but in fact the socialist position fueled much anti-war opposition, especially the growing anti-war feeling among soldiers on both sides that eventually made the war unsustainable (Patterson 2014). Pacifist parties, too, appeared powerless in the face of war, unwilling to support the idea of resistance to conscription or offer any public opposition. Behind the scenes, however, and in neutral Switzerland, anti-war activities and publications continued. Even in Germany, where pacifist parties were effectively suppressed, a new anti-war organization, the New Fatherland League, was founded in November 1914. There were other forms of popular anti-war protest, too, such as the frequent industrial strikes and bread riots, at which crowds of mainly working-class women protested against the effects of the starvation blockade with demands for "peace and bread" (see Stibbe *et al.*: 2017). Unrest was especially acute after the Russian revolutions in 1917 and served to lay the groundwork that allowed the German revolution of November 1918 to spark as rapidly as it did. The revolution itself, which overthrew the imperial order and brought the war to an end in November 1918, can be seen as an act of mass resistance, a decisive popular rejection of the war that rested on the decisions and actions of thousands of individuals.

Despite the enormous difficulties of campaigning for peace during times of war, peace activism by socialists, feminists, scientists, and religious groups continued throughout 1914–18, while humanitarian efforts reached across national boundaries to alleviate the suffering of displaced civilians, prisoners of war, internees, and those millions affected by war-related disruptions to food supplies and the accompanying spread of diseases. There were a number of smaller meetings involving socialist women and pacifist groups keen on maintaining international links, but apart from the Women's International Congress discussed above, no larger-scale gatherings were possible. In Britain, the introduction of conscription in 1916 led to highly public resistance that was widely reported in the national and international press, with the tribunals of conscientious objectors—men who refused to serve in the army on grounds of their objection to war on religious, political, or ideological grounds—highlighting the range of arguments against the war. Although at between 16,000 and 20,000 the numbers were low in comparison with the millions who served, and the press coverage was generally unsympathetic, they had the tireless practical and moral support of the No Conscription Fellowship (NCF, founded in 1914). The publicity they attracted and the consistency of their stance in the face of imprisonment and ill-treatment attracted admiration and emulation, inspiring an international movement, the War Resisters International, founded in 1921. Several important organizations still active in the cause of peace at the time of writing were founded during or in the immediate aftermath of the war—including the Fellowship of Reconciliation and WILPF. In general, peace movements emerged from the war more determined than ever to avoid future conflict, and we see international as well as national campaigns for the control of arms, the regulation of weapons, and strategies of war directed at civilians, such as aerial bombardment, poison gas, and starvation blockades, developing as mass movements across Europe and America in the 1920s.

WORLD WAR I PEACE TREATIES AND THE LEAGUE OF NATIONS

At the Congress of Vienna, French Foreign Minister Charles Maurice de Tallyrand-Périgord, representative of the defeated French nation, had been an active participant in the talks, and France was swiftly readmitted to the international community. In contrast, the various peace treaties after World War I were conducted only among victorious powers,[3] and the League of Nations established in 1920 also excluded defeated nations from membership for some years afterwards: Germany was not admitted to membership until 1926. This exclusion of defeated nations was criticized at the time as undermining efforts to create a lasting peace—notably by British economist John Maynard Keynes—and the fact that an even more devastating war broke out within eighteen years was laid at the door of punitive peace treaties, especially the Treaty of Versailles: "[I]f we aim deliberately at the impoverishment of Central Europe, vengeance, I dare predict, will not limp. Nothing can then delay for very long that final war between the forces of reaction and the despairing convulsions of Revolution, before which the horrors of the late German war will fade into nothing" (Keynes 1920: 209).

The negotiators at Paris in 1919 were very much aware of the Congress of Vienna as the most recent attempt to create a new world order and ensure a sustainable peace, but there were significant differences that made the task even harder. In 1919 there was more public accountability, with public opinion influencing democratic governments, there was greater complexity and a far more global scale: as well as the vastly increased size of delegations—Britain alone sent a staff of 400 compared with just nineteen in 1815—representatives of over thirty nations that had not even existed in 1815 expected to have their say (MacMillan 2000: 5).

There were higher expectations all round, which could not possibly all be met. Many looked to Paris not just to agree settlements between warring nations but to bring an end to war altogether. As British diplomat Harold Nicolson wrote in his *Reminiscences*: "We were journeying to Paris not merely to liquidate the war, but to found a new order in Europe. We were preparing not Peace only, but Eternal Peace. There was about us the halo of some divine mission. We must be alert, stern, righteous and ascetic. For we were bent on doing great, permanent and noble things" (Nicolson 1933, cited in MacMillan 2000: 95). Given the huge difficulties in securing any kind of agreement, the Versailles Treaty was not in fact as punitive as either the Germans themselves or Keynes felt at the time, nor as historical judgement has maintained. According to Margaret MacMillan:

> When historians look, as they have increasingly been doing, at other details, the picture of a Germany crushed by a vindictive peace cannot be sustained. Germany did lose territory; that was an inevitable consequence of losing the war. . . . Even with its losses Germany remained the largest country in Europe west of the Soviet Union between the wars. Its strategic position was significantly better than it had been before 1914.
> —2001: 492

The League of Nations was the cornerstone of the Paris peace negotiations. Although it was not a new idea, the US president Woodrow Wilson was its particular champion at the talks and he steered the discussions in the direction of his own vision. Historical emphasis has been largely on the failure of the League to prevent conflict, notably and most spectacularly World War II (1939–45), or to prevent the build-up of arms during the interwar period, but however imperfect, the League is significant in reflecting changed attitudes to warfare and even a move toward a culture of peace. The aims of the League expressed an understanding that the prevention of war would not be possible without concern for social justice, the recognition of the rights of small nations, and the attempt to limit colonial power through the mandate system. It had a number of associated autonomous bodies, including the Permanent Court of International Justice, and the International Labour Organization, which is still active today, as well as special commissions on such subjects as refugees, slavery, and health, which recognized that these were major international concerns that could not be tackled by individual states. Antony Adolf concludes that "[t]he League's *multipronged approach to world peace* arguably made it actualisable for the first time and is its greatest legacy" (2009: 190).

The League of Nations also enjoyed huge public support by many who saw it as the best hope for bringing the world back from the brink of destruction, and it was welcomed as an expression of a desire for creation of a sustainable peace conceived of as going far beyond the absence or avoidance of war. Peace organizations were critical of many aspects of the League, but yet were able to use it as an opportunity to press for disarmament, social justice, humanitarian intervention, class, race, and gender equality, and a legal framework that supported the rights of nations and individuals.

As we have seen, in 1920 there were powerful forces that stood in the way of social progress and were ideologically opposed to all those factors that were conducive to building a sustainable peace, whether within or between nation states. This was reflected in the nature of the peace treaties, widely perceived as uniquely punitive, self-seeking, and

FIGURE 0.10: US President Woodrow Wilson presenting the dove of peace with an olive branch. Credit: Photo 12/Getty Images.

incompatible with a lasting and sustainable peace. As MacMillan has pointed out, there were many and recent precedents for this kind of treaty (2002: 196), which serves to show that the treaties were backward- rather than forward-looking and thus unable to break through the cycle of bitterness and the spirit of *revanche* that made future wars more likely at international level. Nor did the post-war unrest, inequality, and poverty that characterized defeated nations in particular encourage the stability that would be a sound basis for peace (see Sharp *et al.*: 2017).

CONCLUSION

Yet, despite the dominant discourse that saw war as inevitable and continued to link masculine strength and virility with warfare and military prowess, the wars of the nineteenth and early twentieth centuries were undertaken in the greatest atmosphere of anti-war feeling, public awareness, and accountability in the history of warfare. Colonial and imperial wars apart, the conduct of war was subject to greater scrutiny and control, and rules concerning the treatment of combatants and non-combatants, enemy aliens, prisoners, and wounded soldiers were governed by agreed international standards of humanity, at least in theory. Despite rigid censorship and a nationalistic press, protests against World War I continued throughout the conflict, especially in Britain following the introduction of conscription in 1916, in the French army during the army "mutiny" of 1917, and through the strikes and bread riots that characterized life on the home fronts of Russia and central Europe. The Russian Revolution of 1917, with its promises of bread, peace and land, found adherents and gave hope to war-weary populations in belligerent nations. The revolutions that ended the war in Germany, Austria, Hungary, and elsewhere toppled rulers and dismantled the huge nineteenth-century empires, allowing newly independent nations and republics to emerge. Suffrage was extended to wider social groups, including women, with fewer restrictions in terms of wealth, age, status and property, and in post-revolutionary nations electorates could vote for representation by delegates of both genders and from a wider range of social backgrounds. The aftermath of World War I brought about a fundamental change in attitudes to warfare and led to the rise of mass national and international peace movements, as well as international structures intended to regulate international affairs as a way of preserving peace. While in 1815, peace had been an ideal largely confined to minority religious groups or the intellectual elite, and the preservation of peace between nations had been restricted to high levels of state politics, by 1920 the prevention of war had gathered support, especially in the latter half of the nineteenth century, as an ethical and political, and, above all, a rational and pragmatic concern of all humanity. The rise in international thinking in socialist and feminist movements as well as intellectual exchange and the popular spread of cultures of peace through literary works had led to a shared vision of peace that was rooted in social movements at a grass roots level. The year 1920 reflects a point at which the discourses of peace were in the ascendance at state level, expressed through the covenant of the League of Nations, and also enjoyed huge popular support in nations affected by World War I.

Thus we see a shift in the idea of peace from 1815 to 1920—it had become less religious and more popular and we observe the emergence of a rights-based discourse. Social movements committed to overcoming national and racial as well as class and gender differences had emerged and strengthened from the mid-to-late nineteenth century onwards, and economic arguments stressed the folly of destroying mutually beneficial trade links through conflict, which were further reinforced by the lessons of World War I. As discussed by Stella Ghervas in Chapter 1 of this volume, the understanding of what constituted peace had also moved on from the Congress of Vienna's limited definition of peace as an absence of war between European Great Powers. By 1920, a great deal of discussion, thought and consideration had been given to the question, and there were significant groups and movements dedicated to creating a sustainable peace for the future. The League of Nations, despite its flaws, symbolized internationalists' hopes for a new world order based on understanding and cooperation that later provided the foundations of the United Nations. Present-day definitions of cultures of peace look beyond international relations and at structures of violence and inequality within society, with education and culture playing a major role in social attitudes (see Boulding 2000). Literary and other cultural representations such as the visual arts play an important role in influencing the spread of ideas and allowing psychological and scientific insights to reach a mass population. This is especially clear in the two cases explored in this volume: the novels and essays of von Suttner and Tolstoy. Both authors were highly influential in promulgating ideas of peace and anti-war thinking, mobilizing emotions as well as reason in opposition to war. Despite the uneven developments, many reversals, and the destructive effects of violence and repression, the idea of peace as more than simply the absence of war, the commitment to human rights, to greater equality between races, classes, and genders gathered support throughout the nineteenth and into the twentieth century, and the moral, secular, and even pragmatic commitment to cultures of peace within and between nation states had become firmly entrenched by 1920, remaining remarkably resilient in the face of the internal and external forces that sought to destroy them.

CHAPTER ONE

Definitions of Peace

STELLA GHERVAS[1]

Peace! That is the cry of the earth tired of bloodshed,
Peace, the wish of reason and humanity.
All honest souls should yearn for it in France.
And all enlightened minds in Europe.

—Germaine de Staël, *Réflexions sur la paix*, 1795[2]

INTRODUCTION

Peace has been more than an elusive ideal. It has been, first and foremost, a word with many meanings, liable to evolve according to circumstances, especially after large political upheavals. It is common wisdom that political concepts and events influence each other, yet few centuries exemplified this fact more than the "Age of Empire" covered in this book (1815–1920), which opened with the downfall of the Napoleonic Empire and closed with that of the Central Empires (German, Austro-Hungarian, and Ottoman). The preceding "Age of Enlightenment" had been a time of reflection on peace, particularly with the observation of the effects of the balance of power introduced with the Peace of Utrecht in 1713, which, it was hoped, would reduce the risk of wars in Europe (see Ghervas and Armitage 2020).

In response to the recurring conflicts of the century, a philosophical school imagining "perpetual peace" had grown wary of the eternal opposition of two military alliances and had started speculating about a continental order that would be based on closer institutionalized cooperation. Eminent representatives of this tendency were the French Abbé de Saint-Pierre, who wrote a "Plan of perpetual peace" (1713), followed by Jean-Jacques Rousseau (1761) and Immanuel Kant (1795).

Under the great pressures of new times, the definition and geographic scope of the idea of peace evolved markedly. The first years of the period covered in this volume played the greatest role in this process, as the Congress of Vienna and other treaties of 1814–15 laid a permanent foundation for a new European order on which all later intellectual constructions would rest. The French Revolutionary wars and the spectacular successes of Emperor Napoleon I dealt a definitive blow to the belief that the balance of power could be the specific remedy against imperial tyranny and continental wars, since it had failed to prevent both; indeed, the French Empire had completely jammed the balance of power in its favor, reducing most of the states in continental Europe to subjection.

The triumphant French Empire generated two contrasting views. The first legitimized it as the prolonging of the ideals of the French Revolution and fostering a mystical bond among peoples that previously did not share the same languages and traditions. The Continental System of Napoleon was to be a *Pax Napoleonica*, the modern equivalent of the Roman peace (*pax Romana*) of ancient times, under a benevolent Emperor and the eagles of the French army. The opposing view saw it as a principle of chaos, the negation of the humane values of European civilization; it depicted Napoleon as the "Antichrist" and the struggles against him as "apocalyptic." Progressively, the greater part of European elites agreed that the French Empire should be denounced, and that its downfall would finally bring about a return to peace. This is why the Prussian King Frederick William III, the Russian Tsar Alexander I, and the Austrian Emperor François I were depicted as the "protectors of peace," surrounded by a mystical aura. In this vein, Benjamin Constant in *L'esprit de conquête* opined that "a government that sought today to incite a European people to war and conquests would commit a pernicious anachronism" (1814: 11). Europe, he stated, was a "mass of men with different names and different modes of social organization, but homogeneous by nature" (1814: 6). As such as it was "sufficiently civilized for war to be a burden to it": "its uniform inclination goes toward peace" (1814: 6).

Because it was now widely accepted, even in Paris, that the French Revolution and the Napoleonic order were the foil, the anti-type for the stable disposition of Europe, and the political *acquis* of the eighteenth century was no longer considered sufficient, a question logically followed: What should such a *peace* be? What would be its rationale and its tenets? There existed a vast range of opinions, from the most conservative, favorable to a return to the absolute monarchies of the Ancient Regime, via constitutional monarchism that favored a modicum of political representation, to even republicanism. The individuals at the helm of the foreign policy of the great powers—all absolute monarchs or their directly appointed ministers, except in Britain—realized that something more was required. As much as the eighteenth century had been an age of speculation, the post-Napoleonic one would be one of experimentation and counter-experimentation. In contrast with the estrangement from worldly business that had been the lot of philosophers of the eighteenth century, those who would now think and write would be, more often than not, the very actors in the momentous political events of their time.

To illustrate the momentous shift from the previous era, suffice it to note the expansion of definitions of *peace* in the sixth edition of the French dictionary of the *Académie française* (1835) compared to the fifth edition (1798), where the main—and political—definition long used for peace had been "the state of a people that is not in war."[3] In a more specialized sense, it had been—at least in French and English—"a treaty of peace." Three decades into the nineteenth century, the revised definition included a "state of tranquility of a State, a people, a kingdom that has no enemies to fight."[4] Peace, hence, was no longer the mere absence of war: the word emancipated itself and acquired a status of its own, as a desirable condition to achieve and maintain thereafter, which required the resolution of pending issues with neighbors. In this process, political peace made a semantic return voyage to the original Latin acceptation of *pax* as "tranquility."

It also rejoined a pre-existing (non-political) definition: the "concord and tranquility that exists in families, in communities." This evolution is not fortuitous, but rather an index of the transition from the dominant "modern" conceptions of the eighteenth century toward a remarkable revival of Christian traditions that transcended the established Churches. As we shall see, this goes a long way to explain the departure from the type of peace that the Treaty of Utrecht had inaugurated. The new conceptions of peace would have to rest on a common philosophical foundation, a sort of "lowest common denominator" that would equally satisfy British parliamentarians and supporters of Russian autocracy. From that crucible of diverse opinions was thus born a set of "doctrines" of peace that rested on a monarchical *status quo ante*, but allowed several political regimes to coexist in Europe. Even the revolutionaries of 1848 accepted the necessity of the post-Napoleonic order: their dispute was with the absence of constitutions and parliaments from it. Rather than seeking a single definition of peace in Europe produced in that crucial moment, we should thus rather embrace a range of definitions, as did contemporaries.

PEACE IN THE POST-NAPOLEONIC ERA (1814–53)

Peace as Commissions and Institutions

The diplomatic negotiations during the time of the Congress of Vienna (1814–15) were the crucible for a new forward-looking conception of the order of Europe, and therefore a redefinition of the political conception of peace. As one historian aptly puts it: "At the prior peace conferences, the major order of business had been to agree on the conditions to end war and restore peace. Whereas this implied discussions on the future order of Europe, the major interest was to settle the claims which lay at the origins of the war and the focus was thus largely backwards-looking."[5] This was about to change: the great powers, without denying the virtues of the balance of power (France's ability to cause havoc had been already been reduced by returning it to its *ante-bellum* borders of 1792 and surrounding it with buffer states), recognized the necessity of a new form of cooperation among themselves that had no equivalent in the past. The Final Act of the Congress of Vienna of June 9, 1815 introduced a number of commissions and institutions that later generations learned to consider obvious attributes of "activities in time of peace." A significant step was the foundation of, as well as the essential institutional arrangements and international recognition for, two leagues of states located in the middle of Europe: the German Confederation[6] and the Helvetic Confederation, i.e. Switzerland.[7] Another outcome was the birth of "technical commissions" (at least fifteen working groups were responsible for different issues related to the Congress), which were distinct from and complemented the ordinary work of diplomats; they were tasked with resolving the details of larger matters and setting up a *modus operandi* for the future (see Mayr 1939). A case in point was the Commission on navigation on the Rhine, which obviously involved the riparian states, but later extended to other neighboring ones. The idea that permanent cooperation should exist not only among diplomats of different countries, but also among their public officers, was rather novel.

Another key feature of the post-Napoleonic peace system was the institution, after the Final Act of the Congress of Vienna, of a set of conferences that took place almost every year and came to be known as the *Congress System* (see Jarrett 2013). This was the result of a stipulation of the Quadruple Alliance signed in Paris on November 20, 1815 (art. VI):

> the High Contracting Parties have agreed to renew their meetings at fixed periods, either under the immediate auspices of the Sovereigns themselves, or by their respective ministers, for the purpose of consulting upon their common interests, and for the consideration of the measures which at each of those periods shall be considered the most salutary for the repose and prosperity of Nations, and for the maintenance of the Peace of Europe.

FIGURE 1.1: Participants at the Congress of Vienna in 1814–15, Vienna, by Jean-Baptiste Isabey. Credit: DeAgostini/Getty Images.

In French, the word *maintien* was defined as "to keep in the same state, in a state of permanent stability."[8] In the new spirit of the time, peace was not only an agreement to be concluded at the end of war: its essence had to be preserved as a *status quo ante*. It was a process that had to be discussed and regularly acted upon, at various levels.

Another, apparently anomalous, element was the Treaty of the Holy Alliance, signed two months earlier on the initiative of Russian Tsar Alexander I.[9] Beyond its religious overtones, it squarely placed the metaphor of a peacefully united family in the political sphere. The Holy Alliance considered the three signatory monarchs (the Emperor of Russia, the King of Prussia, and the Emperor of Austria) as united "by true and indissoluble fraternity" and committed to protect "Religion, Peace and Justice." It also claimed that they were "members of a single Christian nation." The convergence of the definition of political peace with that of Christian peace became a distinctive feature of the long nineteenth century, and a departure from the framework of the preceding hundred years (1713–1815). Although the new form of peace was Christian, it was not remotely connected with the former mystique of the alliance between the Holy Roman Emperor and the Catholic Pope of Rome. In the first place, the Holy Roman Empire was already defunct. Second, the Holy Alliance was perceived as a stab in the back for devout Catholics who hoped for a return to the traditional German order, since it put the three major Christian branches on an equal footing. In so doing, it ousted the pope as arbiter of political matters in Europe while leaving aside the question of what would become of the Muslim Ottoman Empire (see Pirenne 1946–49; Ghervas 2015b).

The Peaces of Westphalia (1648) and Utrecht (1713) had expressed tolerance for Protestants, and they were an admission of a new political reality. Yet the idea had never been expressed that a "system of peace" could be anything but a Catholic institution

FIGURE 1.2: The Triumph of the Tsar or Peace, by Louis Léopold Boilly, 1814. Credit: Musée de l'armée/Active Museum/Alamy Stock Photo.

under the aegis of the pope. The Holy Alliance, by relating the monarchs directly to God without the intermediation of the Church of Rome, was such a statement. In that sense, it was wholly secular (see Ghervas 2014a).

While the faith of Alexander I is beyond doubt, the attribution of these elevated ideas to the Scriptures may have been somewhat of a façade, since the text of the Holy Alliance was imbued with two products of the Enlightenment: the political philosophy of the age of Enlightenment, notably the plans of perpetual peace (see Ghervas 2014b and 2020), blended with a spiritual conception called *Illuminism* that sought to reconcile reason and imagination, which had developed at the turn of the eighteenth century outside of traditional Churches (see Jacques-Chaquin 2001; Ghervas 2008: 233–96). That treaty, ostensibly written with a traditional religious phraseology, aimed in reality at establishing an innovative *status quo ante* for preserving peace in Europe. It sought to prevent a repetition of the populist excesses of the French Revolution, while implicitly admitting liberal regimes—since constitutional monarchies and republics were invited to subscribe to it. Though formulated as a mere letter of intent, the Holy Alliance was quite possibly a conscious attempt at establishing an organized political order in Europe based on multilateral cooperation (Ghervas 2014a: 72–5). Hence its purpose may well have been to assert some politically advanced ideas under the guise of traditional beliefs still held by a sizeable part of the population.

Europe was committed to a true "collective contract of general peace," as the French historian Albert Sorel put it, and principles to which most countries adhered, more or less sincerely (1904: 501). I have written elsewhere that the balance of power was replaced by a balance of diplomacy: between the Quadruple Alliance and the Holy Alliance, the new peacetime order that emerged in Europe in 1815 was an active coalition of four Great Powers, which would soon be joined, at the Congress of Aix-la-Chapelle in 1818, by a monarchical France. It should at once be added that the "Congress System" never had the supra-state character of Saint-Pierre's plan of perpetual peace, nor did it establish a formal court of arbitration (Sédouy 2009: 49–68). Tsar Alexander I, although tsar of the autocratic Russian empire, was hailed as a "defender of peace," and even praised by American Quakers (Ghervas 2008: 259).[10]

Peace as Law and Order

The difference between the peacetime order of 1815 and those that had preceded it was not lost on contemporaries. Friedrich von Gentz noted in 1818 that it was "a phenomenon without precedent in the world's history. In place of the principle of equilibrium, or more accurately of counterweights formed by separate alliances ... there has succeeded a principle of general union, uniting all the states collectively with a federal bond, under the guidance of five principal Powers." While he recognized that it had its inconveniences, "it would be ... the best possible combination to assure the prosperity of the peoples, and the maintenance of the peace." He also considered that the question of its duration was the "only important question of our times," on which rested "the peace, the destinies and the future existence of the peoples of Europe" (Gentz [1818] 1876: 354–7).

Unfortunately, the continental Great Powers increasingly confused the peaceful *liberal* voices in Europe, favorable to constitutional monarchy and freedom of the press, with the violent, *revolutionary* ones (the "Jacobins"). Both were considered as equal threats to the peace of Vienna, to be targeted by police repression. This shift was helped by a semantic coincidence. Peace had a further political meaning applied to domestic affairs, which today might be considered somewhat obsolete: according to the early nineteenth-century American lexicographer Noah Webster, it meant also "public tranquillity, that quiet, order and security which is guaranteed by the laws" (see Ghervas 2019: 109).[11] In the French language used for diplomacy, there were actually two words for that notion of security: the first was *sûreté* which was the fact of being removed from harm, as well as objective measures taken by the forces of law and order in that direction; the second, *sécurité*, was subjective and indicated the inner confidence of being safe from harm, which could be either justified or unjustified (*Dictionnaire de l'Académie française*, 1798). The first word came to be progressively replaced by the second over the course of the nineteenth century—not without frowns from the defenders of lexical purity. This distinction had the merit of highlighting two essentially distinct dimensions of the concept of security, objective and subjective, that are often confused in modern discourse: this may contribute to explain why "security" is still charged with ideological connotations. In any case, all those dimensions were wrapped, at the time of the Congress of Vienna, into a single word: *peace*, which could range from the private to the public and also include peace of mind. Tragically the Reaction—with its semantic fixation on "keeping the peace" against the "revolutionary menace"—was a self-fulfilling prophecy, since it left no choice to liberals but to follow the path of insurrection.

"Keeping the peace" soon became interpreted as sending armies to put down revolutions all over Europe. To make things worse, the monarchs even borrowed each other's armies to put down rebellions (ironically, the Abbé de Saint-Pierre had given that very advice to monarchs in his peace plan). At the Congress of Troppau (1820), the Vienna order had completed its transformation into a *directorial system*: that is, a syndicate of monarchs supporting each other against political troublemakers, be they parliaments, rebels, or even a legitimate king who had granted a constitution. The liberal-minded Count Czartoryski, former minister of the tsar, who found himself in 1831 on the wrong side of a Polish uprising against Russia, lamented that while perpetual peace had become the conception of the most powerful monarchs on the continent, diplomacy had corrupted it and turned it into venom (Czartoryski 1830: 276–7; see also Ghervas 2015a). There could indeed be a dark side to definitions of peace.

"PEACE" IN THE WORLD: FROM COLONIES TO THE RISE OF EXTRA-EUROPEAN POWERS

Peace as a Monopoly of "Civilized Christians"?

It was also a time when the notion of "peace in freedom" became largely the preserve of European powers and the United States of America, and more specifically of white people (see Brower 2009: 4–26; Tirefort 2016). In his book *De la réorganisation de la société européenne* (1814), the French economist Comte de Saint-Simon and his disciple Augustin Thierry formulated a design of a European parliamentary system inspired by the Enlightenment and maintaining the "national independence of each country," which placed their vision firmly in the tradition of the Plans of Perpetual Peace. It coincided somewhat with the later versions of the eighteenth century, in that it promoted a representative form of government—though not a democratic one. In any case, it rejected the post-Napoleonic system that the Great Powers were about to establish in Europe, which amply represented their own interests and not necessarily of those of other states or of their own subjects.

Saint-Simon's works marked a departure from the prudent positions of the Enlightenment thinkers and the French Revolution about colonization, heralding the new "age of empires." One of his aims was "to people the globe with the European race, which is superior to all the races of men; to make it [as] travelable and habitable as Europe, there is an endeavour through which the European parliament will have continually to exert the activity of Europe and always keep it alert" (Saint-Simon and Thierry [1814] 1966: vol. I: 204). He considered that, Europe being the space of civilization, the inequality of the "races" or "varieties of man" was self-evident: "During the Revolution, the Heads of state (. . .) established that the Blacks were the equals of the Europeans: this principle was necessarily bad since it is based on a fact the wrongness of which is evidenced by observations" (Saint-Simon [1807] 1966: 129; Piguet 1993: 7–24). Though this idea should not be confused with the eugenic theories of the late nineteenth century, it was nevertheless a mix between a faith in the superiority of the Christian culture, the naturalism of Comte de Buffon, and the theory of climates, as well as an urge to find a rational justification for the disproportionate role of Europeans in the destinies of the world. Alas, one conclusion was implicit: the new system of peace would include non-Europeans but it would not represent them.

Saint-Simon exemplifies a nineteenth-century view that political conceptions or legal systems not derived from a European matrix should be ignored or considered subordinate to colonial rule. It would take a long time before the academic world itself woke up from this axiomatic Eurocentrism; there have been recent efforts to repair at least part of that bias.[12]

Geographical Extension of the Definitions of Peace

Concomitant to this "de-universalization" of the civic rights ideals of the French Revolution, the second decade of the nineteenth century was also a moment when the European definition of *peace* could not help but be extended geographically, in the direction of other continents. The Napoleonic wars also had broad implications for the New World, where the implosion of Spain after the Napoleonic invasion presented an opportunity for liberation to the white colonial elites who were chafing to emancipate themselves from metropolitan rule. Yet the mission of establishing "universal peace" was considered a monopoly for states located in Europe, or at least those established according to the same principles.[13]

This European aloofness was, in fact, a new and transient phenomenon. Since the Middle Ages, the European powers had cultivated by necessity a tradition of diplomatic relations with other powers on their fringes, as well as in the Indian Ocean (where the East India trade had contributed fundamentally to the development of the law of nations) (see Alexandrowicz 1967: 83–96; 2017). Despite ideological intransigence on both sides, diplomatic activity had been particularly intense with the Ottoman Empire, since the European kingdoms around the Mediterranean and in south-eastern Europe had frequently found themselves in a situation of military inferiority, preferring appeasement to confrontation in spite of ideological intransigence (Pitts 2018: 28–67). Furthermore, commercial treaties were necessary so that they could benefit from the lucrative markets of the eastern Mediterranean. From the pivotal moment at the end of the seventeenth century when a large European alliance had managed to turn the tables, the balance of military power had progressively shifted to the detriment of the Ottoman Empire. By the time of the Congress of Vienna, it had become a secondary power: still significant in the grand scheme of things, but no longer any match for the European great powers. As a result, the most pressing issue was no longer an alliance against the Turkish menace. Instead Russia, Britain, Austria, and France competed for acquiring the spoils of the Ottoman Empire, while jealously preventing each other from doing the same. In the course of the nineteenth century, the disproportionate increase in the military capabilities of the Europeans led to a revolution in the practices of peace: matters were first discussed between chanceries (as with the London Protocol of 1828 about the creation of a Greek state), before a treaty was imposed on a non-European power.

In truth, this trend was not a complete novelty. Since the Great Discoveries of the fifteenth and sixteenth centuries, European powers had generally given short shrift to the political legitimacy of peoples without a properly established state, or to states that were in no position to oppose colonization:[14] for example, no American Indians were invited to the Treaty of Paris of 1763 that concluded the Seven Years' War, though they were an interested party. By contrast, the Great Powers of that time had also deigned to treat a few non-European states, notably the Ottoman Empire and Indian kingdoms, with respect and even deference (Pitts 2018: 1–15). The nineteenth century was, however, a period when European dominance established itself over the world with such disproportionate force that, by its end, the quasi-totality of the planet, except for a handful of states, was in the hands of Europeans or of successor states of the European colonial powers. In Africa, the last pre-colonial sovereign state was Abyssinia (merely because it had defeated an Italian army) (see Jonas 2015), while in Asia the political sovereignty of Japan was grudgingly tolerated and that of China violated on a regular basis (see Cassel 2012). The Age of Empire is thus also defined by the fact that the prerogative of peace and war became the exclusive monopoly of states that subscribed to European legal tradition. In the emerging theory of international law, the pre-existing notion that only European states have legitimate existence, by virtue of their Christian civilization and institutions, evolved from an ideological fiction into a *fait accompli* by force of arms: as the British poet Hilaire Belloc aptly put it in 1898: "Whatever happens, we have got / The Maxim Gun, and they have not" (Belloc 1898). Most European lawyers started agreeing that since states or populations outside of Europe (notably natives of America and Australia) did not meet the European institutional standards now considered as "universal," they could not be sovereign and in a position to enforce their rights (Koskenniemi 2009: 11–97). This came to the point of erasing the contribution of non-European actors to the evolution of the *ius gentium*, and thus to peace. Sadly, there was little incentive during the Age of Empire for colonial powers to develop peace through law with non-European peoples, since military victory could be obtained quickly, at a low cost, and without risk.

Peace as a Regulatory Instrument of Colonial Societies

It follows that *peace*, in a colonial context, referred to the establishment of a European system that performed two functions: governing the settlers and regulating the pre-existing societies as distinct from the settlers. The "civilizing mission" rested on a domestic

FIGURE 1.3: France bringing peace and prosperity, November 1911. Credit: Pictorial Press Ltd/Alamy Stock Photo.

definition of peace. Military operations in a colonial context were not legally considered as wars, because they occurred in a territory over which the colonial power claimed to have legitimate sovereignty in the first place. They were considered more in the nature of police operations against rebels, not unlike those performed in Europe against revolutionaries. The word *pacification* became commonly used to describe the military operations against natives resisting invasion, one of the first examples being the campaign in Algeria after the French annexation of 1830.

Paradoxically, it was the accession of the United States of America to independence that re-launched the debate around the rights of native populations. The US Supreme Court (*Johnson v. McIntosh*, 1823) ruled on the rights of Amerindian populations to landed property.[15] *Discovery* was understood as "the original foundation of titles to land on the American continent as between the different European nations by whom conquests and settlements were made here," *recognition* "in the wars, negotiations, and treaties between the different European powers," and *adoption* by the USA. "This principle was that discovery gave title to the government by whose subjects or by whose authority it was made against all other European governments, which title might be consummated by possession." Furthermore, the original inhabitants

> were admitted to be the rightful occupants of the soil, with a legal as well as just claim to retain possession of it, and to use it according to their own discretion; but their rights to complete sovereignty as independent nations were necessarily diminished, and their power to dispose of the soil at their own will to whomsoever they pleased was denied by the original fundamental principle that discovery gave exclusive title to those who made it.[16]

While the Supreme Court wrote, with barely disguised irony, that such claims were "pompous" and an "apology," it nevertheless ruled that under the current legal system, Indians could only *occupy* (not own) the land and were not free to dispose of it as they wished. In other words, they did not enjoy the same rights as the European settlers in the country.

US President James Monroe, when expressing his doctrine of foreign policy before the US Congress in 1823, argued that the allied European powers could not "extend their system to any portion of either continent without endangering our peace and happiness." "Nor can anyone believe,"—he added—"that our southern brethren, if left to themselves, would adopt it of their own accord."[17] This ideological justification of US interventionism in South America certainly expressed an ambition to oust Spain and Portugal as the colonial powers in Latin America; it was also the death toll for Simon Bolivar's own dream of unity and independence, inspired by the European revolutions, within a "greater Colombia"(Lynch 1983: 5–10). As far as Britain was concerned, and according to Benjamin Disraeli, the attribution in 1876 of the title "Empress of India" to Queen Victoria was in reference to the Antonine dynasty which featured (beside Hadrian and Marcus Aurelius) the Emperor Trajan, arguably one of the greatest conquerors of Roman history.[18] It appears that the time-honored European custom of mentioning the benefits of peace and prosperity in such solemn occasions did not apply there—and indeed the Queen's proclamation, a catalogue of formal measures, makes no mention whatsoever of the peoples of India. In the last twenty years of the century, with the ongoing (but amicable) scramble between France and Britain for the expansion of their colonial possessions, colonization was increasingly glorified as bringing peace and prosperity to "savage" nations (see Pakenham 1990).

Pacification as a Military Intervention

A fact nevertheless remains: *pacification*, i.e. establishing *peace* in colonial lands, was understood to require military force. For a sizable part of European public opinion, there was no conflict in terms between colonial peace and colonial war, since both were a consequence of the duty of civilization: the war of "pacification" was a temporary ill, hopefully the last one ever needed before peace could prevail together with "civilization." It is another instance of the "tragic pun": the almost imperceptible modification of peace as a state of tranquility into an apology for military interventions by the great (European) powers to impose unilaterally their own model of societal order. In spite of the reluctance and even scathing criticism of a few dissenting thinkers and political men, the division of humanity into two orders (civilized and non-civilized) was both morally and legally part of the definition of peace in the Age of Empires: its full benefits were thus reserved for the first to the detriment of the second. Historians of peace have little choice but to acknowledge, in that arbitrary segregation of part of humanity and the justification of colonial imperialism as the "peaceful violence of civilization,"[19] a serious logical flaw in what otherwise could have been a coherent set of definitions of peace.

It is ironic that wars against non-Europeans were waged, all the way through the nineteenth century, in a spirit of "civilized" competition among Europeans and the USA, firmly under the umbrella of renunciation of war among themselves. With few exceptions (notably the Spanish–American war of 1898), the colonial powers carefully avoided wars for colonial motives, thus breaking with the practices of the eighteenth century; at the same time they reserved to themselves an unfettered right to wage wars against African and Asian peoples. To candid eyes, it might appear as if the European drive for peace had served as an alliance between colonial powers for partitioning the world. This was true especially in 1899 when a coalition of European powers, the US, and Russia intervened in China, essentially displacing the legally established government, while Russia achieved the conquest of Manchuria. Beyond this Eurocentrism was the difficulty of coherently translating a set of definitions of peace elaborated in a few European idioms into a global spectrum of political contexts, cultures, and languages. This argument of normative "universalization" rested on a contradiction: if its values were truly universal, why were such "police operations" needed to enforce them? While national historiographies have long hesitated before tackling this and several other paradoxes, modern trends of global (and even planetary) history have started shedding a cruel light on the tragic repercussions of this thinking, particularly in the decades leading to World War I (Hippler and Vec 2015: 3–16).

The exertions deployed by mainstream scholars and politicians in the late nineteenth century to use civilizing values such as peace as the foundation of a nation-centric narrative of colonial conquest comes across, in our modern international system informed by the Universal Declaration of Human Rights (1948), as an insidiously schizophrenic act of *doublethink*. Credited for having founded the national education system of republican France, Jules Ferry has also become, with his passionate repudiation of the birthright of all men to legal equality (a cornerstone of the French Revolution)[20] in order to justify a war of conquest and generally the merits of colonial imperialism, a paradigm of the moral and intellectual aporia of "colonial peace." As Ferry had imprudently evidenced, eugenics, and genetic determinism, had become in the 1880s an academic discipline also used to support imperialism, whether in Europe or on other continents (see Levine 2010).

The first years of the twentieth century are, furthermore, a turning point where the dogma of European superiority began to meet its first practical rebuttals: Japan rose to prominence by soundly defeating Russia both at sea (with the destruction of its fleet) and on land in the Far East. The Treaty of Portsmouth (September 5, 1905),[21] brokered by US President Theodore Roosevelt, opened with these words: "The Emperor of Japan on the one part, and the Emperor of all the Russias, on the other part, animated by a desire to restore the blessings of peace ..." The European legalities of peace were being observed, but their implication was reversed: they underscored the precedence of an Asian emperor over a Russian tsar. It is ironic that this reversal of values was achieved with the roar of artillery instead of the peaceful voice of reason. In Russia (a multiethnic empire) the defeat rippled back and the tsarist government, already embattled with its internal problems, faced sedition from within its army and naval forces. Sun Yat-sen, founder of the modern Chinese state, retrospectively wrote in 1941:

> We regarded that Russian defeat by Japan as the defeat of the West by the East. We regarded the Japanese victory as our own victory. . . . What will be the consequences of this driving force still remains to be seen. The present tide of events seems to indicate that not only China and Japan but all the peoples in East Asia will unite together to restore the former status of Asia.
>
> —Sun 1941: 144

Alas, the victories of Japan were no signal of peace for the peoples of Asia, but the revelation that another imperial power had joined the colonial fray.

PEACE THROUGH LAW

Peace as the Law of God

In Europe itself, peace also had to be reinvented against empires. It is a fact frequently glossed over that the young generations that participated in the revolutions of 1848, even though inspired by the Enlightenment, were fervent Christians for the most part. The leaders of peace movements were composed (as the French poet Victor Hugo put it at the opening of the Paris Peace Congress of 1849) of "publicists, philosophers, Christian religious ministers, distinguished writers, several of these great men, these public and popular men who are luminaries of their nation." Their source of inspiration was largely religious: "Sirs," proclaimed Hugo, "this religious thought, universal peace, all nations connected by common a link, the Gospel as supreme law, mediations substituted for war, is that religious thought a practical thought? [. . .] But the law of God is not war, but peace," he stated (Hugo 1851: 17).

In the long nineteenth century (and in stark contrast with the previous ones), Europeans conceived political peace once more as a divine legacy. By 1848, however, it was no longer to be bestowed on humanity through the mediation of anointed kings: among the proponents of the idea that peace had to rest on popular foundations was Giuseppe Mazzini (1805–72), an Italian patriot and a republican, but also founder of the movement *Giovine Europa* (Young Europe).[22] Even while profoundly Christian, he reconnected with the secular stance of Rousseau and Kant that "the people themselves ought to erect the specific institutional structure that will allow future generations to benefit from peace and development for many centuries to come" (Mazzini [1849] 2009: 124). Yet this

FIGURE 1.4: Assembly of Congres de la Paix with Victor Hugo (1802–85) presiding over it, Saint-Cecile Hall, August 21, 1849, Paris. Illustration from the magazine *L'Illustration, Journal Universel*, vol. 14, no. 340, September 1, 1849. Credit: DEA/BIBLIOTECA AMBROSIANA/Getty Images.

foundation took on an extended meaning: "The 'people' to which we so frequently refer is not just an empty concept, but rather the expression of a philosophical and religious idea; it is the *sacred word* of the future" (Mazzini [1849] 2009: 124). He sought a "Holy Alliance of the peoples," a brotherhood of the peoples that would replace that of the kings signed in 1815. Later, in 1901, the French lawyer and peace activist Émile Arnaud (president of the International and Permanent League of Peace) coined the word *pacifism*; its meaning was initially vague, ranging from absolute repudiation of violence to reformism, especially in the direction of peace through international law. Peace congresses, largely inspired by Christian ecumenical principles, became a staple of the second half of the nineteenth century, as well as of the years that preceded World War I. The last Peace Congress took place in Constance, Switzerland, on August 1, 1914. It led to the creation of a "World Alliance for International Friendship Through the Churches," as an "international organization formed to help Christian churches promote peace, disarmament, rights of racial and religious minorities, conscientious objection and arms control."[23] While the membership of this movement did not reflect the world's religious diversity, it still marked a departure from the imperious Eurocentrism that had led the great powers to preclude the greater part of humanity from the benefits of peace. Moreover, it firmly established the connection between universal human rights and world peace.

PEACE AS A LEGAL PROCESS

On a somewhat parallel course, the definition of *peace* as a legal process, i.e., *peace through law*, also grew to prominence in the second half of the nineteenth century.

Though it complements the tradition of perpetual peace promoted by philosophers of the Enlightenment, it distinguishes itself by its distinct cultural origin: as the brainchild of Anglo-American non-conformist Protestant circles (particularly the Quakers) (see Brock 1968: 217–72; Ceadel 1996: 145–51) that then became the creature of lawyers. Its main ideological distinction was that it did not aim at federating states, but merely at regulating their relations through agreements and judicial procedures. During our period, the threads of the peace movements (especially those of a religious inspiration) and those of peace through law ran alongside and often crossed each other.

It should be immediately clarified that the new device of *arbitration*, which developed in the last three decades of the nineteenth century, was different from the earlier system of resolving disputes called *mediation*. The latter, which also required the intervention of a third party (typically a state neutral in the matter), had been practiced for centuries. In particular, the activity whereby neutral diplomats would go back and forth between states in disagreement to convince them to start a negotiation was typically referred to as *good offices*. Mediation did not, however, require commitment from the parties to see the process through and they could withdraw from it at any moment. As such, it was merely an attempt to avert the recourse to war as the "procedure" to resolve the dispute. Two states resorting to such a solution instead of fighting were still technically at peace, yet very near to war. Arbitration was a step further, as both parties committed to defer the adjudication of the matter to a third party, thus obliging themselves not to take recourse to force. It also met a practical need: to enforce arbitration between two states that, as a matter of expediency, did not wish to resort to war in order to solve a technical dispute. It is not surprising that the first cases were between the US and Britain, two countries split by deep-rooted grudges but sharing a common legal tradition.

A key precedent was the "Alabama claims of the United States of America against Great Britain" in the context of the US Civil War: it was prompted by depredations to Union shipping, caused by the *Alabama* privateer as well as other Southern vessels they had repaired in English ports. According to article I of the Treaty of Washington of May 8, 1871, which aimed to settle "complaints and claims on the part of the United States [. . .] which are not admitted by Her Britannic Majesty's Government," both governments agreed to convene an arbitration tribunal. The selected venue was Geneva, Switzerland, and five countries delegated an arbiter. This Treaty was, from a legal perspective, the transposition of the device of an *arbitration agreement* into international law. It did more than merely convening the arbitration body, as the two sides also agreed from the outset on three principles that should govern the attitude of a neutral government toward vessels of a belligerent country—thus establishing valuable jurisprudence. Principles and methods for solving disputes were taking shape (see Bowen 1868). The sentence rendered on September 14, 1872, essentially that Great Britain had failed to exert due diligence concerning the Southern privateers, was hailed as a success for international law. It should be pointed out that peace, in this case, had entirely stemmed from the goodwill of the two parties or, rather, their acute awareness that it would be more expeditious to handle issues that were highly technical but relatively minor in the grand scheme of things through peaceful means rather than by a costly military confrontation. Had either of them decided not to honor its part, though, the tribunal would have failed without recourse. Nevertheless, this arbitration court safely disposed of what could have become a *casus belli* between the two countries; as such, it was undoubtedly a successful experiment in preventing war.

Competing Policies of Peace: Deterrence vs. Arbitration

The Crimean War (1853–6), which pitted a Western coalition against Russia, had caused the collapse of the peace system championed by the Great Powers of the Congress of Vienna. After 1870 Germany and France were constantly at daggers drawn; this heralded a return to a balance of power of the type of the eighteenth century, which Abbé de Saint-Pierre had aptly named a *system of war* (Ghervas 2014b: 52). Compared with the previous century, it was somewhat mitigated by the diplomatic activity of the "Concert of Europe" (see Sédouy 2009; Ghervas 2015a: 458–64). Europe was again divided into two dangerously opposed blocs. However, the demographic, economic, and social consequences of the Industrial Revolution were such that the political configuration of the continent was constantly shifting: witness the breakdown of the entente between the emperors of Russia, Germany, and Austria from the 1870s, notably because of clashes between nationalisms. One of the mechanical effects of a peace of balance—or a peace of deterrence—is that the military might of the opposed coalitions has to remain roughly equivalent. In this age of steam machinery, the rapid improvement of weaponry and the increase of available resources made it necessary for the antagonistic powers constantly to keep up with each other. The inevitable consequence of such a condition is an "arms race," such as that which occurred in 1891, when Britain and Germany engaged in a competition for naval supremacy, notably building "dreadnought ships" (see Massie 2007). In view of the ravages that modern weapons could inflict, the new correlation of peace with disarmament became increasingly self-evident. The attraction of the great powers for disarmament may have carried an idealistic veneer for the public opinion, but it is often forgotten that, in this industrial age that now prided itself on its *Realpolitik*,[24] the motivation was more down-to-earth: a concern that spiraling military costs could eventually bankrupt them. Indeed, the Ottoman Empire, saddled by its "capitulations," was plunging into a chasm of debts in which the modernization and upkeep of its armies played a large role. That very financial preoccupation brought Tsar Nicholas II to invite the other powers to a peace conference that took place on May 18, 1899 (see Eyffinger 1999: 16–41). While it did not lead to effective disarmament measures (presumably because the other powers thought they had enough wherewithal for some more), it had an unexpected side effect: to reinforce the belief that disagreements among the great powers could and should be solved through the use of law rather than force. In 1899, it led the signatories of the First Hague Convention, "animated by a strong desire to concert for the maintenance of the general peace," to resolve that "with a view to obviating, as far as possible, recourse to force in the relations between States, [. . .] to use their best efforts to insure the pacific settlement of international differences" ("Concerning the Pacific Settlement of International Disputes": 108). While encouraging the recourse to good offices and mediations, as well as commissions of inquiry, it importantly established a Permanent Court of Arbitration for the friendly settlement of disputes ("Concerning the Pacific Settlement of International Disputes": 108).[25] That act crystallized the shift from pre-existing mediation to a formal body that provided adjudication in case of disputes. There was, however, no obligation for the great powers to make recourse to it, or to any enforcement of its decisions: the choice between arbitration and war was in the nature of a financial decision between the potential returns and risks of two possible investments. Indeed, among legal authors lower costs were a strong argument in favor of arbitration (see Rogers 1905). Britain, confident in its overwhelming military superiority against the South African Boer states in that same year of 1899, as a matter of course chose the force

FIGURE 1.5: The Peace Palace (The Hague, 1913): Vredespaleis, 1913, Peace Palace, seat of International Court of Justice (ICJ), Hague, South Holland, Netherlands. Credit: DEA/N. CIRANI/Getty Images.

of arms in its bid to turn them into colonies.[26] By contrast, a tribunal was set up in America to adjudicate on an obscure and convoluted case of 1902 between the US and Mexico about sums due to the Catholic dioceses of Alta California in the wake of the Mexican–American War of 1848 (the so-called Controversy of the Pious Fund of the Californias).[27] The Second Hague Conference in 1907—this time on the initiative of the US government—expanded on the technical achievements of the first. In 1913, the Peace Palace opened its doors in The Hague as if to materialize and embody, with its bourgeois decorum (reminiscent of the Burgundian style of the late Middle Ages), the new face of peace.[28]

Despite its recent religious connotations, peace was still perceived, more than ever, as a physical device. The earlier eighteenth century had seen the success of the metaphor of a *European system*, based on the balance of power. This one had seen the success of the *system of peace* that the Congress of Vienna had implemented in 1815. By contrast, the last years of the nineteenth century saw the birth of an engineering metaphor (so germane to this age of steam turbines) of a *machinery of peace* that specifically referred to dispute-resolution procedures. As the British peace campaigner, minister, and lawyer William Evans Darby wrote in 1908: "The machinery of Peace is consequently of as much practical importance as its ideals and impulses. It becomes equally obvious that whatever promotes the definition, development and efficiency of International Law must prepare the way for permanent peace" (Darby 1908: 3).

CONCLUSION

The Great War was the final rebuttal of the prophecy of 1814 by Swiss political writer Benjamin Constant that the spirit of conquest had died. The Age of Empire merely saw a change in the causes of wars: instead of the greedy and ambitious patrimonial kings that both Rousseau and Kant had rightly blamed for war in the eighteenth century, the tyrants of the Age of Empire were industrial states, blindly driven by ethnic nationalism and an insatiable hunger for more land resources. The new balance of power between two opposed coalitions finally grew into the explosive mix that caused the conflagration of 1914. In light of the rise of ethnocentric and imperial ideologies in the last decades of the nineteenth century and the early twentieth, the peace movements can be seen as bold attempts to defuse and reverse the general trend of nation-states toward egoism and the cult of war. It is thus important to make a fundamental intellectual distinction between the republican revolutionaries of 1848 and the ensuing peace movements on the one hand, and the nationalist, state-driven turn of the second part of the nineteenth century— largely monarchical and colonialist in nature—on the other. While the new French Emperor Napoleon III stated in 1852, "some claim that the Empire is war; I state that the Empire is peace,"[29] he was soon to provoke the Ottoman Empire and engage his country in the Crimean War against Russia in 1853 and once again against Austria in 1859, in his effort to support the bid of the Kingdom of Sardinia to unite Northern Italian states. Similarly, after defeating France in 1871, Emperor William I of Germany, in the Hall of Mirrors of the Palace of Versailles, had made a solemn and repetitive commitment to bring peace to Germany:

> We assume the imperial title, conscious of the duty of protecting, with German loyalty, the rights of the Empire and of its members, of keeping the peace, and of protecting the independence of Germany, which depends in its turn upon the united strength of the people. We assume the title in the hope that the German people will be granted the ability to enjoy the reward of its ardent and self-sacrificing wars in lasting peace, within boundaries which afford the fatherland a security against renewed French aggression which has been lost for centuries. And may God grant that We and our successors on the imperial throne may at all times increase the wealth of the German Empire, not by military conquests, but by the blessings and the gifts of peace, in the realm of national prosperity, liberty, and morality.[30]

Alas, those declarations sounded hollow, and the builders of the "machinery of peace" at The Hague were still in the early days of their engineering: they could not harness the enormous pressures that would eventually drive the fatigued European engine to the terrific boiler explosion of the Great War; indeed, they had not been even tasked with that mission. Accounts of the spring of 1914 portray it as peaceful until the July crisis that followed the assassination of the presumptive heir of Austria, Franz Ferdinand, on June 28, 1914 derailed the hitherto-orderly rhythm of international relations and thrust it into a chaotic sequence of events, which ended in the outbreak of World War I. The disaster was due to a much-debated conjunction of factors: certainly involving the clashes of nationalisms, a conflict of imperialistic aims of European powers in the Balkans and the Middle East, a structural risk resulting from two dangerously opposed alliances, the ravages of anarchism (a precursor of modern suicide terrorism), and finally the stunning failure to use mediation or arbitration as a means to avoid the conflict (see Valone 1988; McMeekin 2013). Yet should one blame the operators of that moment, or the planners and maintainers of the European system who—disregarding safety measures and common sense—had let the international pressure rise for over two decades?

The unprecedented murderousness of World War I also had an influence on the cultural perception of war. Trench warfare is among the most mentally devastating forms of conflict. Combatants who lived through an interminably slow routine of daily toil interspersed with sudden deadly action had plenty of time to reflect about the abjection and absurdity of their situation; by contrast soldiers involved in a fast-paced war of movement have often too much on their hands to think at all about anything outside of their immediate missions. Several Great War poets, though not openly anti-war, showed a marked departure from the jingoist drives of 1914; they expressed their disgust at the de-humanizing monstrosity of modern battles in words like these of Wilfred Owen:

> What passing-bells for these who die as cattle?
> —Only the monstrous anger of the guns.
> Only the stuttering rifles' rapid rattle
> Can patter out their hasty orisons.
>
> —Owen [1917] 1983: 19

This disenchantment was not only expressed in subdued poetic complaints, however. From April to June 1917, several mutinies broke out in the French army, in which pacifism (understood now as a disavowal of the conflict) played a role. In Russia, in March 1917, the soldiers also mutinied, hurling the country into the Revolution. In October, hundreds of thousands of Italian soldiers deserted following the defeat at Caporetto, in today's Slovenia. The casualties and privations of the war economy also started taking their toll on the morale of the civilian populations. As an Italian soldier wrote in 1917: "If you get the news that I died, don't say I died for my homeland, but that I died for the masters; in other words for the rich people who were the cause of the death of so many good young people" (Rossi 2014: 44). Pacifism became an active fight for *peace*, defined as the (sometimes violent) rejection of war, which younger generations no longer wanted to have any part of.

The end of World War I was also a period of intense reflection on peace. Out of this carnage emerged, thanks to the Covenant of the League of Nations inserted by US President Woodrow Wilson into the Treaty of Versailles signed on June 28, 1919, a new institution created "in order to promote international co-operation and to achieve international peace and security."[31] This new "machinery of peace" took several pages out of the plans of perpetual peace (notably that of Kant), and promoted a number of essential principles that the Enlightenment thinkers of the eighteenth century, as well as the monarchs of 1814, would have subscribed to: "obligations not to resort to war," "open, just and honourable relations between nations," and scrupulous respect for the treaties.[32] It was, on the other hand, more democratic in nature than that of Vienna, embracing the contribution of the peace movements that followed the revolutions of 1848; it also acknowledged "international law as the actual rule of conduct among Governments,"[33] thus confirming the effort of the lawyers toward "peace through law." Its tone was still paternalistic toward the colonies and territories "which are inhabited by peoples not yet able to stand by themselves under the strenuous conditions of the modern world."[34] It opened, however, a tenuous door to the process that would eventually lead them to state sovereignty, though peace and prosperity would remain distant prospects.

The amount of ground covered by the definitions of peace since 1814 is, therefore, enormous: from a cessation of hostilities, it became the foundation of institutions, commissions, a Congress System, a Holy Alliance (first of the Kings and then of the peoples), and then a judicial machinery. Peace also met its disheartening failures, with the suppression of the popular movements of the 1820s and 1848, the reneging on two major principles of the French Revolution (the equality of men of all colors and the renunciation of self-aggrandizement), the imperial adventures inside and outside of Europe, and finally the collective suicide of a world war. The word *pacification*, with its connotations of military brutality, summary executions, and exactions, became a terror of civilian populations. The world that emerged in 1919 out of the "War to End all Wars" was markedly different from what it had been a century before. On the top of this, the conditions of the Treaty of Versailles did not offer bright perspectives for peace between France and Germany (see Cohrs 2006; Ghervas 2020: ch. 3).

All in all, the newly born League of Nations—a stronger "machinery" of peace, it was hoped—was intended to institutionalize the inheritance of the actor-writers of the nineteenth century who had contributed to new definitions of peace as something to be preserved, practiced, and established, and to a rapidly growing body of practices. The novelty of the new age was that peace was progressively escaping the momentary European monopoly of the nineteenth century to become, by 1920, a common standard to be extended to humankind. It is not particularly an accident, thus, that the Covenant for the new peace organization of the 1920s was laid out under the guidance of an American president who was both a devout Protestant and a political scientist, any more than it should be surprising that the Holy Alliance of 1815 had been the brainchild of an Orthodox Russian tsar nurtured with Enlightened readings (De Traz 1936: 47–97). The age of machines had taken its toll: the next "era of peace" would be as secular as the earlier one had been religious.

CHAPTER TWO

Human Nature, Peace, and War

Jane Addams and Evolutionary Psychology

INGRID SHARP

During the nineteenth century, beliefs about human nature, peace, and war were influenced by factors such as religion and philosophy as well as by shifts in international politics and radical new ideas, such as Charles Darwin's (1809–82) evolutionary theory and the rise of international socialism; ideas that fed into a view of human society as something that was subject to change and development. Literature and popular science also played a major role in expressing and influencing ideas about the capacity of human nature to overcome aggression and encourage cooperation, aided by emerging fields such as psychology and new ideas about education. These ideas coalesced into a view of human nature as not immutable, but as something that could change and develop within a human society imagined as moving toward a new era of civilization, or alternatively as moving toward degeneration and decline (see Pick 1989).

A major category of analysis in considering this question is gender, as most commentators throughout the nineteenth century posited a fundamental and innate difference in men's and women's relationship to war, based on a belief that there were distinct and polarized characteristics innate to the sexes, indeed that men and women inhabited "separate spheres."[1] At the same time, however, as Stephan Dudink, John Tosh, and Karen Hagemann have pointed out, "politics and war have become the seemingly 'natural' homelands of masculinity—a masculinity that sometimes has been quite explicit, but more often has been elided in the equation of 'man' with 'human' and 'mankind' which conceals masculinity behind discourses of 'general interests' and 'universality'" (Dudink *et al.*: xii). During the latter half of the nineteenth century, women's movements emerged in the US and Western Europe that challenged male supremacy and questioned men's fitness to govern in the best interests of both sexes. The arguments put forward by these groups, too, often rested on the dominant discourse of the complementarity and polarity of the sexes. While early campaigns revolved around issues such as men's monopoly of education, employment, and representation, as well as their control over women's bodies, liberty, and property, the question of war as a gender issue emerged toward the end of the nineteenth century. Attracting international interest due to the treatment of Boer women and children by British forces during the Boer War of 1899–1902, it came to a head during World

War I, which for some feminists represented the catastrophic failure of masculine rule and demonstrated the urgency of women's inclusion in international politics.[2]

While there was a strong belief throughout the nineteenth century that war was a natural human instinct and to a great extent inevitable in international relations, there were also voices that questioned this and put forward suggestions for overcoming the urge for aggression and violence in human interactions through social justice, education, and the regulation of international relations. Influenced by the ideas of Darwin, a strong justification of war as being of evolutionary benefit to nations was articulated and indeed was held by many to be at the heart of German militarism (see Le Bon 1916; Chickering 1975; Crook 1994), but this was countered by a belief in evolutionary biology that placed war, aggression, and violence in the camp of atavistic urges that could be overcome by a more highly developed moral society and more highly evolved individuals. This in turn was underpinned by the optimistic belief that both society and humanity were moving in the direction of more civilized, enlightened relationships (see Sluga 2013; Quataert 2014). British journalist and anti-war campaigner Norman Angell's international best seller, *The Great Illusion* of 1910, expressed the view of significant numbers of influential thinkers: "The warlike nations do not inherit the earth; they represent the decaying human element. The diminishing rôle of physical force in all spheres of human activity carries with it profound psychological modifications" (xiii).

There were national variations, however, as well as developments across time during the period. In Germany, Prussia's military prowess was marked by its defeat of Napoleon during the wars of liberation in 1813 and consolidated through the wars of unification in 1866 and 1871. After unification in 1871, the military was held in the highest esteem throughout Imperial Germany and a conservative, masculinist militarism hostile to progressive ideas pervaded civil society: in his study of peace movements in Germany during the nineteenth century, Roger Chickering has argued that pacifist ideas had a particularly difficult time gaining traction in Germany due to the ascendancy of the military and of militarist values in society, politics, and religion (1975: 384–419, see also Frevert 2001: 103–20). Other liberal ideas such as internationalism, socialism, and feminism had to develop cautiously in Germany under conditions of deep mistrust and repression.

Peace movements, unknown until 1815 (see Martin Ceadel's Chapter 6 in this volume), proliferated in Europe and America in the late nineteenth and early twentieth centuries, so much so that an International Peace Bureau was set up in 1891 in order to "keep track" of their diverse activities and visions (Quataert 2014: 14). The late nineteenth century was an era of unprecedented anti-war sentiment and activism at both national and international level, with arguments against war ranging from the religious to the pragmatic and legalistic to the evolutionary. Yet even within the peace movements themselves, the possibility of entirely eradicating war from human relations was contested, while the idea of educating boys for peace rather than preparing them for war was a distinctly minority position.

Although the peace movement itself often consisted of mixed groups led by men—in Germany, for example, two-thirds of members and all its leaders were men (Chickering 1975: 74–5), for the general public the anti-war position was more naturally associated with women and there were a number of women's organizations that laid claim to women's higher nature in this area (see Sandi Cooper's Chapter 3 in this volume, and Cooper 1987, 1991) and their consequent responsibility for intervening in men's affairs to preserve the peace. This was cemented by the publication of Bertha von Suttner's internationally successful *Lay Down Your Arms* (discussed by Laurie Cohen in Chapter 5 of this volume)

FIGURE 2.1: Jane Addams (1860–1935) in 1910. Credit: Hulton Archive/Getty Images.

in 1889 and the adoption of a commitment to a rhetoric of peace and sisterhood within the international women's organizations, the International Council of Women, founded in 1888, and the IWSA, founded in 1903. It was further reinforced by the outbreak of World War I in 1914, which was vigorously opposed on gender lines by international groups of women working across national and sometimes across ideological and class boundaries to challenge militarism. Many of the pacifist women were committed to an exclusively female view of peace, seeing women as more advanced than men in evolutionary terms, operating at a higher level morally, and innately programmed for cooperation and peace-building. However, there were also key thinkers such as US peace activist and social theorist Jane Addams (1860–1935), who was awarded the Nobel Prize for Peace in 1931, and German campaigner for human and reproductive rights Helene Stöcker (1869–1943), who put forward ideas about human nature that included both women and men in their vision of evolutionary development toward a more peaceful global society. This chapter will consider ideas of human nature, war, and peace from a gender perspective, exploring some of the psychological explanations offered for war in particular in Addams's writings and the suggestions she put forward for creating cultures of peace.

A GENDERED VIEW OF HUMAN NATURE

Separate sphere ideology, which developed in the late eighteenth century, dominated beliefs about human nature during the nineteenth century, with women placed in the domestic and men in the public sphere, and with "natural" characteristics such as aggression and nurturing associated with these spheres.³ Women embodied the domestic virtues of the home while men provided for and protected their families from the harsh realities of commerce and politics. Although this was a lifestyle only possible for the affluent middle classes, the ideology itself was pervasive and underlay laws, workplace regulation. and social norms throughout the nineteenth century in Western industrialized nations. At the same time, ideas about masculinity were formed, consolidated, and reinforced through politics, education, and religion that posited a desirable form of manliness based on leadership, resolve, stoicism, and racial superiority: in his historiographical survey of recent literature on masculinities in war and peace, Robert Nye notes that according to scholars, societies have valued military masculinities and "the personal characteristics of manliness that it comprises more highly than civic virtue and its masculinities" (Nye 2007: 418). In most European nations, universal male conscription played an important role in reinforcing the role of war-preparedness in defining masculinity and in establishing military masculinity as a dominant model (see Frevert 2001; Hagemann 2004; Geva 2014).

Although the concept was subject to shifts over time and local and class variations, and the characteristics associated with masculinity and the key formative role played by war and the military varied over time and across cultures, there is a remarkable consistency between the US and Western European ideas, and these will be the focus of this chapter. R.W. Connell's concept of hegemonic masculinity is helpful in making sense of this as it posits masculinities that are neither universal nor fixed, but contingent, shifting, relational, and highly dependent on cultural context (see Connell 1995). Indeed, nineteenth-century masculinity was far from monolithic but defined and constructed in relation to competing versions of masculinity, as can be clearly seen in the construction of masculinities in war, which depend on construction of inferior, "non-martial," masculinities and on constructing the effeminacy of the enemy (Connell 1987: 183). Jessica Meyer (2009) and Stefan Dudink, Karen Hagemann, and John Tosh (2004) note that war is a dominant identity-forming activity for men: war plays a role in making men and thus reflects and expresses but also forms masculinity in fundamental ways. Twin pillars of masculine identity during the nineteenth century were constructed around providing for and protecting the family, and public service in politics and the military within an imperialist context. In all the Western societies these attributes were developed through education and training specifically geared toward preparing boys for leadership roles in the military, civil life, and the Church. In Britain, elite boys were prepared for imperial leadership roles through schooling in single-sex boarding schools that separated them from their families at a very young age and placed emphasis on loyalty to their class, school, nation, and race. The experience of the Boer War (1899–1902) which had found so many British young men to be physically under par (Winter 1980) led to an increased emphasis on health and fitness, so that non-elite boys were also encouraged to engage in team sports and activities in organizations such as Scouting, founded in 1907, to develop discipline and physical fitness (Tosh 2005). In Germany, the shape of the nation was defined by a series of wars between 1813 and 1871, and it remained dominated by a distinctly Prussian militarism that permeated civil society. As Hagemann (2004) has shown, the German cult of military masculinity coalesced around compulsory conscription, introduced in 1813, that positioned military service as a rite of passage into a shared fraternal masculinity that supposedly transcended class boundaries (see also Frevert 2001). From 1870, military service was explicitly intended as a moral and physical antidote to the effeminacy and degeneracy of urban society, in particular to the "creeping 'poison' of social democracy" (Frevert 2001: 274).

War, then, was widely accepted as a gendering and gendered activity (Higonnet *et al.* 1987: 4): it was waged by and in turn shaped men. But this "natural" relationship between masculinity and war was also problematic. Increasingly, as the century progressed, masculine characteristics such as aggression that underlay men's role in war were open to feminist critique, and men's natures were being held responsible for the continuance of destructive wars. South African intellectual and anti-war campaigner Olive Schreiner in 1911 set out the gendered arguments associating men with aggression and war. In chapter 4 of her influential book *Women and Labour*, she argued that men are innately programmed to destroy life, women to preserve it: "'It is a fine day, let us go out and kill something!' cries the typical male of certain races, instinctively. 'There is a living thing, it will die if it is not cared for,' says the average woman, almost equally instinctively" (1911: 176). This was not because of an innate moral superiority but because, in the case of war, women have special knowledge born of the flesh, a knowledge to which men have no access; "the knowledge of woman, simply as woman, is superior to that of man; she knows the history of human flesh; she knows its cost; he does not" (1911: 170). For this reason, she argues, women's inclusion in the affairs of the state was necessary to bring about the end of warfare: "[w]ar will pass when intellectual culture and activity have made possible to the female an equal share in the control and governance of modern national life; it will probably not pass away much sooner; its extinction will not be delayed much longer" (1911: 178).

Schreiner's chapter clearly articulated the key elements of a feminist pacifist position that gained traction in response to the outbreak of World War I in 1914. For her, only women can truly value human life because of their childbearing capacity and experience. This gives women an innate and instinctive urge to preserve human life while men have the urge to kill; consequently women pay a higher price in war than men. The dangers of childbearing and the fact that women are responsible for providing manpower to wage war entitles women to speak on the subject and work toward removing war from the world. Underlying the argument was a belief in human progress, in which war belonged to an earlier stage of human development. Schreiner's position is problematic as it associates all women by definition with an anti-war position, assumes that women's political influence would overcome war, places maternity at the core of all women's identity, and does not allow for "maternal thinking" in pacifist men.[4]

In Germany, the most outspoken feminist peace campaigners were Lida Gustava Heymann and Anita Augspurg. Through their campaigns against the state regulation of prostitution in the 1890s, these women had formed a view of men as the irrational sex, slaves to their baser instincts unless checked by the greater moral power of women. Even in peacetime, they saw women as the victims of male violence and sexual incontinence, and the outbreak of war in 1914 was for them the ultimate demonstration of men's enslavement to their atavistic urges and further evidence of their unfitness to govern: "The world war has proved that the male state, founded and built up on force, has failed all along the line; we have never seen clearer proof of its unfitness. The male principle is divisive and, if allowed to continue unchecked, will bring about the total destruction of humanity" (Heymann 1917/1922: 65).

Because they saw women's influence in affairs of state as essential for preventing war, Heymann and Augspurg were part of a small group of women who continued their campaign for women's suffrage throughout the war, when most mainstream women's organizations had stepped back from this position in favor of supporting their nation's war effort (see Wiltsher 1985). Heymann and Augspurg's conviction that women in their natural state had an innate love of peace that made it impossible for them to support killing remained intact throughout the war despite all evidence to the contrary: in all nations, women's organizations and the vast majority of their members engaged in activities that supported the patriotic war effort and often attacked the pacifist women as the enemy within alongside the external enemy (Sharp 2013b). Yet in 1919 they wrote: "Women are, just because they are women, against all forms of brutal force that seek to pointlessly destroy what has grown, what has become. They want to build up, to protect, to create anew" (Heymann and Augspurg 1919: 1). There were, however, other views within the German women's peace movement; for example, the ideas of Helene Stöcker, equally committed to bringing about lasting and sustainable peace, did not rest on a theory of innate and insuperable gender differences, but rather on the possibility of moral development for the whole of humanity (see Wickert 1991).

The relationship between masculinity and war was also problematic in that, if war was masculine identity-forming around ideas of heroism, endurance, duty, and patriotic service, this view was undermined by experiences of warfare such as soldier breakdown, reluctance to kill, and refusal or unfitness to serve, and by the effects of injury and disability caused by war on key elements of masculine identity: autonomy, adventure, and independence. In fact, war disrupts as much as it confirms the gender order and, as Meyer has noted, war is not just able to make masculinity but to break it as well: "the physical and psychological damage wrought on men by trench warfare was demonstrating that war could destroy as well as make men" (Meyer 2009: 3).

In particular, World War I called these values into question because of the scale of the armies involved, their nature as largely conscripted or volunteer rather than professional forces, the shift to an industrialized war using technologically advanced weaponry, and the high incidences of psychological and physical injury among the combatants. Winter (1980) records high levels of rejection on the grounds of unfitness after conscription was introduced in Britain in 1916, and this is mirrored by statistics from Germany and France, suggesting that military vigor was far from being the natural state of all young men and raising questions about the masculine identities of those who were rejected. Lois Bibbings (2009) has written about the negotiation of masculine identities among those men—an estimated 17,000—who objected to killing on grounds of conscience and became conscientious objectors. Notwithstanding arguments that reinforce the idea of men as naturally well equipped for and even enjoying killing (Ferguson 1998: 357; Bourke 1999), one of the most powerful and enduring images of the solder to emerge after World War I is that of the soldier victim (Meyer 2009: 5). Many men emerged from the wars broken in body and spirit, their ability to function as men in civilian society diminished rather than enhanced by their experience of combat. The huge numbers mobilized during World War I, and the protracted nature and extraordinary conditions under which it was fought, meant that the instances of psychological damage were so numerous that they were impossible to ignore and difficult to reconcile with the idea of masculine relish of danger and violence. Paul Lerner (2008), Michael Roper (2009), and Edward Madigan (2013) have written about psychological survival in these conditions, while Edgar Jones's analysis has found that, contrary to contemporary assumptions that it was the tension of immobility that caused the strain, and that engagement in active combat secured psychological release, men who kill were not in fact protected from damage but rather suffered more than those not so exposed (Jones 2006). This echoes reports that many men do not shoot to kill in battle (see, for example, Hochschild 2011: 162), and require intensive training to desensitize them sufficiently to overcome the taboo of killing another human being. These factors undermine the "natural" alignment of masculinity with warfare and call into question any assumptions of the evolutionary benefits of warfare for men and self-consciously masculine societies structured on military virtues and military prowess.

Jane Addams certainly saw war as evolutionary backsliding, including men within her ideas about evolutionary peace biology and seeing them as victims as much as perpetrators of war. Her experience of the war, especially her encounter with the women from warring nations at the Women's International Congress at The Hague in 1915 and through her visits to war-torn countries, convinced her more than ever that war was a tragedy for humanity that in its reversion to a primitive violent destruction would tear down the social bonds that had taken generations to build up (see Addams 1922 and Addams et al. 1915). For Addams, war represented the dominance of forces that worked against progress—nationalism, tribal loyalty, hatred of the enemy—and reversed progress toward her goal of internationalism, cooperation, and mutual care.

Addams was an important and original thinker as well as a social activist who reflected seriously on peace from 1899 until her death in 1934. A well-known and highly popular public figure for much of her life, she wrote ten books and hundreds of articles, and was awarded thirteen honorary degrees and the Nobel Prize for Peace. By 1914, she had already published numerous articles and made various speeches setting out her ideas about peace as well as writing an influential book, *Newer Ideals of Peace* (1907).

As soon as war was declared in 1914, Addams prioritized her work for peace, initiating the founding of the Women's Peace Party in New York in 1915. She accepted the role of president of the Women's International Congress at The Hague in April/May 1915 and led a delegation of forty-two US women who sailed through dangerous seas to attend. This congress, which was jointly planned by suffragists from belligerent and non-belligerent countries, brought together over a thousand women to discuss how best to stop the current war and prevent future wars. The only major international peace meeting during the war, the congress was followed up by delegations of women visiting the heads of states of warring and neutral nations to discuss the possibility of mediation. It has been the subject of a great deal of scholarship especially by women's historians and its resolutions are credited with inspiring Woodrow Wilson's fourteen points of January 1918.[5] Addams was highly influential in setting up and shaping a new transnational women's peace organization, the Women's International League for Peace and Freedom (WILPF), which remains one of the most effective forces advocating for women's role in bringing about a sustainable peace in the twenty-first century. Although increasingly the subject of feminist scholarship,[6] Addams has often been omitted from historical accounts of peace history and is not often credited with the originality and scope of her intellectual engagement with peace. In fact, her thinking anticipated many of the approaches and concepts important for peace studies later in the twentieth century: it was based on an understanding of human nature rooted in evolutionary biology, pragmatism, and cultural feminism which she blended, as US social historian Katherine Sklar puts it, to "build a bridge between two heretofore distinct discourses: those related to peace, arbitration, and antimilitarism on the one hand, and those related to social democracy, social ethics, and government on the other" (Sklar 2003: 80). Addams can be placed within the traditions of nineteenth-century thought, and drew inspiration from British and Russian thinkers such as Beatrice and Sydney Webb and Petr Kropotkin, who stayed at Hull House during visits to America, as well as from American philosophical traditions. Like her contemporary, the influential US psychologist William James (1842–1910), she was a pragmatist who placed experience at the heart of understanding and referred to human instincts adapting to shifts in human social experience. Mary Jo Deegan describes her as a "critical pragmatist" who combined "American thought with radical emancipatory practice and goals" (1990: 266). For Addams, human nature was not fixed, and she saw hopeful signs that war values were outdated in the new industrial society she experienced through her work with and life alongside some of the poorest groups in Chicago. As Sklar (2003) has shown, her ideals were rooted in practice rather than at the level of international arbitration and regulation from above. The same is true of her understanding of human nature, and how this relates to the violence and aggression of war.

Central to her model for peaceful coexistence was her experience of immigrant communities at Hull House, the settlement house that she had set up in 1892. Their lives together demonstrated that there were certain conditions where tribal loyalties could be overcome and mutual support and compassion could develop out of a mix of altruism and egotism: to avoid crushing or being crushed, cooperative cosmopolitanism had developed. She saw this forced cooperation of different national groups among the poorest of the city as carrying the germs of an international, cosmopolitan order that would form the basis for a sustainable peace:

> a deeper and more thorough-going unity is required in a community made up of highly differentiated peoples than in a more settled and stratified one, and it may be logical that we should find in this commingling of many peoples a certain balance and contending forces; a gravitation towards the universal. Because of their difference in all external matters, in all of the non-essentials of life, the people in a cosmopolitan city are forced to found their community of interests upon the basic and essential likenesses of their common human nature; for, after all, the things that make men alike are stronger and more primitive than the things that separate them.
> —Addams 1907: 12

In 1915, Austrian psychologist Sigmund Freud (1856–1939) published his response to the war, *Thoughts for the Times on War and Death*, in which he argued that the shock and disappointment expressed about humanity's sudden descent into barbarism reflected an incomplete understanding of the primitive forces that raged below the very thin veneer of "civilization" that kept them in check. In fact, humanity had not descended to the beasts, but had never really risen much above them:

> We may already derive one consolation from this discussion: our mortification and our painful disillusionment on account of the uncivilized behaviour of our fellow-citizens of the world during this war were unjustified. They were based on an illusion to which we had given way. In reality our fellow-citizens have not sunk so low as we feared, because they had never risen so high as we believed.
> —Freud 1915: 285

How did Jane Addams's view of human nature and her optimism about the possibility of progress toward a world without war fare in the face of the news from Europe and her own first-hand observations? Addams's belief in progress through evolutionary biology had always been social as much as individual. She saw human society as progressing from militarism toward humanitarianism, with older moral judgments being superseded by newer ones to adapt to the new context. She had always recognized the powerful urges that underlay the appeal of war and had set her faith in overcoming these by creating social structures that brought other, equally strong, urges to the fore. Despite

FIGURE 2.2: Sigmund Freud (1856–1939) with his sons Ernst and Martin in 1916. Credit: Hulton Archive/Getty Images.

characterization of her as unworldly, she was far from naive about human nature and knew that strong aggressive urges needed to be overcome, and recognized that humanity's warring instincts are especially difficult to reconcile during wartime. Nor was she, as some have claimed, a biological essentialist who believed that women were either innately superior to men or naturally more committed to peace. For example, Deegan claims that Addams practiced "a female chauvinism based partially on a biological explanation" and that this weakened her arguments (1990: 242). However, as Marilyn Fischer points out:

> [W]hile Addams at times used maternalist rhetoric, her pacifism was not based on a belief in women's essential pacifist nature. Instead, it was grounded on her understanding of democracy, social justice, and international peace as mutually defining concepts. For Addams, progress toward democracy, social justice, and peace involved both institutional reform and changes on moral intellectual and affective sensibilities.
>
> —2006: 1

Addams did, however, operate in a highly gendered society where women were excluded from politics, were economically and socially subordinate to men, and bore primary responsibility for caring within the family. As such, women had a long tradition of managing, nurturing, and preserving that was relevant both for running the new cities and for creating conditions for peace. Addams's view of human nature was necessarily gendered because of the fundamental divergence of male and female experience, especially in wartime, but she was also committed to a belief in the moral progress of men as well as women and hoped for a world in which gender differences would be less important. Responses to her as a woman involving herself in politics and in war show how far off that position was and explain perhaps why she was predominantly active within women's organizations. Women's voices for peace were excluded and silenced, she herself had experience of being attacked by a press campaign in which she was variously dismissed as a "silly, vain, impertinent old maid . . . who is now meddling with matters far beyond her capacity" and a "foolish, garrulous woman," who, according to the *New York Times*, as a woman was incapable of understanding war and soldiers (Knight 2010: 204). Addams knew that women's experiences and priorities formed a vital aspect of peace building and that women's relationship to war as waste, loss, and damage was a key insight and absolutely necessary in making progress toward a world without war. Although highly committed to gender justice and the equal representation of women in civil life, Addams's view of human nature transcended the gender dichotomy. Addressing the all-male House Committee on Military Affairs in January 1917, Addams reminded the audience that men were "much more likely to catch this war spirit" than women and to get carried away by their emotions as a result (quoted in Knight 2010: 212), but this did not mean that she considered this susceptibility to be innate or insurmountable. She made it clear that the gender differences she observed were in her view gradually being eroded, and that men's different experiences in the modern industrial age meant that, for younger men, war as a means to settling international disputes was anachronistic and incomprehensible:

> We had been much impressed with the fact that it was an old man's war, and that many of the soldiers themselves were far from enthusiastic in regard to actual fighting as a way of setting international difficulties. War was to many of them much more anachronistic than to the elderly statesmen who were primarily responsible for the soldiers presence in the trenches.
>
> —Addams 1922: 51

Although Addams subscribed to the idea of social progress and evolutionary biology, she did not think that moral progress to overcoming war was inevitable—it was a process requiring human energy and human agency as "we know in our hearts that the best results of civilisation have only come about through human will and effort" (Addams 1907: 117). Her ideas about creating conditions for a dynamic and active peace had been set out in a speech to the Universal Peace Congress in 1904 and further developed in *Newer Ideals of Peace*, and were based on the understanding that some elements of war were "psychologically attractive: it appealed to a basic human desire for self-sacrifice and adventure" (Schott 1993: 246). However, as Addams herself had put it in 1899, this was a result of "the mistake of confusing moral issues sometimes involved in warfare with warfare itself . . . The same strenuous endeavour, the same heroic self-sacrifice, the same fine courage and readiness to meet death, may be displayed without the accompaniment of killing our fellow men" (Addams, quoted in Carroll and Fink 2003: xxvii).

In 1910, William James published a pamphlet "The Moral Equivalent of War" in which he put forward proposals for finding alternatives to war that would offer "rival excitements" and allow young people to develop the same essentially military virtues of comradeship, physical and mental toughness that war would have encouraged. However, as Schott notes, James's vision was not only firmly in sympathy with those who advocated war as a moral teacher, but his suggested program of national service did not as he claimed embrace "the whole of the youthful population," but only men and indeed only affluent young men who stood in need of having "the childishness knocked out of them" (Schott 1993: 253). Addams's vision was formulated earlier than James's, and differed from his in ways that can be seen as arising from her gendered experience as well as her greater exposure to different social classes: from her Hull House experience, Addams knew that the different experience of women had created a different relationship to war, and unlike James's model that perpetuated separate sphere ideology and "sought to maintain a

FIGURE 2.3: US psychologist William James (1842–1910). Credit: Bettmann/Getty Images.

society dominated by wealthy men" (Schott 1993: 253), she put forward a far more socially inclusive model of cooperation that broke down gender as well as class barriers, finding common purpose in rising to the challenges of communal living.

In her various leadership roles as well as in her writings, Addams put forward ideas of cooperation and reconciliation based on what would now be seen as a human rights agenda, emphasizing the human need for security, transparency, democracy, and equality, and advocated what would be seen now as cultures of peace, moving away from the systemic violence of an undemocratic system based on secret diplomacy where class and gender divisions reinforced entrenched inequalities. Addams was particularly committed to transcending the nation state and expressed optimism that, given the right national and international structures in which to thrive, human biology carried within it the seeds for overcoming aggression and finding ways of living in harmony. This rested on her experiences of cooperation across national and class boundaries and in her faith that the instinct to protect the young and vulnerable would in the end overcome the atavistic urge to wage war.

Her often uncomfortable and challenging experience of war as a pacifist activist, including dispiriting visits to warring and neutral nations, and her experience of profound isolation when the public mood turned hostile after her return from the Hague in 1915 and even more so when America entered the war in 1917, caused her to reflect on and refine her ideas. However, unlike the response described by Freud, Addams's view of human nature, rooted as it was in practice, was not shattered by the unexpected outbreak of a global war, although there were certainly aspects that took her by surprise. During a concerted press campaign against her that misrepresented her pacifist views, she was taken aback by the power of propaganda to arouse powerful emotions and utterly drown out rational voices (Addams 1922: 56; Knight 2010: 214–20). Those who stood out against the war such as the conscientious objectors in Britain and the women who attended the Hague Conference were a tiny minority in all belligerent countries and had to find ways of coping with press and public hostility as well as legal measures formally directed against silencing and prosecuting dissenting views. According to her account, Addams suffered desperately from her unpopularity and the accusations that she lacked patriotism, drawing strength only from her sense of international community, the support of like-minded thinkers, and a strong sense of being on the right side of history (Addams 1915: 65; 1922: 50–7). Her experience of profound isolation during this time if anything reinforced her belief in the power of the group: forced by conscience to go against the majority view, "literally starved of any gratification of that natural desire to have [her] own decisions justified by [her] fellows" (1922: 57), she wrote to a friend: "I feel as if a few of us were clinging together in a surging sea" (quoted in Knight 2010: 215). She recognized the high price paid by those who challenged majority convictions—pacifists died early as a result of the strain of going against the grain (Addams 1922: 56), and in the past prophets had been vilified and killed for insights that the majority were not yet ready to adopt (Addams 1922: 53–4).

Her reflections on the loneliness she felt when forced to take up a position against the mainstream of thought in her national community is revealing of her understanding of the importance of social bonds to human happiness as well as her Darwinian sense that variation was necessary for evolutionary change:

> We could not, however, lose our conviction that as all other forms of growth begin with a variation from the mass, so the moral changes in human affairs may also begin with a differing group or individual, sometimes with the one who at best is designated as a crank and a freak and in sterner moments is imprisoned as an atheist or a traitor.
> —Addams 1922: 53

Addams was also instrumental in shaping WILPF, and her ideas are clearly expressed in the resolutions of The Hague and Zurich conferences, which put forward the fundamental principles for what we would now call "positive peace" (Galtung 1964: 1991) in which war was more than just combat, peace more than simply the absence of war. These include preventing violence, education for peace, sustainable economic development, respect for human rights, equality between men and women, democratic participation, tolerance of difference, and the free flow of information and disarmament, which clearly anticipate many of the ideas key to present-day peace theory and cultures of peace as set out on the UNESCO website as "a commitment to peace-building, mediation, conflict prevention and resolution, peace education, education for non-violence, tolerance, acceptance, mutual respect, intercultural and interfaith dialogue and reconciliation" (unesco.org). WILPF embraced the idea of the League of Nations, although Addams saw its practice as a missed opportunity to demonstrate by practical compassion the benefits of internationalism in an interconnected world. Instead, the League failed to rise above nationalism and seemingly ignored the humanitarian catastrophe of famine and displacement that blighted post-war Europe and was "a disgrace to civilisation" (WILPF 1919: 1).

Addams, then, in her writings and her activism made an important and distinctive contribution to the understanding of human nature and war within nineteenth- and twentieth-century thought. In particular, she added the dimension of using the practice of marginalized groups—poor immigrant communities and women, excluded from but intimately affected by policy decisions politics—as a model for government and policies. Her analysis of the causes and prevention of war challenged the view that war was an

FIGURE 2.4: Jane Addams at a press conference in 1935. Credit: Bettmann/Getty Images.

essential and inevitable aspect of human nature, stressing instead the social and political factors that led to wars. Her experience of cooperation at local level showed her that ethnic groups could be educated to overcome longstanding and apparently ingrained national antipathies and cooperate. Because her ideas were pragmatic, rooted in practice and experience rather than in abstractions, she did not give way to despair at the outbreak of the war, but used the insights gained to argue even more strongly for social structures that would bring out the cooperation and mutual interdependence that she continued to see as fundamental human needs. Her ideas were developed and refined in the light of her experience in World War I and her intensive engagement with ideas of peace, but essentially can be seen as the forerunner of many ideas central to twentieth- and twenty-first-century peace theory (see Sharp 2013a).

CONCLUSION

While for much of the nineteenth century, war was largely viewed as an inevitable and—for some—even beneficial consequence of human nature in interaction with others, there were strands of argument that challenged this and stressed instead the possibility of educating human beings for peace while overcoming the social factors that led to war. Ideas about human nature and concepts of masculinity were subject to variation within and between nations and overlaid by enduring colonial views of a hierarchy of races as well as persistent class and gender stereotypes. Equally, the interpretation of the meaning of war for humanity was fragmented, and attitudes to war and openness to the ideas of the peace movement were stronger in some nations and at some times than others. In general, however, the move was in the direction of the growing interest in and influence of pacifist ideas toward the end of the nineteenth and beginning of the twentieth centuries.

Before 1914, progressives such as Norman Angell had argued that the economic fates of developed Western nations were so strongly intertwined that war between them had become impossible. At the same time, even those who were in favor of war as a way of regulating international affairs recognized that technical advances in weaponry had made war a far more destructive and costly business and that therefore wars in future would be, according to even German general and war enthusiast Heinrich von Treitschke, "rarer and shorter" (quoted in Mueller 1991: 15). International developments such as the rise of the peace movements in industrialized nations and The Hague congresses of 1899 and 1907 suggested that the world was more ready to find ways of overcoming wars than at any time previously. From 1899 to 1902, the British had to conduct the Boer War in an atmosphere of international as well as domestic disapproval and endure open criticism of the conduct of the war and its consequences, which did much to promote anti-war feeling in Britain (Hochschild 2011: chapter 3, especially 34–7), while World War I was the first major war to be conducted following a long period of anti-war agitation (Mueller 1991: 11–12). During this period, many were encouraged by scientifically backed ideas of progress to believe that aggression could be overcome by education and socialization or channeled into more productive activities, and some feminists also used essentialist arguments that equated masculinity with aggression and violence to argue for women's inclusion in the life of the state. Optimism about human progress was starkly challenged by the outbreak of World War I in 1914, which seemed to reinforce pessimistic ideas about human psychology, such as those expressed by Sigmund Freud during the conflict, that aggression was innate to human nature and could never be truly eradicated.

While the majority of the women's movement retreated into patriotic war service and abandoned at least the public articulation of claims for women's rights during the war, a small but committed group within the international movement banded together across national boundaries as far as this was possible under wartime restrictions to campaign for peace. While some remained wedded to essentialist ideas equating men with war and claiming peace as a female sphere, there were influential thinkers such as Addams who placed claims for women's equality within a broader democratic framework of economic, political, and social justice and called for international structures designed to overcome the self-interest of the nation states. Addams shared many of Freud's ideas about the importance of primitive urges in understanding human nature, but remained optimistic that the instincts of nurturing the helpless young could be mobilized to overcome and override the more destructive combative instinct, while her conversations with soldiers reinforced her conviction that the younger generation of men too saw war as an outmoded means of settling international disputes. Before 1914, she argued consistently that human nature could find more positive and constructive ways of satisfying the desire for adventure, challenge, excitement, and competition that seemed to be met by war. After World War I, she suggested that the ability to rise to the logistic challenges of global war showed humanity's potential ability to overcome challenges of poverty, disease, hunger, and mass displacement that the post-war world was faced with, along with the huge challenge of rebuilding the towns, cities, and countryside the war had destroyed.

These ideas were reflected in the resolutions of the International Women's Congress at The Hague, which argued along similar lines to those put forward by peace movement progressives, but also explicitly bound up progress toward a more peaceful world order with women's inclusion in the life of the state. Addams envisaged a global order structured in such a way as to overcome the factors that led to war, and that would promote democracy, equality, and justice and the inclusion of women in political decision-making at national and international level. These ideas represent a major challenge by feminist thinkers such as Addams to widespread pessimism about the link between men and war— as something men need and even enjoy in order to express their masculine natures and preserve the masculine strength of the nation.

CHAPTER THREE

Peace, War, and Gender

The Evolution of Women's Voices

SANDI E. COOPER

Convulsed by twenty-five years of war and revolution that ended in 1815, the victorious European coalition that defeated Napoleon met in Vienna from September 1814 to June 1815. Besides restoring the Bourbon monarchy to the French throne, the meeting determined to shape a long-term European peace by establishing a stable balance among European powers and agreeing to suppress revolutionary uprisings everywhere. Count Klemens von Metternich, who orchestrated much of the meeting, realized that traditional dynastic wars among European powers would undermine inherited monarchical authority. For official Europe, therefore, the purpose of peace was to conserve the social and political parameters of the Old Regime.

For a small group of Protestants, mainly Quakers, and humanitarians in England, the end of what was then the worst bloodshed in human memory inspired very different peace thinking. The unrelenting violence among Europeans utterly contravened the presumed Christian culture that bound them. The dead and wounded toll from the wars of the French Revolutionary and Napoleonic era, 1792–1815, was a historic cataclysm. The (London) Society for the Promotion of Permanent and Universal Peace, founded in 1816, grew out of impulses similar to those inspiring anti-slavery societies and groups backing criminal justice reform. War was declared to be inconsistent with Christian teaching. Overall the group did not preach total nonviolence but argued for the establishment of international, official institutions to preserve peace via negotiation, arbitration, mediation, and good offices—essentially the modes that peace organizations urged throughout the nineteenth century.

Nearly simultaneously, a peace society was founded in New York. These groups became the ancestors of the British Peace Society (founded in 1816 as the Society for the Promotion of Permanent and Universal Peace) and the American Peace Society, founded in 1828.[1] As citizen lobbies grew in the nineteenth century, issues such as public health, workers' rights, sanitary reform, urban amenities, and women's equality increasingly demanded the attention of the educated middle classes. International peace quickly joined the roster of public causes. However, while the major European powers managed for decades to heed Metternich's warning about war, the revolutionary message of the French Revolution periodically produced popular uprisings for either political rights or national unification.

In Paris and Geneva during the 1820s peace societies concerned with humanitarian issues—prison reform and the end of the death penalty—were formed respectively by the

Duc de Rochefoucauld-Liancourt (Société de la morale chrétienne) and Jean-Jacques, Comte de Sellon (Société de la paix).[2] Much like the London society, these groups insisted they were a-political, committed to Christian principles and humanitarian goals. They largely functioned as small discussion organizations and published broadsides and pamphlets. Apart from Valentine de Sellon, the Count's daughter, women seemed to play no part and indeed, in the 1840s when the first international congresses of peace societies began to meet, women watched from balconies.

It was Eugénie Niboyet (née Mouchon, 1799–1883), a follower of the French socialist reformers, Saint-Simon and Fourier, who introduced a different dimension into the peace discourse.[3] Niboyet launched the first newspaper devoted to peace in 1844, *La Paix des Deux Mondes*, followed by *L'Avenir*. Her advocacy was unlike the exclusively male Anglo-American groups. It was practical, she argued; since 1815 peace had produced a period of invention, prosperity, economic expansion, and global trade. Progress was not promoted by imperialist adventures such as the French occupation of Algeria (1830) nor by squashing the Polish revolutionary desire for a nation.[4] "Our definition of peace is based on freedom of all peoples and classes to enjoy the benefits of expanding prosperity," she wrote in opposition to the apparent fears of the upper classes against those beneath them (Niboyet, June 27, 1844: 1–2). "Friends of peace must morally denounce all usurpation, all violence, as the source of trouble and of war," she proclaimed (Niboyet

FIGURE 3.1: Fredrika Bremer (1801–65). Credit: Kean Collection/Getty Images.

July 4, 1844: 1). When she finally closed down her papers in 1845, it was with the sad note that the powers had kept the peace via ever escalating armament and had done nothing to alleviate the brutal social divisions within their states.

Niboyet's advocacy of peace presaged themes later common to women's arguments. Peace was tied to social justice, individual rights, the abolition of misery, and a demilitarized international community. Unlike those of male-led peace groups, her proposals did not depend on legal international modes such as arbitration.

Niboyet had not specifically called on women to initiate peace actions, but the Swedish novelist and feminist Fredrika Bremer (1801–65) did. In an "Invitation to a Peace Alliance" published in *The Times* (Bremer, August 28, 1854) she called on women to break their silence and protest against the Crimean War (1852–6). Bremer had escaped a patriarchal childhood, and traveled through Europe and the United States where slavery especially horrified her. In *Hertha* (1856), the novel that inspired changes in the patriarchal rule of males over unmarried female members of the household, the heroine rejects parental control that prevents a marriage based on love. Bremer's public eminence established by her successful career as a writer is possibly what persuaded the London newspaper to publish a call to women that urged Christian women's groups everywhere that served the poor to ally to oppose "the direct effect of war" and to stop the impending Crimean war and, indeed, all future wars:

> At a time like this, when the Powers of the West arm themselves against those of the East and enter into a struggle threatening to spread over several of the countries of Europe like a large bleeding wound, tearing men from their homes, leaving thousands of widows and fatherless children, destroying harvests, burning cities, filling hospitals, calling up bitter and hateful passions, laying shackles on commerce, embittering life in many thousand quiet, industrious families—a struggle, the sorrowful effects of which possibly may be felt by most of the nations of the earth—at such a time we have ventured a thought, a hope that through women a peaceful alliance might be concluded embracing the whole earth . . . opposing the direful effects of war, and contributing . . . to the development of a state of peace, love and well-being to come forth once the terrors of war shall be over, and the time of devastation has passed away.
> —Bremer 1854

Bremer's call for an international alliance of women did not materialize, but her vision of the impact of large-scale warfare was indeed prescient.

From the mid-century revolutions of 1848 through the wars of national unification (Italian and German) as well as the American Civil War, peace voices were hard to hear.[5] However, in 1867 a group of liberals organized a peace conference in Geneva. Many opposed the incumbent (second) Napoleonic dictatorship and they created the Ligue international de la paix et de la liberté. The organization launched a long-term publication, *Les Etats-Unis d'Europe*, which came out in English, French, and German. The congress agreed upon a platform of self-determination, free speech, the right to work, public education, and religious toleration, the end of standing armies, and the establishment of a permanent organization that would support a United States of Europe.[6] It avoided social issues. At the second meeting, in August 1868, an even more radical project was introduced: Geneva-born Marie Goegg (1824–99) presented a resolution to include women in all peace societies and discussions on behalf of her newly founded group, the Association internationale des femmes. The Ligue supported her in an August 1868 vote. Goegg realized that women needed a serious education to become engaged in politics. In her speech to the Ligue she observed: "Men have paid dearly for their mistake and their descendants still suffer. By denying women as their equal, arrogant men lowered their own stature. If women had been called from 1789 to develop their own abilities, . . . society . . . would have progressed"(1878, 4–5).

Marie Goegg founded the first feminist organization in Switzerland to work for women's emancipation, including a campaign to open universities to women. The *Journal des Femmes* launched in 1869 reported on the variety of women's groups created in the US and Europe. The looming crisis in 1870 between France and Prussia led Goegg to convene a meeting of the Association Internationale des Femmes (April) to try to prevent a conflict, but when it occurred, she lashed out at an executive committee meeting of the Ligue international:

> Men love and want war . . . they know that women on the other hand, want peace. This reason alone . . . would be sufficient for them to impose their undivided authority and suffices, in effect, to create a . . . condition conducive to kings and the sycophants who surround them. Thus the non-involvement of women . . . makes possible in our time, the revival of an act whose outcome will be to ruin, demoralize, cripple and butcher the best of both nations.
> —Le Comité de la Ligue allemande de la Paix (Section des Femmes),
> August 1870: 66

After 1870, Goegg focused on women's organizing. Hers was the first woman's voice that tied international violence to male behavior. Concerned with improving the status of women she hosted a meeting in Geneva (1877) in conjunction with British efforts against prostitution, led by Josephine Butler, that brought women from half a dozen nations together (see Summers 2006).

By the 1870s, the Peace Society in Great Britain, the oldest European peace group, had formed a Ladies Auxiliary, led by Mrs. Henry Richard, wife of the eminent religious peace crusader from Wales. The religious, a-political evangelism of the Society eschewed feminist concerns and the Auxiliary apparently obeyed (Brown 1913: 60–4). Feminists therefore moved to build their own organizations and journals. In the pages, for instance, of *The Englishwoman's Review*, published between 1866 and 1910, war, peace, militarism, and social reform received regular coverage. Connecting the vote with the potential for a peaceful foreign policy emerged as a common theme. The Franco–Prussian War was presented as the blundering, brutal result of dynastic politics by Lydia Becker in the *Women's Suffrage Journal* (see Brown 1913: chapter 2).

In the last third of the century, women's engagement in peace expanded significantly. The American Julia Ward Howe (1819–1910), known for her American classic "Battle Hymn of the Republic," despite her support for the Union in the US Civil War became sickened by the war and campaigned for a mothers' crusade against all war. Violating all social norms, she left the prison of her marriage to a husband who fumed at her fame as a writer and activist (see Showalter 2016). In September 1870, in Boston, she issued a "Mother's Day Proclamation" which opened with a bitter denunciation of the fact that "great questions" were decided by irrelevant agencies. "Our husbands shall not come to us, reeking with carnage for caresses and applause. Our sons shall not be taken from us to unlearn . . . all that we have taught them of charity, mercy and patience." Women from one country must not allow their sons to hurt those of women from another. For too long women's role had been to bewail and to support, to commemorate, but now, Howe wrote, "I earnestly ask that a general congress of women without limit or nationality be appointed and held at some place deemed most convenient and at the earliest period . . . to promote the alliance of the different nationalities, the amicable settlement of international questions, the great and general interests of peace" (Howe 1870).[7] The 1873 Woman's Peace Festival in Boston received considerable publicity and similar meetings occurred in St. Louis, across Great Britain (Howe herself spoke at a big London event), and in Geneva, and were reported in *La Donna* (Venice), the first Italian women's paper.

Increasingly women challenged male-led peace movements to expand their vision. From Algeria came a new voice calling on women to demand peace and a cessation of violence. Virginie Griess-Traut (1813–98), who engaged in a number of feminist reform activities in France, published a cry to women: "[D]emand to be counted! We are half of the human race, that half on which the heaviest weight of household anguish and national miseries fall. . . . Drive away the false doctrine of the necessity of war, . . . Banish from our children's lips that inconceivable prayer to 'the God of Arms'" (Griess-Traut 1870: 79).

Independently wealthy, Griess-Traut was a socialist, feminist, and pacifist who chose to live with Jean Traut in a "citizen couple" arrangement. A participant in nearly every women's meeting that occurred up to the end of her life, Griess-Traut repeatedly called for women to denounce war and militarism (November 1879, *Le Travailleur*, 11–12). In her will she left a legacy to the newly created International Peace Bureau (1892) which insured its survival—donations from Nobel and Carnegie did not come until at least a decade later (reported in *La Correspondance autographiée* 1895: 1).

The year 1889 was a watershed for organized peace movements. It was the centennial of the French Revolution, the year that Gustave Eiffel unveiled his lacy iron tower on the occasion of the major Parisian Exposition, a World's Fair bringing peoples from everywhere to see the sparkling French recovery from its humiliating defeat of 1871. Peace societies and members of parliaments used the occasion to found the Universal Peace Congress and the Interparliamentary Union.[8] Coincidentally, in Germany it was also the year when Austrian author Bertha von Suttner's novel *Die Waffen Nieder* (*Lay Down Your Arms*) appeared. To its publisher's surprise, the novel became a runaway bestseller, and by 1914 had appeared in every major language and sold millions of copies. It portrayed the tragedy of the fictional Martha Trilling who lost two husbands in the wars of the late 1860s and included graphic portraits of battlefield carnage.[9] Von Suttner's high-profile work for peace in the Universal Peace Congresses and the peace societies she inspired in Austria and Germany are discussed by Laurie Cohen in Chapter 5 of this volume.

The increasing numbers of women engaging in the peace movement in the quarter-century before World War I included those working in local groups as well as those attending large congresses. The Quaker Ellen Robinson (1840–1912), who led the English Peace Union, wanted to build an international network of women's peace societies. Robinson succeeded Priscilla Hannah Peckover had (1833–1931) as head of the (Wisbech, Cambridgeshire) Women's Local Peace Association. A devout Quaker, Peckover had used her own personal fortune to build peace networks in Britain and on the continent. During the 1880s she founded a journal, *Peace and Goodwill*, and worked energetically to expand women's membership in the venerable British Peace Society. The society in Wisbech actually grew to over 4000 members under her care, a significant leap from the 150 women members of the peace society in 1879. The International Peace Bureau connected Robinson to French women's groups. She wrote:

> We English women ask when we can call on ancient ties between our two nations. The current state of Europe appears hardly susceptible to universal harmony. Each nation

feels threatened by the continued growth of its neighburs' military forces. [The tension] encourages the most insignificant incident to become a serious cause of confrontation. But the French and English, so close, with so many common interests, could live in peace and show mutual sympathy, offering an example to the rest of Europe which might, perhaps, shape the union of all nations.

—Robinson *et al*. 1895

Her appeal referred to the growing use and success of international arbitration as the means for reducing tensions and, ultimately, weaponry. Women, Robinson argued, have a personal, educational and social role. In Paris she connected with Eugénie Potonié-Pierre (1844–98), a feminist-pacifist who demanded the vote and total civic equality: as secretary of the Cercle de la solidarité des femmes, she crusaded for equal education and political and civil rights, and attacked socialists for their lame concern about women. Their group, the International Women's Peace Union, organized branches in half-a-dozen nations (Brown 1913: 103). Potonié-Pierre wrote:

> L'Union internationale des femmes pour la paix is developing very well. I have just received the backing of Madame Belva Lockwood. . . . Committees have formed in Italy, England, Belgium and we have the moral support of Swiss women. In Austria, Denmark, America and probably Norway, Sweden, Greece and Australia, we expect support. The most difficult thing is, without a doubt, to persuade Germans to support the Union.

She concluded by saying that the Union's main objective was "general disarmament" and to "examine the means by which the powers can agree on such a step" (Potonié-Pierre 1895).[10]

German women from the Ligue allemande de la paix sent "their French sisters" a carefully worded manifesto of support, emphasizing the importance of furthering arbitration, admitting that a modern war would be a "massacre" and a major setback to civilization but omitting talk of arms control. The German women who promised to "work with all their strength to accomplish the noble aim of universal peace" featured Bertha von Suttner, who by the mid-1890s had won international name recognition for her anti-war novel *Die Waffen nieder (Lay Down Your Arms)*, as their main signatory. The others included a number of doctors, academics, the editor of the *Deutsche-Hausfrauenzeitung*, social workers, artists, and socially prominent women (Le Comité de la Ligue allemande de la Paix (Section des Femmes) 1895). The Union internationale des femmes pour la paix, unlike the cautious leadership of the International Peace Bureau and such groups as Passy's Société française pour l'arbitrage entre nations or the Association La Paix par le droit, sang out squarely for disarmament and an end to the arms race. The women ignored the charge that disarmament campaigns were unpatriotic, if not treasonous.[11] It is noteworthy that the British–French connection that Robinson and Potonié-Pierre established preceded the formal Anglo–French Entente by a decade.

With the August 1898 Russian invitation proposing a conference of the major powers to consider arms reduction, women swung into action. At a meeting of the Federation of German Women's Associations in the fall of 1898, Margarethe Leonore Selenka (1860–1922), an eminent zoologist, proposed a mass petition campaign to support the initiative. In Germany, the feminist-pacifist Anita Augspur (1857–1943) undertook the job of organizing the campaign.[12] By May 1899, when the actual diplomatic conference assembled at The Hague, the international campaign had gathered over a million signatures (see

FIGURE 3.2: Anita Augspurg (1857–1943). Credit: Ullstein BIld Dtl./Getty Images.

Selenka 1900). Selenka proudly observed that women's emergence from public shadows to agitate for a successful Hague Peace Conference inspired the first public meetings of women in Spain, Russia, and Japan as well as over 560 simultaneous meetings in dozens of countries. "Are not," she asked, "the Peace Question and the Women's Question akin in the origin of their being? Both of them . . . contain a strong ethical element, firmly bound up with the most pressing social and economic needs" (1899, quoted in Chatfield *et al.* 1994: 92).[13] It was no wonder that she made the German ambassador's list of the "worst social elements" present at The Hague. In fact, women peace activists were entering a stage in which they increasingly challenged male dominance in policy issues and were prepared to go much farther in their demands than the more cautious male-led peace organizations.

Concomitantly in Paris, the Ligue des femmes pour le désarmement international, founded by the Polish Princess Marie-Gabrielle Hortense Hugo Wiszniewska (1836–1903),[14] launched an international mailing campaign which collected thousands of signatures supporting the Hague meeting. It went on to agitate for arms reductions, a position modified under pressure from male peace leaders. In 1900 her group changed its name to L'Alliance universelle des femmes pour la paix par l'education (Universal Alliance of Women for Peace through Education). The executive committee contained well-known writers, wives of political leaders, leaders of anti-alcohol campaigns, organizations for the care of orphans, teachers, and people from Catholic, Protestant, and Jewish organizations, as well as women from various political backgrounds. Groups were organized outside of Paris in the provinces as well as in Sweden, Norway, Italy, Rumania, Russia, Finland, Spain, and Egypt (see Marya-Chéliga 1900: 76–88). Shortly before her death in 1903, the princess proposed to the tenth international feminist congress meeting in Paris that "Pacifist feminism will remain an empty shell as long as women do not occupy the majority of seats in the Society of Nations."[15]

Inspired by Bertha von Suttner, the Dutch aristocrat Johanna Waszklewicz-van Schilfgaarde (1850–1937) hosted a salon during the meeting of the diplomats in 1899 where officials mingled with peace campaigners, including von Suttner, discussing the day's negotiations—diplomats among pacifists! Waszklewicz-van Schilfgaarde went on to create a peace society and published *Vrede door Recht* (*Peace Through Law*) (1900–2) and, unlike the neutral positions of delegations to international conferences of peace societies, she organized actively against Great Britain during the Boer War.

In France at the end of the nineteenth century, women writer-activists openly split with traditional peace movements to confront the Dreyfus case and the culture of militarism. In the pages of the feminist journal *La Fronde*, Clémence Royer (1830–1902), acclaimed for her scholarly work and her translations of Darwin's opus, laid bare the ways in which the military class supported itself on public funding by constantly manufacturing specters of war or thrilling ordinary people with colorful flag waving displays (Royer 1898).[16] She pointed to the huge budgetary allotment—about a billion francs per year atop billions spent on reorganization—with no public accounting. Were a war to break out, she predicted, at least 100,000 combatant casualties could be expected and no likely victory, given the rough equality of the sides.[17] Unlike the male-led peace movement, Royer attacked European policy overseas, particularly the intervention in China. European armies sent to punish the fighters of the Boxer Rebellion (1900) were treading a delusional path. In the twentieth century, the billions of peoples beyond Europe who were outraged by British and European arrogance would erupt to throw out the imperialists. To expect a civilization as old as China to embrace Christianity was a fantasy and an insult, and, she wrote, "[t]he war in China . . . is very likely to cause more destruction than ten medieval crusades and will only set civilization back" (Royer 1900: 1).

Her co-journalists pointed their pens at the military as the second Dreyfus trial in 1899, at Rennes, made clear that the military court had deliberately ignored the exculpatory evidence in order to shield their brother officers. The journalist Séverine (pen name of Carolyn Rémy) denounced the proceedings in a series of articles, "Notes d'une Frondeuse," which described the generals as "flatulent, self important and hypocritical" and the chief judge, General Mercier, as "the rampart of the nationalists." "What inspires some men to be more evil than others?" she asked (quoted in Cooper 2011: 18). The lower-ranking officers, she stated, perjured themselves out of fear for their careers and the trial raised questions about military justice. Royer, too, called the five judges contemptible and demanded the abolition of military tribunals. The editor and writers of *La Fronde* provided their readers with an undiluted diet of invective from August through September as the rigged trial proceeded, alarming the moderate male-led peace movement. Frédéric Passy, the doyen of the French and European peace movement, was fearful that these outspoken women would only stoke nationalist hostility against pacifism and add weight to their charge that it was utopian or treasonous. Moderate women activists, such as those in the International Council of Women which coordinated movements from various national cultures, trod lightly on the suffrage issue but the organization's commitment to peace was straightforward. An American, May Wright Sewell, was appointed to head its Peace and Arbitration Committee, which campaigned for a menu of legal international initiatives.[18] Sewell traveled and lectured widely in an effort to engage largely well-off women in the cause.

The outbreak of the Boer War in 1899 was an outrage too horrific to ignore, especially since Britain had been a major supporter of arbitration at The Hague Conference just a few months earlier. For British pacifists to protest against the war was dangerous; when a small group of British peace activists gathered in Trafalgar Square in September 1899 to urge that the new Hague arbitration arrangements be employed, they were surrounded by 40–50,000 pro-war demonstrators who threw sticks, rotten fruits, pipes, books, and knives. The police looked on for a time before they reluctantly moved in to rescue the small protest group, as reported in *Concord* on October 1, 1899 ("The Battle of Trafalgar Square," 165–7).

Word of British atrocities against civilians in South Africa aroused suffragette and social welfare reformer Emily Hobhouse (1860–1926). Hobhouse joined a committee to oppose the war, raised money, and collected supplies to bring aid to the women and children who were brutally victimized. At a meeting of over 3000 women in London in June 1900 a series of resolutions condemned the war—the loss of young British lives, the expenditure of millions when at home the poor could have benefited by those funds, and, particularly, the brutish treatment of civilians who were not dark-skinned colonials but rather peoples of European descent. Doubtless the overtly racist appeal helped further the cause (see Hobhouse Balme 1998). British tactics against civilians included scorched earth, destroying farms, and herding families into camps to confront the guerilla tactics of the Dutch Boer farmers. When reports reached England of Boer families, particularly women and children, being subjected to horrific conditions in concentration camps, Hobhouse went to South Africa, sailing in December 1900 and arriving by Christmas. In South Africa, the writer Olive Schreiner (1855–1920), who had been campaigning against British imperial and military moves, was silenced by the censorship but Emily Hobhouse received authorization to travel to distribute supplies and was able to file reports. However, the reports she filed about the conditions in the camps, the epidemics, lack of rudimentary sanitation, starvation, people sleeping on the ground under no shelter or blankets, enraged the government (see Liddington 1989, chapter 3; Fry 1919). Hobhouse described pregnant women lying on the ground, mothers and children dragged from their homes with nothing but the clothes on their backs in the summer of 1900—then winter in South Africa—typhoid killing children whose faces were shriveled with starvation. Her estimate of over 25,000 dead was not news that the London government welcomed atop reports of the bravery of the Boer farmer-soldiers (van Reenan 1984: 51).

Her request to the government to return in spring 1901 was rejected and instead a "Committee of Ladies" was sent, including Millicent Garrett Fawcett, chair of the leading British suffrage organization, and a select group of conservative women. Fawcett's report rejected Hobhouse's claims and indicated that conditions in the camps were quite acceptable. In a way, this division among English feminists presaged a similar split in 1914. Hobhouse discovered—as von Suttner had and others would—that women hardly presented a unified anti-war position, if that position involved criticism of one's own government. In fact, stories about the behavior of British soldiers was more likely to be blamed on poor upbringing by their mothers rather than the orders of their officers. Hobhouse refused to be put off and sailed again to South Africa in October 1901, but was

FIGURE 3.3: International Women's Suffrage Alliance including Millicent Garrett Fawcett. Credit: Universal Images Group/Getty Images.

arrested on arrival. Returned to England under martial law, Hobhouse prepared a blockbuster of an exposé, published in 1902 as *The Brunt of War and Where It Fell*. She portrayed a war on unarmed civilians, women, children, and the elderly who were either carted off to camps or told to go find people to care for them. *The Brunt of War* was a presage of twentieth-century total war and contributed to turning British public opinion against the war, despite the Fawcett commission whitewash.

Women activists continued to challenge the male leadership in the peace movement by attacking the arms race. An impatient French woman, Sylvie Flammarion (1884–1919), determined that the disarmament message needed a wider audience than those able to afford attendance at peace congresses. She addressed working-class women in market places and at a crowded public meeting at the Société des Savantes in Paris on "Feminine Humanity Against War," showing gruesome slides of a South African battlefield to a majority woman audience (Rambaud 1901). Her campaign against armaments was echoed by writers in *La Fronde* who publicized US atrocities against women and unarmed civilians in the Philippines, expressed outrage at British peace terms in South Africa, denounced

French mistreatment of the Annamese (Vietnam), and rejected the militarized patriotism of those crying "treason" against pacifists who opposed armaments and arms spending increases.[19] Women peace activists, particularly in France, denounced militarism. The costs of sustaining the armed peace, noted by Royer, became a major theme of Flammarion's impassioned speeches: at 22 million francs a day in military spending, she argued, France and other nations would soon only be paying taxes to fund the military. In a speech to a meeting of La Paix et le Désarmement par les Femmes, reported in *La Fronde* on June 8, 1903, she argued that the consequences to civilized society would be apparent—the nation would be weakened, not strengthened. In a public speech in a large hall in Lille on April 29, 1905, Flammarion reminded the audience that the 1789 Revolution had established the fundamental principle placing sovereign authority in the people—the people who work, suffer, and pay. "The current condition of Europe . . . affects the soldier more than the officer; during peace, he is taken from his work; during war, he is led to butchery. This is what women must understand. If . . . women of the people finally would see the truth, none of them would support the military edifice" (reprinted in *La Paix par les Femmes* May 1905: 15).

At the end of the 1890s, Italian feminists joined in. Paolina Schiff (1844–1926) and Irma Melany Scodnick (1847–1920), active in the Lega dei interessi femminili, returned from the Parisian women's peace congress in 1900 determined to engage women in the Italian peace movement. Their second strategy was to launch campaigns to reform the educational curricula in primary schools, to reach out to the growing cadres of young women teachers, and to press for an anti-war-toys campaign. Before Maria Montessori (1870–1952) launched her famous new model for primary school education around 1907, women activists in Italy had initiated a move toward reforming the content of what was taught in order to achieve an end similar to Montessori's—humanizing the teaching of children as the foundation for a larger vision of democratic citizenship. Their campaign soon had to confront the problem of mass illiteracy among the poor and working class, worse among women. Here again, peace activism was tied to a broader swathe of social reform.

Schiff and Scodnick had come to an anti-war position through their anger at their government's 1896 invasion of Ethiopia which produced the first major humiliating defeat of a European imperialist state when the Italian army was beaten at Adua. The war mobilized both middle-class and socialist women, who were outraged that the state they had struggled to create during the *Risorgimento* was killing its own young men, leaving poor women to struggle with children, doing nothing to decrease poverty and disease, while building a navy and expanding a conscript army. Moreover, reports of the behavior of Italian soldiers in their colonial enclaves were horrifying. Scodnick bitterly described the murder, rape, and pillage by the so-called "carriers of civilization to the colonies" (1907, quoted in Scriboni 2008: 35). Another Italian feminist, Camilla Baricelli, founded the journal *L'alleanza* where she wrote in September 1906 that peace was the future of human destiny and predicted "human and rational law will rise invincibly against the irrational behavior of a handful" (*Per la pace universale*, ivi September 15, 1906, cited in Scriboni 2008: 34).

The socialist feminist *alma dolens* (pseudonym of Teresita Pasini dei Bonfatti) brought the energy of a crusader to Italian peace circles, attacking the movement's silence about the social consequences of military spending. Her attack on Italian peace activists was blunt—their refusal to campaign against military spending made them responsible for the hunger of children and the miasma of poverty. A passive, intellectually focused peace movement was useless. When the Messina earthquake (1908) destroyed huge numbers of lives and homes, she demanded that peace activists volunteer, deliver supplies, and support medical and emergency help—in short, become activists (*Per la pace universale* 1, January 5, 1909, cited in Scriboni 2008: 38).

dolens attacked peace groups for their silence on women's rights but a real split occurred in 1911 when the official leadership of the Italian movement backed the invasion of Libya[20] whereas, with a few exceptions, educated women rejected the move. Their vocal protests evidently provoked the nationalist writer Filippo Marinetti into publishing his *Futurist Manifesto*: "[w]e want to glorify war—the only cure for the world, militarism, patriotism . . . the beautiful ideas which kill, and contempt for woman" (1909: #9 of the manifesto, widely available online in English).

His dashing and noisy exhibitionism attracted a following, often young men who wanted the thrills of motorcars, airplanes, speed, and action. Women, in Marinetti's statement, needed to remain silent, homemakers, out of the public space. Women who campaigned against the war were ridiculed and told to mind their own sphere which included supporting men at war. The novelist Sibilla Aleramo took up the challenge and made it very clear that if men wanted to play at virility, there was little that women could do to stop them but that they (women) bore absolutely no responsibility for what clearly was the outcome—death and misery (Aleramo 1911: 1).

Women's activism attacked the French educational system too and curricula content for school children became an important target. In France, two schoolteachers, Madeleine Carlier and Marguerite Bodin, launched the Société d'Education Pacifique which campaigned among teachers in favor of a new form of patriotism. The organization grew to twenty-three sections across the country and was focused on history teaching. "Who will write the small, truly international, history manual?" asked Odette Laguerre in *La Fronde*, May 6, 1903. Then, answering her own challenge, with Madeleine Carlier, Laguerre co-authored a handbook intended for the training of potential teachers in normal schools (Laguerre in *La Fronde*, May 6, 1903), The manual emphasized the positive attainments that science and industry brought during peacetime and redefined patriotism as a positive sense of being in a nation—not an emotion shaped by enmity toward others. As Niboyet had once argued, peaceful progress improved food supplies and produced manufacturing marvels; violent warfare did not (Clinton 1998, 207–10).

Similarly in the United States a former teacher, Fannie Fern Andrews, established the American School Peace League in 1907, promoting a curriculum of internationalism and positive patriotism. Andrews lectured around the United States, convinced that school curricula could engage children of immigrants and native-born citizens in a broad understanding of peace and collaboration (see Howlett n.d.; Zeiger 2002). In Boston, Lucia Ames Mead (1856–1936), with her husband, Edwin Mead, emerged to become a well-known name in the movement and founded the Boston School Peace League in 1910. In addition, with members of the US committee, she protested against increases in the US naval budget and campaigned against Admiral Mahan, whose influence on both US and German policy makers effected significant naval expansion (Mahan 1890; Mead [1890] 1910).

Ineluctably women moved toward a critique of patriarchy, though the word was not used. For a young, new peace crusader, Jeanne Mélin (1877–1964), socialism, suffragism, women's equality, and peace formed an inseparable matrix. As a child, her grandmother's descriptions of the dying and wounded in their home during the Franco–Prussian War had turned her against all war (Mélin (alias Thalès) 1957: 1) and by 1903 she claimed to have become "irrevocably a feminist" along with her other commitments (Mélin (alias

Thalès) 1957: 19). Her life became a round of meetings—campaigning for arbitration, for women's right to vote, for benefits to support working-class women, for disarmament— and Mélin emerged as an accomplished public speaker and a familiar figure at congresses. Years later, she wryly observed that the period called the "belle époque" was indeed beautiful for the privileged, of which, she admitted, her family was part (Mélin (alias Thalès) 1957: 4). By 1910 she was a central figure on the French national council of peace societies, a delegate to the international congresses, and a journalist who worked to tie peace circles to socialist and feminist groups.

In the United States the work of Jane Addams, particularly her book *The Newer Ideals of Peace* (1907), provided a pointed attack on patriarchy. Described as "[t]he most important and innovative work of peace theory in the first decade of the twentieth century" (Carroll *et al.* 2007: xiv), Addams rejected standard peace bromides, emphasizing legal internationalism. Expanding on her social work model in Chicago, Addams argued that peace could only emerge from a totally different political culture shaped by the democratic engagement of disparate ethnic groups. As discussed by Ingrid Sharp in Chapter 2 of this volume, her vision of peace was based on a grassroots set of practices which included women, immigrants, and the poor, trained in local governance practices instead of the top-down, controlling masculine models that typified most nations. In this instance, peace education—broadly understood—and a new vision of peace theory reflected a distinctive women's approach. Addams clearly connected the historical traditions of militarism to the authoritarian structures of state institutions. Her argument for inclusiveness in the political process was independently echoed by the Swedish Nobel Prize winner (1909 for literature) Selma Lagerlöf (1858–1940) who addressed the International Suffrage Congress in Stockholm in June 1911. It was women and men, she argued, who created the home, but men alone who created the state. Until women participated equally in the state, public life would not erase violence, strife, and class struggle. Only with women's equal participation could the state and the public sphere reach a higher plane (Lagerlöf 1911: 14). The International Peace Congress, also meeting in Stockholm, voted for a large project, a Code de la Paix which proposed establishing legalistic and diplomatic means for resolving disputes.[21] Lagerlöf, however, essentially dismissed such projects, insisting that the exclusion of women from the political process meant that only half the human race was making decisions. Until women fully entered the political process, she maintained in a speech to the International Suffrage Association in 1910, militarism and war preparation would dominate (Howard (trans.) 1911: 3–5)

Women activists came to the peace movement also from a concern with women's control of their own bodies. Dr. Aletta Jacobs in the Netherlands, for instance, worked to help poor women manage pregnancies. She moved into suffrage and peace groups, and in 1915 became the prime organizer of the women's peace congress at The Hague. The nexus between birth control and citizenship seemed clear to her. If women remained overburdened with endless childcare and drudgery, the likelihood of participation in the public space would remain impossible and, without women's citizenship, the pressure to preserve peace was unlikely and women would only be creating cannon fodder.

In France, Nelly Roussel (1878–1922), an active campaigner for a woman's right to control her body and her pregnancies, eventually also realized the tie to anti-war movements. She ran straight into French anxieties about population size relative to Germany. The call to French women to furnish the nation with a fit population prepared to defend *la patrie* butted head on into the radical Rousselian project that privileged women's bodies and health.[22] With the outbreak of war in 1914, speeches and publications

FIGURE 3.4: Dr. Aletta Jacobs, Dutch suffrage leader and coordinator of the Women's International Congress at The Hague, April 28–May 1, 1915. Credit: Heritage Images/Getty Images.

advocating birth control were prohibited, as women's bodies became a contested space in a nationalist project that assumed warfare was inescapable (Accampo 2006: 171 ff.). Roussel understood that women's health and equality would only be respected if the warfare state was abolished. This issue became far more than an intellectual discussion after World War I when France, followed by Italy and Germany, outlawed birth control and abortion with severe criminal penalties. Conversely women who produced large families would receive medals and various public subsidies.

After 1900, escalating international crises over colonial possessions, the naval race between Britain and Germany, the introduction of more murderous weaponry—the machine gun, for instance—were met with increasing alarm among peace activists. Pre-1914 peace groups never assumed that war was either inevitable or totally avoidable, but they predicted that if it did happen it would be unlike any previous experience of war on the European continent. The sense of impending violence impelled Bertha von Suttner's six-month, coast-to-coast lecture tour of the United States in 1912 at age sixty-nine. Addressing peace and women's groups, she bluntly called the Department of War a "department of hell," urging American women to mobilize for international disarmament with all their energies. Like many Europeans, she saw America as a land of promise for progressive causes and peace (see Cohen 2009).

The German-born, naturalized US citizen Anna Eckstein (1868–1944) became a noted peace activist in her adopted country and was equally fearful of a coming war. From 1911 to 1912, she collected signatures for The World Petition to Prevent War Between Nations to encourage use of the Hague conventions, and began a petition campaign to convene the promised third Hague Peace Conference (cancelled in 1913) which amassed about six million signatures on the eve of the war. Eckstein, initially drawn to peace campaigns by Bertha von Suttner, became an active member of the Massachusetts peace society and an ardent anti-war campaigner. Fluent in German, French, and English, she was uniquely placed to understand the powder keg in Europe which she expected to explode.

Frances Hallowes, a British pamphleteer, also pleaded with the European powers to convene the promised Third Hague Peace Conference. At the May 1914 meeting of the International Council of Women, Hallowes described the murder of over 4000 women and 15,000 children in the South African war alone. She vividly portrayed the mutilation and mass rape of women in the Balkan Wars (1911–13) and the huge destruction to homes by General Sherman in the US Civil War. For her, war unleashed a bloodthirst in men, a legitimization for latent violence among largely young, unmarried males. Practically speaking, she insisted, the cost of the arms race was the direct source of endless poverty among the world's most advanced societies.

The largely legalistic approach of the organized, male-led, international movement was significantly expanded with the publication of Norman Angell's *The Great Illusion* (1910), which became a bestseller on both sides of the Atlantic. Peace activists could draw on very practical anti-war arguments based on the globalized interconnectedness of European economies: investments and productions crossed all borders in Europe; banks were transnational in some cases.

Bertha von Suttner died on June 21, 1914, a week before the Sarajevo assassination that eventually triggered the Great War that she had feared. By August 1, 1914, the powers abandoned Metternich's 1815 warning and plunged the continent into the miasma which undermined its global ascendency, overturned four empires, produced a massive revolution and devoured 10,000,000 young lives. The decimated post-war generation also included an army of crippled veterans and governments unprepared to care for them. Weakened civilian populations were easy prey to the global influenza pandemic that wiped out millions more. The social and personal upheaval and the political consequences for the twentieth century cannot be exaggerated.

About five months after the bloodbath began, it was clear that the promise of a quick victory was a chimera and that the war demanded total civilian and military mobilization. It was women who foresaw the coming years of death and human misery and who took the first steps toward trying to roll back the massive mistake of their male leaders. By 1914, European and American women were totally comfortable in organizing, publishing demands, holding conferences, lobbying governments, and reaching out to public opinion. Women had campaigned for civil rights, the right to higher education, and admission to professions hitherto male only. Some taught poor women to control their bodies and plan their motherhood. A handful of places accorded them the vote and from Oregon, the first

FIGURE 3.5: Jeanette Rankin (1880–1973) in 1918. Credit: Bettmann/Getty Images.

woman to be elected to the US Congress, Jeanette Rankin, took her seat.[23] By the end of 1914, women began to realize that the dreaded prediction about mechanized, industrial warfare had come to pass. Early in 1915, from the German socialist Clara Zetkin, the Swiss-American Clara Guthrie d'Arcis, and the Dutch Dr. Aletta Jacobs, came forth calls to end the bloodbath and organize peace—not as an interlude between wars but as an organized interstate system where women and men made political decisions. Their foremothers in the nineteenth century had provided the foundation for their initiatives. They envisioned a world order composed of constitutionally organized nation-states where all adults shaped public policies, including social and economic justice, gender equality, and peaceful international relationships. Instead of the old motto *si vis pacem, para bellum*, they would substitute *si vis pacem, para pacem*.

CHAPTER FOUR

Peace, Pacifism, and Religion

CLIVE BARRETT

"THE FRIEND O' GOD AN' PEACE"

Introducing a Poet

Picture a packed Riverside Church, New York, April 4, 1967. A frisson of anticipation greets the civil rights leader the Revd. Martin Luther King Jr., standing to deliver his address "Beyond Vietnam, a Time to Break Silence," his first speech opposing US military engagement in Vietnam. The gathering, Clergy and Laymen Concerned about Vietnam, hears King proclaim a once-in-a-lifetime opportunity and responsibility to stand for that which is right, for that which will be vindicated by God. He cites verses from a "noble bard of yesteryear":

> Once to every man and nation
> Comes the moment to decide,
> In the strife of truth and falsehood,
> For the good or evil side;
> Some great cause, God's new Messiah,
> Off'ring each the bloom or blight,
> And the choice goes by forever
> Twixt that darkness and that light.
>
> Though the cause of evil prosper,
> Yet 'tis truth alone is strong;
> Though her portion be the scaffold,
> And upon the throne be wrong:
> Yet that scaffold sways the future,
> And behind the dim unknown,
> Standeth God within the shadow
> Keeping watch above his own.

A culture of peace exists from which the peace movement of any generation can draw, as it in turn adds to that culture. The reconciliatory teaching and nonviolent being of Jesus of Nazareth is the basis for Christian opposition to war. There are saints, official and unofficial, in the cause: the fourth-century Martin of Tours, who refused to go into battle, saying, "I am a soldier of Christ. It is not lawful for me to fight"; Francis of Assisi; Wyclif, and the Lollards, whose New Testament-based opposition to war influenced fifteenth-century Bohemian reformers, from Hus to Chelčický.[1]

It is a late twentieth-century misapprehension that the so-called "just" war theory had any significant impact on the Churches' critique of war in the previous two centuries, at least outside Catholic circles, and with Catholic emancipation only granted in 1829, that community had other priorities (Fisher 2014: 28).[2] It was little in evidence in 1914 (or 1939), and even less so in the nineteenth century. Protestants were more comfortable with references to Scripture, and, as we shall see, those in the Peace Society from 1816 who drew on Christian tradition were more likely to look to the pacifism of the early Patristic period, the first four centuries of the Christian era, or to the writing of reformers such as Erasmus. The literature and lives, sayings and stories from peace people of the past inspired and enthused those who resisted different wars in later ages.

Our focus here will be on the words and actions of individuals and groups from diverse traditions who resisted war as a direct consequence of their faith in God, their trust in the values expressed in Christian scriptures, and their hope in an order which transcends the transitory whims of political argument. For Christian "pacifists," an evolving term, longing to deepen their relationship with the founder of their faith who was seen to counter violence in his very being, opposition to war was part of what it meant to be loyal to Christ. For members of the Society of Friends, with a long-standing peace testimony, such a position was at the heart of Quaker identity. As Nonconformist Churches became larger and more mainstream, their radical edge was diminished; pacifists within such Churches would generally be a minority, albeit sometimes a substantive one. The established Church of England identified strongly with the state, even seeing the Empire as God's agent for the conversion of the world; in that context, questioning the military and its motives smacked of treason, even blasphemy. Church of England pacifists were rare, but potentially more subversive.

We will consider three phases of Christian peace campaigning: the middle years of the nineteenth century, turn-of-the-century Victorian and Edwardian internationalism, and, finally, with the failure of what Martin Ceadel terms "pacificism," we will explore the faith and witness of Christian pacifists during the war years 1914–18. Our guide will be an American poet, whose verse drew from and interpreted Christian scripture and tradition. That poet, King's "noble bard," is James Russell Lowell (1819–91). The verse King cited was penned during the US war with Mexico, 1846–8. Lowell's anti-war sentiments would transcend generations and continents.

Lowell was one of a group of New England romantic writers known popularly (but not always flatteringly by literary critics) as the "Fireside Poets," a description Lowell embraced in his 1864 collection *Fireside Travels* (Burt 2008: 509). They wrote on American themes in accessible, popular, easily memorized, standard verse for recitation by families around the fireside. Lowell's diverse peers included Henry Wadsworth Longfellow, Oliver Wendell Holmes, William Cullen Bryant, and John Greenleaf Whittier, the latter being an anti-slavery Quaker who, in the *Brewing of Soma*, was the unwitting author of what became an establishment hymn, "Dear Lord and Father of Mankind," symptomatic of all he despised in organized religion.[3]

The lawyer son of a wealthy Unitarian minister in Cambridge, Massachusetts, Lowell was encouraged by his wife Maria White, herself a poet and active abolitionist, to become actively involved in the anti-slavery movement in the US in the 1840s (Duberman 1966: 71–2). In 1845 the US, following a policy of western expansion advocated by the Democratic president James K. Polk, annexed Texas then the following year occupied New Mexico and California before invading parts of what is now recognized as Mexico. The war ended with the US parting with $15 million (equivalent today to $500 billion) but expanding its area by the size of Western Europe. Internal opposition to the war came from those within anti-imperialist or anti-slavery movements, such as Abraham Lincoln,

FIGURE 4.1: James Russell Lowell (1819–91). Engraving with handwritten poem, "Death and Bereavement," 1860. Credit: Archive Photos/Stringer/Getty Images.

who feared the increase of slavery lands and with it the associated growth in influence of southern slave-owners. Henry David Thoreau (1817–62) was imprisoned for a night for refusing to pay his war taxes, leading him to write his essay *Civil Disobedience* which later influenced Tolstoy and especially Gandhi in their struggles with authority.[4]

In December 1845, Lowell's poem "The Present Crisis" was published in the *Boston Courier*. It was a call to conscience, to stand up against tyranny and for the cause of right. It explicitly opposed slavery and implicitly urged resistance to the prevailing war spirit, whatever the personal cost to one self. Those who took such a stand would ultimately be justified.

> Once to every man and nation comes the moment to decide,
> In the strife of Truth with Falsehood, for the good or evil side.

The poem was adapted and published as a hymn in Nonconformist hymnbooks (sung to the stirring Welsh melody "Ebenezer"). Note the final lines of this verse from Lowell's original:

> Hast thou chosen, O my people, on whose party thou shalt stand,
> Ere the Doom from its worn sandals shakes the dust against our land?

> Though the cause of Evil prosper, yet 't is Truth alone is strong,
> And, albeit she wander outcast now, I see around her throng
> Troops of beautiful, tall angels, to enshield her from all wrong.

This was what so moved Martin Luther King, one hundred and twenty years later.

Attempting to make a living by writing poetry and satire, in 1848 Lowell published *The Biglow Papers*, which, with hindsight, the Grolier literary club of New York described as the most influential book of that year.[5] It was singled out for praise when Lowell was awarded a DCL at Oxford University in 1873 (Duberman 1966: 263). A critique of the 1846–8 Mexican–American War in particular, and of war in general, the first edition of fifteen hundred copies sold out in a week.

In *The Biglow Papers*, Lowell gives a voice to a rural young man, Hosea Biglow, speaking in Yankee dialect. Having been accosted in the nearby town by a recruiting sergeant in full military uniform, Biglow had a restless night and wrote down what he really wanted to tell the soldier. In the morning he showed his verses to the parson. They combined critique of Southern slavery with Christian opposition to any form of war. Biglow's position, simply, was that war is wrong and cannot be justified by recourse to Christian scriptures.

> Ez fer war, I call it murder,—
> There you hev it plain an' flat;
> I don't want to go no furder
> Than my Testyment fer that;
> God hez sed so plump an' fairly,
> It's ez long ez it is broad,
> An' you've got to git up airly
> Ef you want to take in God.
>
> 'Tain't your eppyletts an' feathers
> Make the thing a grain more right;
> 'Tain't afollerin' your bell-wethers
> Will excuse ye in His sight;
> Ef you take a sword an' dror it,
> An' go stick a feller thru,
> Guv'mint ain't to answer for it,
> God'll send the bill to you.

This is a key sentiment on personal responsibility to God for one's own actions. One cannot justify one's actions by saying others, even the government, made one do something that is wrong, in this case sticking a feller through with a sword, as each individual is personally liable to God for the consequences of his or her own actions: "God'll send the bill to you."

> Wut's the use o' meetin'-goin'
> Every Sabbath, wet or dry,
> Ef it's right to go amowin'
> Feller-men like oats an' rye?
> I dunno but wut it's pooty
> Trainin' round in bobtail coats,—
> But it's curus Christian dooty
> This 'ere cuttin' folks's throats.

Biglow gives the message he wants to hear from the Northern states:

> "I'll return ye good fer evil
> Much ez we frail mortils can,
> But I wun't go help the Devil
> Makin' man the cus o' man;
> Call me coward, call me traiter,
> Jest ez suits your mean idees,—
> Here I stand a tyrant-hater,
> An' the friend o' God an' Peace!"

Lowell's verse will guide us through selected periods of the Christian pacifist story, from 1815 to 1918, beginning with the mid-century peace movement in England, acknowledging its roots in the aftermath of Waterloo.

"EZ FER WAR, I CALL IT MURDER"

Elihu Burritt

When Lowell was at his poetic peak, other Americans were making waves on the eastern shores of the Pond. A briefly significant figure was Thomas Pyne (c. 1802–73), formerly an Episcopalian rector in the US. In 1840 Pyne wrote an address for the Peace Society in England noting "the contrariety of all war to the Gospel," the avoidance of bloodshedding by the Apostles, and the appalling evils of war—including implications for the soul as "every moral act puts forth consequences permanent as eternity" (Pyne 1840: 1–2). Pyne linked national and individual attitudes and behavior: "The nation is but the individual multiplied. The passions of the mass are the passions of the man. The duties of the mass are the duties of the man." Thus he argued that everyone should "put away the unholy spirit of strife from him with all its pride, narrowness, evil-speakings, covetousness, cruelty, and revenge." Let each person, he said, "be as cautious of becoming a party to national acts of tyranny or inhumanity, as he would to private conduct of a like kind . . . Let him discourage books, prints, pictures, statues, &c. of a warlike tendency" (Pyne 1840: 4).[6]

More influential was the Congregationalist Elihu Burritt (1810–79). With Britain gripped by fear of French invasion, and militia bills being presented to Parliament—provoking a Quaker retort from the 1846 Meeting for Sufferings that military preparations, even for defense, were likely "to precipitate the very events against which they profess to guard"—Burritt's League of Universal Brotherhood attracted ten thousand signatories to its pacifist pledge in its first year, of whom six thousand came from Britain (Hirst 1923: 245). This wordy 1847 pledge, forerunner of the influential peace pledge of Canon Dick Sheppard (1880–1937) in the 1930s, opened with a homage to the aims of the Peace Society: "Believing all war to be inconsistent with the spirit of Christianity and destructive of the best interests of mankind, I do hereby pledge myself never to enlist or enter into any army or navy, or to yield any voluntary support or sanction to the preparation for or prosecution of any war" (Brock 1991b: 104–5). It considered the end of all war and "the abolition of all institutions and customs that do not recognize and respect the image of God and a human brother in every man, of whatever clime, colour, or condition of humanity" (Peace Pledge Union 1938: 6).

FIGURE 4.2: Elihu Burritt (1810–79). Credit: Encyclopaedia Britannica/Getty Images.

Burritt made it a priority to engage women and children in his peace movement and, through the League, helped to establish Olive Leaf Circles, enabling genteel women to discuss peace issues and correspond internationally with similar women's groups. Quaker women were prominent, but Burritt also noted participation by well-connected Church of England women (Liddington 1989: 15; Brock 1991b: 109–11).

The Peace Society

The roots of the Peace Society lie in earlier anti-slavery movements on both sides of the Atlantic. In his 1812 volume *War Inconsistent with the Religion of Jesus Christ*, David Low Dodge (1774–1852), a Presbyterian and an opponent of the slave trade in the US, cited research on the pacifism of the early Church Fathers by Thomas Clarkson (1760–1846), a Church of England deacon at the heart of British anti-slave trade campaigning. Three years later Dodge became the founder of the New York Peace Society (Mead 1905: xx).

The following year, 1816, in London, the Society for the Promotion of Permanent and Universal Peace (the Peace Society) was founded, in order to publish tracts showing that "War is inconsistent with the spirit of Christianity, and the true interests of mankind; and to point out the means best calculated to maintain a permanent and universal Peace, upon the basis of Christian principles" (*Rules of the Society*). The Peace Society was a strictly and overtly Christian grouping, with membership open to persons of every denomination "who are desirous of uniting in the promotion of Peace on earth, and good-will towards men." It aimed to influence faithful Christian living; in an avowedly Christian nation, that in turn might influence national policy. The relationship between the nineteenth-century peace movement and the Christian culture and language of the age is so intertwined that the peace movement cannot be understood separately from this Christian milieu.

Early pamphlets published by the Peace Society included: *A Solemn Review of the Custom of War*, by Noah Worcester (1758–1837), Unitarian founder of the Massachusetts Peace Society; Thomas Clarkson's work on the Fathers, *An Essay on the Doctrines and Practice of the Early Christians as they Relate to War*; and a translation of the peace writings of Erasmus.

One of the earliest publications was a reprint of the 1796 tract *War Inconsistent With the Doctrine and Example of Jesus Christ* by J. Scott of Islington. This clear sense of inconsistency between war and the core tenets of the Christian faith has regularly been reaffirmed in Christian peace history. So, in 1852, Quakers argued that "The whole system of war is so directly at variance not only with the plain precepts of our Lord, but with the whole spirit of his gospel" (Hirst 1923: 246). Two years later, the Society of Friends reiterated its "continued unshaken persuasion that all war is utterly incompatible with the plain precepts of our Divine Lord and Lawgiver, and with the whole spirit and tenor of His Gospel" (Hirst 1923: 264). After a series of similar pronouncements by the global ecumenical movement at Stockholm and Eisenach in the 1920s, describing war as "incompatible with the mind and method of Christ, and therefore incompatible with the mind and method of His Church," there was substantial endorsement by the 1930 Lambeth Conference of Anglican Bishops in their Resolution 25 that "War ... is incompatible with the teaching and example of our Lord Jesus Christ" (Jasper 1967: 94; Barrett 2014: 225).

The international ecumenical movement often traces its origins to the Edinburgh Missionary Conference of 1910. I would argue that its origins may be traced almost a century earlier, to the founding of the Peace Society. Unusually for the time, this was a trans-denominational initiative, clerical and lay, male and female, mainly but not merely the preserve of those with an historic peace tradition (Quakers), or dissenting Nonconformists accustomed to independent thinking, but embracing several members from the Church of England, two of whom, Thomas Clarkson and his brother John Clarkson, the first treasurer, were in positions of leadership. The latter may have been part of the religious establishment, but they were prepared to work alongside the Society of Friends, whose 1815 Yearly Meeting was told of ten adherents still undergoing prison terms for refusing military service (Hirst 1923: 244).

The inter-denominational constituency of the Society would alone have been challenging for many potential Church of England members, though it would have broken down barriers for those who did become involved. Although the committee at the heart of the Society was pacifist, completely opposed to war—a challenge for those in the established Church who felt constrained by war-permitting Article XXXVII of the Thirty-Nine Articles, "It is lawful for Christian men, at the commandment of the Magistrate, to wear weapons, and serve in the wars"—there was no requirement for ordinary members to be anything other than "desirous of uniting in the promotion of Peace on earth" (Barrett 2014: 3–6). Local groups, called "auxiliaries," were established around the country, with the first female auxiliary formed in Lymington followed in 1823 by two others in Leeds and Guisborough (Peace Society 1822: 6; 1823: 6).

Mid-century Internationalism

By mid-century, the scene was changing. Burritt's pledge of individual Christian commitment was counter to the prevailing trend of increasing the breadth of support of those committed to peace, even at a cost of diluting the core message that *all* war was contrary to Christian precepts.

At Burritt's suggestion, the Peace Society cooperated with plans for an international Peace Congress in Brussels in 1848, and there was a growing sense of a dynamic, but much broader, international peace "movement," using language that was more political, less pacifist, and less religious. A series of international peace congresses took place in subsequent years. In his *Journal* entry for August 21, Burritt noted the powerful impression created by a group of Quaker women among the delegates arriving in Paris for the 1849 Congress: "The soldiers that marched up and down before the entrance of the station threaded their monotonous way through the strangers, and seemed to tread timidly among the Quakeresses, and the busy crowd of peace men and women as if half ashamed of their muskets." At the London Congress of 1851, over twenty-one percent of the delegates (207 out of 969) were Quakers.

In Britain, the Friends of Peace established a Peace Congress Committee, run by a Congregationalist minister, Henry Richard (1812–88), soon to be joined by Richard Cobden (1804–65), popularly regarded as the "Champion of Peace." Cobden, who worshipped at St. John's, Deansgate, in Manchester, had spoken against the Afghan War of 1842 and was riding the crest of a political wave after his triumph in Anti-Corn Law campaigning. Cobden acknowledged his debt to the Peace Society, and in a private letter of September 19, 1853, observed that "The soul of the peace movement is the Quaker sentiment against all war. Without the stubborn zeal of the Friends, there would be no Peace Society and no Peace Conference" (Morley 1903: 608–9). He acknowledged that his own motivation was more politico-economical and financial, but even that was counter-cultural at a time when the military spirit was rampant among the influential classes. He relied on those "whose undying religious zeal" would bring eventual success while looking to build a broader peace movement that embraced all "men who desire to avert war" (Ceadel 1996: 374).

For Cobden, meaningful campaigning required grasping unpleasant nettles, not least British complicity in the slave trade, and the nation's underlying culture of war. In a January 1853 letter to a clergyman he wrote that the peace party would never rouse the conscience of the people, "so long as they allow them to indulge the comforting delusion that they have been a peace-loving nation. We have been the most combative and aggressive community that has existed since the days of the Roman dominion". There was a culture of war, added Cobden, with John Bull, a preference for the history of Agincourt, a fondness for monuments to warriors, and for bridges and streets named after battles, "but above all in the display which public opinion tolerates in our metropolitan cathedral, whose walls are decorated with bas-reliefs of battle scenes, of storming of towns, and charges of bayonets, where horses and riders, ships, cannon and musketry, realise by turns, in a Christian temple, the fierce struggle of the siege and the battlefield." These were worse than anything in Europe, said Cobden, and compared solely to monuments from Ninevah (Cobden, 1903: 376–7).

As the peace movement grew into political awareness and action, the Quaker Meeting for Sufferings sent a delegation to Tsar Nicholas in St. Petersburg in 1854 in an eleventh-hour attempt to avoid war in the Crimea. Joseph Sturge, Robert Charleton, and Henry

FIGURE 4.3: "Two Persuasions," *Punch*, 1878. Artist: Joseph Swain. This cartoon shows John Bright (1811–89) offering a genuine olive branch of peace, while the proffered olive branch of his opponent, Lord Beaconsfield, contains a sword. Credit: Print Collector/Getty Images.

Pease were received by the Tsar, but to no avail (Hirst 1923: 256–9). The visit was criticized by the bellicose British press, but a precedent had been set for future Quaker diplomacy.

Cobden's Anti-Corn Law partner, the Quaker John Bright (1811–89), took the lead when the peace movement was crushed by national war spirit. Britain's imperial adventurism in the Crimea led Bright to impassioned parliamentary speeches, not least that of February 1855 when he famously spoke of the angel of death being abroad throughout the land.

A High Church voice opposing war in the Crimea was that of Alfred Bowen Evans (c. 1811–78), curate of St Andrew's, Enfield. On the national Fast Day of Lent 1855 he argued that war was murder, that "What is morally wrong can never be politically right," and that "What is individually wrong can never be collectively right." Article XXXVII allowed for war that was just, he said, but believing wars to be just did not make them so. Rather, "Is it not more probable," he asked, "that all War is unjust, than that any particular War is the reverse?" (Evans 1855: 9). Evans was impressed neither by a war in which "Christian" England joined with "infidel" Turkey against "Christian" Russia, nor by claims that the process would convert the Turks. "Is it likely that Turks will be convinced of the truth of the Christian religion, when they see its professors tearing each other to pieces? We had better convert ourselves; and turn to the Lord our God, with all our hearts" (Evans 1855: 20). He affirmed the words of Jeremy Taylor (1613–67), "War is as contrary to the Christian religion, as cruelty is to mercy, tyranny to charity" (Evans 1855: 20).

A positive addendum was added by one of the Fireside Poets. Following the 1854 bombardment of the Finland coast by the British navy, Quakers in 1856–7 sent £9000 of practical relief to suffering Finns. Whittier responded to the act in verse:

> And so to Finland's sorrow
> The sweet amend is made,
> As if the healing hand of Christ
> Upon her wounds were laid!
> Then said the grey old Amtman,
> "The will of God be done!
> The battle lost by English hate
> By England's love is won!
>
> —Hirst 1923: 262

"GOD'LL SEND THE BILL TO YOU"

Exhibiting Hopes for Arbitration and the End of War

When the world's first peace museum opened in Lucerne in 1902, the artefacts on display were, surprisingly, implements of war. The inspiration for the museum, Polish railway engineer Jan Bloch (or Jean de Bloch, 1836–1902), wrote huge tomes on the industrialization of the means of war, indicating that the human cost of any future European war would be so high that no such war could be contemplated rationally. The weapons of war, therefore, should be consigned to a museum, to educate and chasten the visiting public.

The Lucerne museum was one of many international institutions developed around the turn of the century. In Britain, the broader peace movement was less rooted in faith than previous generations had been, and more focused on political relationships. Establishing international arbitration to prevent violent conflict was a prominent popular concern, which the Peace Society welcomed—promoting arbitration had been one of its founding aims—forming several local International Arbitration Associations.

Still working to promote peace through the churches, in 1889 the Peace Society instituted the Fourth Sunday in Advent as an annual "Peace Sunday," to encourage peace preaching. The take-up was mainly by Nonconformists, but the number of participating Church of England clergy grew steadily. In April 1894, William Benham (1831–1910), one of several leading churchmen appointed by American Churches to serve on a British committee to promote a permanent Court of International Arbitration, commended the stance of Quakers and claimed that "the time is near when people will realise that you cannot reform the world with muskets and guns" (Peace Society 1894a: 31; 1894b: 61–2).

On Advent Sunday that year, Septimus Buss (1836–1914) preached on Isaiah 2.4 (swords into ploughshares). The people should be consulted about war, he said, "for it is they who have to go forth to war, to kill and to be killed; they also who, in the taxes, have to provide the sinews of war; they also who must perforce endure nearly the whole of the resulting evils." He looked forward to swords and spears, rifles, guns, and bayonets being relegated to a museum of antiquities where children could look at amazement at the implements people once used, with little reason, for fighting and destruction. War would cease, argued Buss, when minds were disabused of the glamour of war, and eyes opened to the miseries and wrongs of war, and to the inestimable blessings of peace (Workmen's Peace Association 1895: 7).

Several senior clerics, including Basil Brooke Foss Westcott (1825–1901) from Cambridge University, subscribed to the middle-class International Arbitration and Peace Association. Westcott was initially commended by campaigners for encouraging ecclesiastical councils to pass resolutions supportive of arbitration. Not that persuading bishops at the core of the establishment was ever easy; when Westcott was appointed Bishop of Durham he would only sign an 1894 petition on arbitration "on the understanding that the Government does not think it inopportune" (Peace Society 1894c: 81).[7] By 1897, however, even the Lambeth Conference of 185 Anglican bishops from around the world spoke of "the duty of promoting by earnest prayer, by private instruction, and by public appeal, the cause of International Arbitration" (Peace Society 1897a: 286; 1897b: 303). It was the fourth time the bishops had met in this way—the first was in 1867—and the first time they had addressed issues of peace. Followers, not leaders, they commented on contemporary social trends rather than considering any prophetic theology of peace. With the aim of addressing that, two years later, a sufficiently emboldened Peace Society affixed fourteen theses for peace—essentially biblical references—to the doors of Canterbury Cathedral, St Paul's Cathedral, and Westminster Abbey (Peace Society 1899b: iv).

The scale of the Peace Society's task was revealed at the 1908 Lambeth Conference, taking place soon after the second international gathering at The Hague. In Resolution 52, the Lambeth bishops stated that "The Conference, while frankly acknowledging the moral gains sometimes won by war . . . records . . . its deep appreciation of the services rendered by the conferences at The Hague." Patronizing sentiments of "appreciation" were drowned by such extraordinary assertion of the supposed "moral gains" of war (Grane 1912: xli).

None the less, the cause of international law and arbitration was becoming fashionable within liberal-minded middle-class circles. John Percival, Bishop of Hereford, addressed the 1904 Universal Peace Congress in Boston, and a tranche of senior Anglican clerics consented to become Vice-Presidents of an increasingly establishment Peace Society (Peace Society 1910: 2–5; 1911: 2–5; 1913: 2–5.). Such expansion of activity reached a peak in 1909–10 when the Peace Society sent out over forty thousand invitations to ministers of religion to take part in the 1909 Peace Sunday, resulting in over five thousand sermons, with the distribution of more than half a million papers, pamphlets, and other forms of literature (Peace Society 1910: 14–15). There was even a Church of England Peace League founded in 1910, chaired by the Bishop of Lincoln, Edward Lee Hicks (1843–1919), with a long list of worthy vice-presidents but little impact in the pews.

Lowell Revisited

At the height of this internationalist fervor, one cleric challenged the underlying philosophy of the age and proposed an alternative approach to peace, based on conscience. In the unlikely setting of an Earl's Court Military Exhibition in London, in 1901, Arthur John Waldron (1868–1925), Curate of St Luke's, Camberwell, delivered a lecture on ethics, illuminated by the anti-war writings of Carlyle, Tennyson, and Longfellow. He dared to ask rhetorically whether the soldier could give not only his life but his conscience. Waldron answered his own question with reference to Lowell.

> You may remember Hosea Biglow's saying:–
>
> "Ef you take a sword and dror it,
> An' go stick a feller thru',
> Guv'ment ain't to answer for it,
> God'll send the bill to you".
>
> Personally, I believe that the ethics of the question ought to be applied to the individual soldier. I know what will be said—that it is impossible to allow the soldier the right to the exercise of his individual conscience; that whatever the Government decides the soldier is bound to do. If the Government makes war, the soldier is not to ask any question; and if the Government murders, the soldier is to be exonerated. Personally, I hurl that from me. I believe—and, I think, the feeling is growing in this country—that no Government in the world, no tribunal in the world, can answer for the individual conscience, that every man is responsible, to himself if not to some higher power, for the right of the faculties which he possesses . . . I know the argument adduced is, that, if he did, he would leave the Army. Then so much the worse for the system. It is condemned on the face of it . . .
>
> But the question is: Is the soldier responsible for the acts of the Government? I hold that no man has any right, by any system, legalised or not, to hand over his personal responsibility to any Government, or to any other power. And therefore, he, the man, intelligent and moral, should be allowed to be the judge of what is right for him to do in any war . . .
>
> —Peace Society 1902b: 265–7; 1902c: 270–2

Waldron's assertion that each individual was a responsible being, and that ethical issues concerning war were not confined to the morality of arbitration and other matters of international politics, was unusual, especially for a clergyman of the Church of England. According to Waldron, opponents of war must do more than complain about a Government that engaged in that war; they must themselves refuse to participate in it. This would be the defining issue for the peace movement in the years ahead. Lowell's verse helped keep such thinking in the public domain.

War in South Africa

As Waldron implied, international institutions alone were insufficient to guarantee peace. Turn-of-the-century internationalism had little impact on British imperial wars and expansionism which were often backed by the Churches, not least for the evangelical adventurism they might offer. By 1896, the Peace Society had counted thirty-eight imperial wars during Victoria's reign (Peace Society 1896b: 136). War in South Africa was another to add to the list.

Inevitably, popular emotion and the established Church was with the imperialists. But as one local study reveals, "the Church of England also provided a home, however submerged, for a more reflective discourse that had left the certainties of Victorian theology behind" (Allen 2012: 31). A few clerics even openly opposed the war. Canon William Barker (1838–1917) of Marylebone addressed five hundred people in Acton in 1900, calling the recourse to force "a reversion to savagery and barbarism" (Peace Society 1901). Some members of the Christian Social Union, principally Charles Gore (1853–1932) and Henry Scott Holland (1847–1918), publicly opposed the South African conflict on the grounds that it was an expression of British imperialist arrogance (Peace Society 1902a: 248–50). Percival was shocked by revelations from Emily Hobhouse (1860–1926) that nearly two thousand children had died in brutal British-run concentration camps (Koss, 1973: 228–30). Hicks, dubbed "Pro-Boer" by the press, preached a Manchester Cathedral sermon on *The Mistakes of Militarism*, published by the Manchester Transvaal Committee (Evans, 2014: 65).

Successive Deans of Winchester, G.W. Kitchin (1827–1912) and William Stephens (1839–1902), joined the South Africa Conciliation Committee, Stephens being severely criticized across his diocese for suggesting that the Jameson Raid was "a crime and a blunder" (Allen 2012: 24–6). Kitchin, who became Dean of Durham and President of the Tyneside International Arbitration and Peace Association, gained a reputation as a formidable opponent of the war, and was denounced as unpatriotic and pro-Boer by a judge from the bench (Peace Society 1900: 47). Kitchin, and Canon Samuel Augustus Barnett (1844–1913), the warden of Toynbee Hall, with other "influential and well-known leaders of thought," signed a statement claiming there was "a special duty laid on those who disapprove of the war to express their disapproval . . ." (Peace Society 1900).

Barnett had "something of the Quakers' craving for the soul's rest in secret peace" (Scott Holland 1915: 94) and was probably the most outspoken of all senior Anglican clergy. As co-founder of Toynbee Hall, with his wife Henrietta, he had insight into the squalid living conditions of East London. In 1899 he protested about the misuse of taxes and about the social impact of the culture of war:

> whenever there is a talk about war, and when men are worshipping the heroes of war, and when they are thinking about what war is going to do, they themselves are more easily inclined to brutal pleasures, and are themselves more proud of being brutal.
>
> In the name, therefore, of the people, of my neighbours, who are capable of being tender, who are capable of being considerate for the weak, who are capable of the highest pleasures of thought and feeling, who are capable, at any rate, of following the Prince of Peace, and of admiring Him, I protest against this light talk about war, which allows them to live a more degraded life than they ever meant to live.
> —Peace Society 1899a: 234

Barnett continued his protest after being appointed a Canon of Bristol, arguing that the people were not being led by the Spirit of Christ, "and the war is their war, and the war is not Christian . . . The fault for the war, if it lies with anyone, lies with the Christian teachers—with us who, being commissioned to teach the unity of power and love, have let the minds of the people worship the power without love" (Peace Society 1900: 45–6).

The World Alliance

The Churches' contribution to the age of international institutions was the World Alliance for Promoting International Friendship through the Churches, later to be incorporated into the World Council of Churches. Its foundations were laid in 1907, when several denominations prepared presentations for the Second Hague Conference. The World Alliance arranged a substantial exchange program between Christians in England and Germany, including the 130 German Church dignitaries—Lutheran, Roman Catholic, and Nonconformist—who attended the Seventeenth Universal Congress for Peace, in London in 1908 (World Alliance 1915: 3; Brittain 1964: 27). Over one hundred British Christian dignitaries returned the visit the following year, and were received by the Kaiser. One of their guides was the secretary of the German Committee, Friedrich Siegmund-Schültze (1885–1969) (Brittain 1964: 27–8). From this continuing program evolved the Associated Councils of Churches in the British and German Empires for Fostering Friendly Relations between Two Peoples, launched in London in February 1911, and which attracted seven thousand members in its first year (Wilkinson [1978] 2014: 23).[8] Their journal, *The Peacemaker*, achieved a circulation of 67,000 by 1914 (Robbins 1976: 18). With an endowment from the Scottish philanthropist Andrew Carnegie (1835–1919), for "uniting the Churches of Christendom for Peace, and in promoting Conferences of their representatives," the vision grew beyond Europe (World Alliance 1915: 4; Wallis 1991: 3). Provisional committees were formed to organize two international conferences—the Churches of Christendom were not that united, even for peace—the first for Protestants at Constance on August 2–4, 1914, and another for Catholics at Liège the following week. The latter was cancelled, but around ninety delegates did gather briefly in Constance, as war was commencing.

A peace movement myth surrounds two of the attendees, Henry Hodgkin (1877–1933), a British Quaker, and Siegmund-Schültze. They traveled back from Constance to Cologne on the same train, probably in separate carriages. Shaking hands on Cologne station platform, Siegmund-Schültze apparently declared, "Whatever happens, nothing is changed between us. We are one in Christ and can never be at war." This was not, as myth has it, the founding event of the International Fellowship of Reconciliation, but it did inspire Hodgkin who told Siegmund-Schültze that their friendship could not be broken by the war.[9] The content of a personal letter to that effect was similar to a public "Message to Men and Women of Goodwill," largely written by Hodgkin and published on August 7, 1914 by the Friends' Meeting for Suffering, stating that the "war spells the bankruptcy of much that we too lightly call Christian . . . If we apportion blame, let us not fail first to blame ourselves and to seek forgiveness of Almighty God" (den Boggende 1986: 57). Altogether, 475,000 copies were printed in Britain and 50,000 in the USA.

The carnage would last four bloody years. "Pacificism," the respectable peace of diplomats and institutions, had failed; they had opposed hypothetical wars, but would support a real one. The insufficiency of internationalism, of reliance on political structures, was starkly revealed. It was time for a rediscovery of deep pacifist commitment, not only by Christians but also by those with humanist or socialist philosophies, who would provide a (costly) and ultimately vindicated personal critique of war.

"ONCE TO EVERY MAN AND NATION"

A New Pacifism

With war, the whole world view of the Edwardians fell apart, every philosophy was challenged and its adherents divided. The left split—some supporting the war, others opposing it; the women's suffrage movement was divided, as were the Churches. Even Churches with dissenting traditions were swept along by war fever in 1914; the Society of Friends found one-third of its membership joining the army (Wilkinson [1986] 2010: ch. 2). The pre-war peace movement had failed. New groups now emerged, including the Union of Democratic Control and the Women's International League. Accurately predicting that the state would eventually compel men into the army, Lilla Brockway encouraged her husband Fenner Brockway (1888–1988), sometime editor of the *Christian Commonwealth*, to form the No-Conscription Fellowship (NCF). This became the foremost organ of opposition to the war. Its primary appeal was to socialists, but its broad membership included many motivated by religious commitment, and its Statement of Faith had a religious ring: "The No-Conscription Fellowship is an organization of men likely to be called upon to undertake military service in the event of conscription, who will refuse from conscientious motives to bear arms, because they consider human life to be sacred, and cannot, therefore, assume the responsibility of inflicting death."

Hodgkin was not the only Christian pacifist struggling to make sense of the war. Richard Roberts (1874–1945), Presbyterian minister in Hornsey, approached Christian intellectuals including William Temple to critique the war, only to discover they held a range of incompatible attitudes. Maude Royden (1876–1956), who would also be prominent in the Women's International League, received a tirade of abuse for an autumn 1914 *Challenge* article asking, "We are all agreed ... that war is an evil; but to what purpose, if we justify each war as it arises?" (Fletcher 1989: 110.) She cited Tertullian's third-century argument (*De Idolatria*: 19) that in disarming Peter in Gethsemane, Christ disarmed every soldier. A hastily arranged conference in Cambridge in December 1914 led to the formation of the Fellowship of Reconciliation (FOR). Royden once again echoed Tertullian in her presentation to that conference: "Christ taught His disciples that they must not be overcome with evil, but must overcome it with good; and by 'good' He does not seem to have meant swords and other arms but love and patience and kindness and meekness. He rebuked a disciple who imagined that he might defend his Master with the sword" (Royden 1915: 38–43).

Some, including Roberts, leaned toward a more pietistic religious order; others like George Lansbury (1859–1940), *Daily Herald* editor and organizer of a Trafalgar Square anti-war demonstration, wanted a more overtly political campaign group. The outcome was a Fellowship "Basis" that stated "That Love, as revealed and interpreted in the life and death of Jesus Christ, involves more than we have yet seen, that it is the only power by which evil can be overcome, and the only sufficient basis of human society"; the unambiguous corollary was "That therefore, as Christians, we are forbidden to wage war" (Wallis 1991: 72).

This was the new pacifism, not dependent on institutional arrangements between nations but rooted in the faith and conscience of individuals. It was more than hope for the nations; it was personal commitment to stand for and to bring about in one's own person that which was hoped for. With the NCF and the FOR, "pacifism" changed its definition. The word "pacifiste," first coined by Émile Arnaud at the Glasgow Peace Congress of 1901, was no longer a description of the well-meaning who still upheld petty nationalisms and who would fall away when confronted by war. The new pacifists were not naïve idealists; they actively resisted war, and resisted governments that made war, taking upon themselves a commitment to peace, not leaving peace to be submerged by the complex priorities of governments and by the false "realism" that had led to war.

Was there a unifying theology within FOR? If so, it probably related to conceptions of the Kingdom of God. Some would have internalized the concept into a quietist spirituality, inwardly directed, "the Kingdom of God is within you" (Luke 17:21). More would have looked for a transformation of society, in line with the righteousness of God, with God and humanity working together toward the fulfilment of the Kingdom on earth.

Christians from all traditions looked to a new, post-war social order. FOR was both a religious order for spiritual support and an active campaigning body, not only against war but against a variety of social evils. Those minded to be spiritual were jolted into action by the war; those minded to be active came to see the value of the faith on which their actions were based. Christian spirituality could have no place for war, as indicated by the Bermondsey doctor Alfred Salter, writing a 1914 article for the *Labour Leader* which was reprinted a million and a half times on leaflets around the world:

> Look! Christ in khaki, out in France thrusting His bayonet into the body of a German workman. See! The Son of God with a machine gun, ambushing a column of German infantry, catching them unawares in a lane and mowing them down in their helplessness. Hark! The Man of Sorrows in a cavalry charge, cutting, hacking, thrusting, crushing, cheering. No! No! That picture is an impossible one, and we all know it.
> —Salter [1919] 1940: 10

Conscription and Conscience

The NCF's fears proved justified, and conscription into the armed forces was introduced with the Military Service Act from March 1916. Lansbury's *Herald* marked the occasion with a Frederick Carter (1883–1967) cartoon on the Feast of the Annunciation (March 25) depicting Mary at the foot of the cross. The caption was, "The Mother of the First Conscientious Objector."

There was, however, a chink in the legislation, the result of pressure on Lloyd George by Quaker MPs Edmund Harvey (1875–1955) and Arnold Rowntree (1872–1951), a clause allowing exemption on "the ground of a conscientious objection to the undertaking of combatant service"—subject to the approval of a Tribunal (Graham ([1922] 1969): 55).[10] The prime minister may have thought the clause would only apply to a few Quakers, but by this time the NCF alone had around fifteen thousand members, united in their commitment to resist a call to arms yet expressing diverse anti-war convictions that tribunal panels of local worthies, responsible for assessing the validity of claims of conscientious objection, struggled to comprehend.

Some conscientious objectors (COs) did indeed come from the historic peace churches, principally the Quakers. Others were atypical Christians from mainstream Churches—Congregationalists, Presbyterians, Methodists, Baptists, Church of England—motivated by faith and inspired, more than their Churches, by the pacifist teaching and example of Jesus. There were Christadelphians, Brethren, Jehovah's Witnesses (known then as the International Bible Students Association, IBSA), and other religious groups.[11] There were many humanists, socialists, and anti-capitalists too. Some accepted duties in the Non-Combatant Corps (NCC) or the Royal Army Medical Corps. Others would only countenance a civilian alternative, and were arrested when this was not offered. "Absolutists" were not prepared to cooperate with a state at war in any circumstances. Many COs were imprisoned with hard labor, some for two years, often in brutal conditions. The consequences for their physical and mental health were severe; over seventy died in prison or soon after leaving prison.[12]

Richmond Castle

The first cohort of imprisoned absolutist COs from Yorkshire and the North East was incarcerated in the cell block of Richmond Castle, Swaledale, adjacent to the Castle's

FIGURE 4.4: Richmond Castle. Credit: Heritage Images/Getty Images.

medieval keep. Ironically, other COs in the NCC were also based at Richmond Castle. The diversity of the prisoners can be gauged from their fragile graffiti, penciled on their cell walls, much of which is still extant.

Some graffiti is general: "CONSCIENCE" and "The conscientious would not go." Verses from Christian scriptures abound: "Thou shalt not kill," "Love your enemy," "Do to others as you would have them that they should do unto you," "Perfect love casts out all fear," and "Love one another and I have loved you." Isaiah 35:10 is written out in full, probably by Charles Herbert Senior of IBSA who gave a talk on Isaiah 35 to other imprisoned COs a few weeks later (Perkins 2016: 51–2). There are two graffitied crucifixion scenes, one captioned "The First Conscientious Objector," the other drawn by a Methodist, John "Bert" Brocklesby. In his drawings, Brocklesby named the Fellowship of Reconciliation, to which he belonged and from whom he received support.

There are several hymns. One 1868 verse from the New York hymn writer Horatio Richmond Palmer (1834–1907) was a standard invocation to Jesus to give one the strength to resist individual sin. Frequently used by the temperance movement, it is here applied to the temptation to succumb to the corporate sin of society, by taking part in war.

Yield not to temptation, for yielding is sin;
Each vict'ry will help you some other to win;
Fight manfully onward, dark passions subdue;
Look ever to Jesus, He'll carry you through.

A socialist prisoner penciled verses from the *People's Flag* on his cell wall; curiously, another Richmond graffiti version contained alternative final lines with "Christ's banner" flying instead of the red flag. One envisages song wars between COs, as religious and socialist prisoners were inspired, or annoyed, by each other's musical repertoire.

Lowell seen in Stone and Song

A West Riding CO, Ernest Lawson, was responsible for several pieces of graffiti, one of which returns us to familiar territory.

"If you take a sword & dror it,
To run a fellow through . . ."

Almost seventy years after Lowell penned his *Biglow Papers* verses, they were not only remembered but regarded as inspirational by an absolutist World War I conscientious objector in his prison cell. Even a committed socialist like Lawson understood the significance of personal responsibility for one's actions, as he repeated Lowell's line, "God will send the bill to you."

Lowell's verse appears once more in the Richmond graffiti, and it is a line we have seen before:

Though the cause of evil prosper,
Yet 'tis truth alone thats strong . . . (sic)

That, recalled from memory, is the great call to conscience,

Once to every man and nation comes the moment to decide,
In the strife of Truth with Falsehood, for the good or evil side.

The context fits perfectly. There comes a time—for Lowell, 1845, for conscientious objectors, 1916—to take a stand for one's beliefs, even if they are completely contrary to mainstream thinking in society and the consequences are personal ignominy and suffering. Implicit also is the expectation that society will eventually recognize the validity and truth of what the person of conscience has stood for. From within a Richmond Castle cell, there was no doubt about the just cause of conscientious objection; doing God's work meant resisting war and this would receive ultimate, eschatological vindication. It was a premeditated stand, encouraged by and expressed in Lowell's memorized poetry.

Lowell, and, to a lesser extent his Fireside colleagues Whittier and Longfellow, were a major influence on British conscientious objectors. Their works, set to music, were widely known from the song books of the Co-operative Movement and the Fellowship movement, rooted in Congregationalism. These strands came together in a modest Manchester NCF 1916 publication, the *CO's Song Book*.[13]

Lowell figures largely in this *Song Book*. The frontispiece is from Lowell—"Count me o'er earth's chosen heroes—they were souls that stood alone"—as are one tenth of the songs. One Lowell verse suggested that those unwilling to take a stand were the ones who were really imprisoned:

PEACE, PACIFISM, AND RELIGION

> They are slaves who fear to speak
> For the fallen and the weak . . .
> They are slaves who dare not be
> In the right with two or three.

There was irony, mid-war, in "Once to every man and nation" being set to Haydn's tune "Austria." Whittier's "Song of Peace" gave the command to "Sing out the war vulture and sing in the dove," and to

> Blow, bugles of battle, the marches of peace;
> East, west, north, and south let the long quarrel cease.

One can speculate as to whether the author might actually have tolerated "Dear Lord and Father of mankind," also featured in the *Song Book*, being used in this anti-establishment context.

Songs of the Frenchmen

When the first cohort of sixteen Richmond COs departed the Yorkshire castle at the end of May 1916, they knew they were being taken to France, possibly to face execution.[14] Norman Gaudie, a Congregationalist, recalled that at Darlington station, accompanied by COs in the NCF, "We indulged in hymn singing, which was joined in by the Non-Combatants with much zest" (Gaudie n.d.: 12). At Waterloo station, London, the singing continued, "'Simply trusting' being a prime favourite" (Gaudie n.d.: 13). Meeting up with conscientious objectors from other parts of the country on the *S.S. Viper* from Southampton, boosted morale further. "'We soon were at one with each other & the spirit manifest now

FIGURE 4.5: Conscientious objectors at Dyce Work Camp, 1916. Credit: Hulton Deutsch/Getty Images.

was beyond description, & we, although being a very mixed gathering Agnostics—Artists—Christians of different sects, joined in our hymn singing with great fervour" (Gaudie n.d.: 14). Under military supervision in France, their treatment, like that of a cohort from Harwich who preceded them, was brutal. Arriving at a Boulogne parade ground, surrounded on three sides by hundreds of uniformed soldiers, each CO was hauled out individually to learn his fate. They would be sentenced to death (pause) . . . confirmed by General Haig (longer pause) . . . and commuted to ten years penal servitude. They had shown they were prepared to die for their conscience. Subjected to intense political pressure at home from MPs Edmund Harvey, Philip Snowden, and others, the government and the military had relented at the last (Graham [1922] 1969: 123; Ellsworth-Jones 2007: 173–4).

SUMMARY

From a twenty-first-century perspective, it is hard to justify any British military action—and there was a lot of it—in the nineteenth and early twentieth centuries. Indeed, John Bright had argued that every war since the accession of William III should have been avoided (Hirst 1923: 276–7).

Arnaud's 1901 "pacifistes"—well-meaning, patriotic, liberal internationalists, or "pacificists"—argued against hypothetical war until the opportunity arose to support a real one. Theirs was a failed realism. The new pacifists, the war-resisters, the conscientious objectors, motivated by deep personal faith—religious, humanist, or socialist—and prepared to uphold it at considerable personal cost, were the true realists.

Christian pacifists from 1816 broke through denominational barriers to reclaim ancient Christian opposition to any war. They renounced war on principle but worked with those whose opposition to war was more pragmatic and partial. We have seen this tradition through the mid-century broadening of the peace movement, to the necessary but insufficient structures of internationalism, which passed responsibility for war-prevention to diplomats, politicians, and international organizations. We have seen Christians and others, individual pacifists standing true to their conscience before the full weight of the militaristic state, who took a costly personal stand, even to the point of hearing sentence of death. Outside of the Society of Friends, and smaller groups like the International Bible Students, most religious pacifists were standing apart from their own Church. They never anticipated being in such a substantive movement of conscientious objectors that the government would have to abandon policies toward war—that was a passing suggestion in the late 1930s. For Christian pacifists, the motivation was simply being true to their faith, true to Christ, believing that to be the only sure foundation upon which to build the values and the reality of lasting peace.

Through it all, our guide has been a poet, James Russell Lowell. His expressions of the primacy of conscience and the stand against war, underpinned by his own religious belief, inspired and encouraged future generations of pacifists. The stories and the literature of past pacifists are a living resource for peace. They are as applicable now as ever, to inspire those who continue that story today.

CHAPTER FIVE

Representations of Peace

Bertha von Suttner, Activist and Visionary on Dreams, Peace, and Justice

LAURIE R. COHEN

Don't always call our peace-plans a <u>dream</u>. Progress towards justice is surely not a dream, it is the law of civilisation. The amount of savagery and stupidity in the world is certainly still very great, but the amount of kindness and gentleness and reason is growing every day.

—Bertha von Suttner to Alfred Nobel, original emphasis[1]

In 1911, the Austrian Peace Society, which Baroness Bertha von Suttner had cofounded two decades earlier, sponsored a public lecture at the University of Vienna. The speaker expounded on a typical topic for the society: the value of arbitration courts as the best means for settling conflictual differences between nations. Indeed, "arbitration" had by then become a catchword among the international peace movement community, not least since its codification at the Second International Hague Peace Conference in 1907.[2] In the Q&A section of the talk, however, a member of the audience, Rudolf Großmann,[3] commented that another means of preventing war was also possible: namely, to abolish the military. Suttner, who was also the president of the society, began clapping her hands enthusiastically. This was followed by a scandalized outcry from a third member of the audience: "You seem to be unaware that the man who made that remark is a known anarchist!" To which Suttner coolly responded: "If that is how anarchists speak—hating war and wishing to combat it by any means possible—then I would proudly accept being called an anarchist myself" (quoted in *Wohlstand für Alle* 1914: 6).[4] This incident, it seems to me, illustrates in a nutshell Suttner's unconventional if not rebellious approach to peace advocacy and her remarkable leadership during the second half of what Eric Hobsbawm dubbed the "long nineteenth century."

This chapter focuses on the personality and political relevance as well as the influence of Bertha von Suttner, née Kinsky (1843–1914), a woman who has made history: by publishing an international bestselling anti-war novel in 1889 entitled *Die Waffen nieder! Eine Lebensgeschichte* (Lay Down Your Arms: A Memoir);[5] by co-founding the Austrian Peace Society (1891) and other peace societies in Europe and other parts of the world; by serving as editor-in-chief of the monthly peace journal *Die Waffen nieder* (1892–99); and by receiving the well-endowed Nobel Peace Prize in 1905, the first of (only) three women

FIGURE 5.1: Bertha von Suttner (1843–1914). Credit: Imagno/Getty Images.

laureates in its initial fifty years. An extremely prominent and active member of the international peace movement until her death on June 21, 1914, Suttner has been called the "creator" of Austrian pacifism (Fuchs 1949: 258), "the most popular pacifist in the world" (Schwimmer 1913), and the "grandiose Cassandra" of her time (Zweig 1943: 203). Suttner also served as one of "the greatest inspirations" to many of the pioneering pro-suffrage peace activists who founded the Women's International League of Peace and Freedom (WILPF) during World War I (Hertrampf 2006: 74). By exploring Suttner's ideas on pacifism and her influence on the trans-Atlantic peace movement, I hope to demonstrate how this courageous utopian embodied some of the zeitgeist of her era and continues to provide inspiration for ours as well.

The Baroness's success can be attributed to her collaboration and communication skills, not least with leading (mostly male) scholars, journalists, philanthropists, diplomats, and, especially, peace advocates, which in turn can in part be put down to her social status and the gender norms of her time (i.e., how aristocratic women, without even having the vote, were commonly treated). Yet Suttner also convincingly internalized Immanuel Kant's Enlightenment motto: "*sapere aude*" (dare to know), which could be interpreted as: have the courage to challenge dogmatic beliefs and stereotypes. Rising to the challenge of attempting to confront the world's problems, Suttner distinguished herself as an accomplished organizer, fundraiser, speaker, writer, women's rights activist, and world traveler. The celebrity she obtained during her lifetime would last for a quarter of a century, exemplified as well by dozens of featured appearances in satirical political journals. Since then, at least in the German-speaking world, her name lives on in numerous schools, streets, stamps, and on the Austrian two-euro coin. Her undertakings resonate, because she succeeded in helping to break two significant contemporary taboos: that war was a natural phenomenon (a law of nature), and that the female sex was incapable of making competent political contributions, especially in international affairs. Whereas the former taboo had been regularly challenged throughout human history (e.g., by Aristophanes' "Peace," Hussite King George of Podiebrad's Peace League, the Quaker movement, Kant's "Eternal Peace," 1795), Suttner's ability to break the latter taboo may actually be more outstanding.

Divided into four sections, this chapter first introduces Bertha von Suttner's upbringing and formative years. It then spotlights her contribution to the international peace movement, focusing specifically on her historical fiction, *Die Waffen nieder*, along with another nonfictional work published the same year. The third section addresses Suttner the Organizer: her cofounding of both the Austrian Peace Society and a monthly peace journal, her political articles and speeches, her associations with philanthropists, and her second breakthrough, the 1899 Hague Peace Conference. The final section offers critical insights on her still palpable post-war and contemporary legacy.

YOUTH AND FORMATIVE YEARS

Bertha von Suttner was born Countess Bertha Sophia Felicita Kinsky von Chinic and Tettau in Prague, Bohemia, on June 9, 1843. Her father, retired Habsburg Imperial General Count Franz Joseph Kinsky, died during his wife's pregnancy, and her young mother, Sophie Kinsky, née Körner, moved away from the Kinsky family and brought up her newly born daughter and five-year-old son in Brno, the capital of Moravia. Kinsky never remarried.

In her memoirs, first published in 1909, Suttner recalled a happy childhood. As befitting her birthright, for example, she was educated by a number of governesses who, apart from her native tongue, German, nurtured her fluency in foreign languages: English, French, and Italian. Some days she spent with her mother at European spas; other days she passed the time playing the piano—she strove to become an opera singer—and reading at home with her cousin Elvira. The girls pored over works by classic German writers Kant, Schiller, and Hölderlin as well as French writers Claude Fleury, Victor Hugo, and Georges Sand, and British writers Emily Bronte, Florence Nightingale, and William Shakespeare. "The literature put me into another world, a second world in which I lived," Suttner reminisced (1965: 75): "I was always a hungry devourer of books" (1965: 46). Successive European wars of the time played little to no role in her childhood. "Politics," Suttner recalled, "did not interest me in the least; I did not even read any daily newspapers" (1965: 75).

By 1873, however, having failed in musical talent and marriage (despite a number of suitors, including young Prince Adolf Sayn-Wittgenstein-Hohenstein, who had tragically died onboard a ship bound for New York; Suttner 1965: 116), Bertha Kinsky considered it necessary to accept work as a governess. She became a foreign language and music teacher to the four teenage daughters of Baron and Baroness von Suttner, whose residences alternated between Vienna and Schloss Harmannsdorf (in Lower Austria). It was here that

FIGURE 5.2: Bertha von Suttner. Credit: Imagno/Getty Images.

she also met her future husband, the "utterly charming" Arthur Gundaccar von Suttner (1850–1902) (Suttner 1965: 82), who was seven years her junior. The two fell in love.

When Arthur Gundaccar's mother discovered their liaison in late 1875, she pressured the countess, who lacked a dowry, to seek employment elsewhere. This led to a brief but life-changing contact in Paris with the Swedish inventor of dynamite, Alfred Nobel (1833–96), which sparked a friendship that would last until Nobel's death. Bertha Kinsky and Arthur von Suttner bravely decided to marry against their parents' wishes, secretly, in June 1876. They then headed directly off to the Caucasus on a longstanding invitation from Kinsky's motherly friend, Mingrelian Princess Ekaterina "Dedopoli" Dadiana (1816–82). The von Suttners remained in the area for nine years, which included witnessing some of the drama of the Russian–Turkish war of 1877–8 (see Cohen 2005a). In their self-chosen exile, Bertha and Arthur eventually earned their main living as professional authors. Bertha von Suttner explained that watching her husband write deeply inspired her, and her first printed short story, appearing in Vienna's *Neue Illustrierte Zeitung* in 1878, left her intent on never putting down her pen again (Suttner 1896). Both selected (male) pen names for themselves. Arthur's was M. A. Lerei,[6] and Bertha picked B. Oulot.[7] The couple returned to Austria in 1885 and never revisited the Caucasus; nor did they ever have children.

Living in Schloss Harmannsdorf, accepted by now by the elderly von Suttners, Bertha von Suttner pursued her writing career. She attained modest success with her first novels, still signed B. Oulot, all of which dealt to a certain extent with aristocratic life, evolution, humanitarian rights, and peace: *Inventarium einer Seele* (Inventory of a soul), *Ein schlechter Mensch* (A bad person), *Daniela Dormes*, clearly inspired by George Eliot's *Daniel Deronda*, and *High Life*. Her breakthrough came in 1889 with the publication of the two-volume *Die Waffen nieder!* (Lay Down Your Arms). The novel became an overnight sensation.

THE PACIFIST WRITER (1889)

Die Waffen nieder!

As Stefan Zweig explained: "With the title of her book—just three words—[Suttner] said everything she wanted to say: *Die Waffen nieder*" (1918: 2). This novel was the first sustained rendering of Suttner's principled idea of peace, which gradually evolved out of her critique of war, and it involved a systematic change in the organization of states: from a (violent) war culture, which included everyday militarism (from giving boys toy soldiers as presents and ritually and unconditionally praising present and former army generals, to producing more and increasingly dangerous armaments), to an active and international peace culture, one based on ideas rooted in enlightened values, which included the promotion of peace education, humanitarianism, women's rights, and an international arbitration court.

Twelve times publishers rejected the manuscript as dangerous and potentially treasonous (see Suttner 1888: 149). Suttner persevered, and in 1889 E. Pierson, a publisher in Dresden, Germany, who had previously printed a few of her essays, finally accepted it. The first edition sold out immediately, and by 1914, forty German-language and sixteen translated editions had been published. Not only did this unexpected worldwide dissemination galvanize the European peace movement by helping to initiate a broad conversation about the presumed necessity of war and the vast differences between a military and a peace culture, it also personally reset Suttner's own life path.

What is striking about this *Bildungsroman* is that its main voice is a bright and courageous young aristocrat, Countess Martha Althaus, who gradually begins to criticize, and ever more forcefully, the repetitive calls to arms and the waging of wars by the leaders of her country (the Habsburg Empire). We first meet Martha at age seventeen, marrying young Count Arno Dotzky. She has been raised by her father, a retired officer who proudly served Austrian–Bohemian war hero Field Marshal Josef Radetzky (1766–1858). Dotzky, also an officer, is just about to enthusiastically enlist to fight in Austria's war against Italian unification (1859). Although very much in love with Arno, a happy wife, and mother of their one-year-old son Rudolf, Martha embraces her conventional gender role: she resolves to be quietly patriotic on the home front.

Everything changes once Dotzky dies, suddenly and tragically, at the brutal Battle of Solferino.[8] Heartbroken and widowed, Martha begins to openly voice her doubts about the utility of war, especially to solve territorial disputes which, according to her father, are the main reasons to go to war in the first place (e.g., Suttner [n.d.]: 36, 43, 122). In these discussions she also comes to realize and then criticize how crimes that are legally punished in order to safeguard the citizenry in peacetime become redefined and even promoted in wartime: "Killing is no longer murder, robbery becomes requisition, and arson means 'taking positions'" (Suttner [n.d.]: 70).

Martha falls in love again and marries Baron Friedrich Tilling, an officer who fought beside Dotzky and has now become somewhat critical of calls to war. For Suttner, Tilling represents a male (manly) partner, sharing Martha's anti-war positions. A key moment in the novel is when Martha's father presents his grandson with a sabre and Martha objects, to which he responds, "You want him to be a mother's boy? ... The best job in the world is to be a soldier and you want to forbid it to him?" (137–8). Martha's aunt intervenes, suggesting that Martha merely wants to protect her one and only son and has forgotten that fate decides whether one dies in bed or on the battlefield. To which Martha responds: "Oh, so when 100,000 men die in war, these would also have died in peace?" (138). Yes, responds her father, to which Martha answers: "What if the people were smart enough to not start a war?" (138). To which her father responds: "That's impossible." At this point Suttner ably lists six conventional justifications for the existence of war (via Martha's father):

1. Wars are established by God himself, Lord of hosts; see the Holy Scriptures.
2. There have always been wars, and thus it also follows that there will always be wars.
3. Without this occasional decimation, humanity would multiply too much.
4. Permanent peace softens and mollycoddles; like stagnant marsh water, it results in degeneracy; that is, moral decline.[9]
5. Wars are the best ways to activate self-sacrifice and heroic courage: in short, to mold a steely character.
6. Since people will always fight, since total unanimity in all demands is impossible, and since differing interests must always collide, permanent peace is therefore an absurdity. (138)

Suttner (via Martha) demonstrates the deep inconsistencies underlying these justifications which quickly become apparent upon closer scrutiny (139). Later she uses the character of a certain Dr. Bresser to articulate another aspect: "Humans have no enemy other than humans, who can be severe indeed. But no other friends, either" (191). Far from seeing war as noble and justifiable, as making "real men" out of young boys, Suttner's novel repeatedly pinpoints both the sacrifice healthy young men and their families had to make and the many long-lasting social (not merely personal) losses: "The next war will not be victory for one party and loss for the other, but *a disaster for everyone*," Martha exclaims (427, original emphasis).

One of the novel's most dramatic passages follows Martha's search for Tilling at the front (after the Battle of Königgratz in 1866), believing him to be wounded and lying at a field hospital. Readers of the novel become eyewitnesses to the death and sufferings, which soon include cholera and reach the home front civilian population (killing Martha's younger sisters and aunt).[10] As Suttner (again via Martha) states, it is unfathomable that the sight of war does not end in all people kneeling and swearing an oath *against* any future war (197). When the Franco–Prussian War of 1870 begins, Tilling is again conscripted, quite unwillingly. He deserts and dies tragically, (wrongfully) shot as a Prussian spy.

Die Waffen nieder!, as narrated by an intelligent and sincere young woman and covering forty years of actual successive European wars—defying, too, a current myth of the "long peace" between 1815 and 1914—touched its readers on many levels and engaged the public in discussing the supposed inevitability of war. Was it really a law of nature, or rather human-made, like the death penalty, and thus preventable? Could not human society find other means than killing—mass murder sanctioned by the state, as Suttner and many pacifists declared—to work out territorial differences or economic disputes? In the novel's final pages, Suttner promotes the actual International Arbitration and Peace Society, founded in 1880 by Hodgson Pratt (1824–1907)—whom she had first met in Paris in 1886—as a pragmatic path toward universal peace.

Machinenalter: Zukunftsvorlesungen über unserer Zeit

In the very same year that *Die Waffen nieder* first appeared, Suttner published another book, this time anonymously (as *"Jemand"* or "someone").[11] Her nonfiction *Das Maschinenalter. Zukunftsvorlesungen über unserer Zeit* (*The Machine Age: Future Lectures About Our Age*), republished a third time in 1899 with a slightly revised title (*Das Maschinenzeitalter*) and under Suttner's own name, was written with educated and professional male readers in mind. The chapters are broken down into essays on sociology, religion, politics, arts and literature, women, love, and war. With clear World War I foreshadowing—and using similar skills as in *Die Waffen nieder* to articulately depict human destruction—the author warned of the next, "the *last* war of civilized Europe," with firearms that would shoot 500 rounds a minute, with an "electrical death machine" that in one blow would eradicate an entire army, burn up every village, and turn every city into a pile of rubble and every meadow into a field of corpses (Suttner 1899). Suttner wrote as well of mass weapons of destruction: submarines that would fire torpedoes at powerful steamships, and manned and armed dirigibles (Zeppelins) that would take part in air battles and drop explosives "that would destroy an entire city within a few minutes" (Suttner 1899: 275). As Suttner explained, war not only threatened "the healthy, strong, and able soldiers," but also civilians and their cultural and social structures: in short, civilization itself (Suttner 1899: 278).

The Machine Age also explicitly demonstrated Suttner's feminist advocacy: in it, for example, she ridiculed and condemned the biologically deterministic norm of the day that equated weak muscles with a weak mind or vice versa. She criticized as absurd the truism that "women have just as little thinking power as brawn; she is incapable of qualified mental labor" (Suttner 1899: 85; cf. Scott 1986: 1073). Indeed, Suttner's vision here of an appropriate peace organization encouraged the respectful and equal participation of women and men, irrespective of ethnicity or social class (Suttner 1899: 94; cf. Shepela 2005).

THE PEACE WORKER

She [Bertha von Suttner] is doing it exactly right: being stubborn and tenacious in her idealism.

—Jean Jaurès, quoted in Zweig 1916: 3

The Austrian Peace Society (1891)

Suttner's first public appeal to initiate the Austrian Peace Society (first called the Society of the Friends of Peace), to be headquartered in Vienna's prominent first district, was printed on September 3, 1891 in the Vienna daily *Neue Freie Presse* and entitled "The Next Peace Congress in Rome." She wrote that the peace movement's main goal was to encourage disarmament and arbitration. To this end, it was their task to disseminate information to the public, and especially to the youth, via journals, public lectures, demonstrations, and congresses. As she had successfully done in her anti-war novel, the society should continue analyzing and opposing the "horrible future scenario of destruction" propagated by those who considered war as "holy" (Suttner 1891: 1). Two later appeals (October 13, 1891, and December 22, 1891), published in the same newspaper, furnished more concrete details: The society "will not be a political one, because its aim is to promote the principle of permanent peace among the peoples" ("Ein neuerlicher Aufruf" 1891: 1). Furthermore, its core objective was to work towards "recognizing and improving the simple principle that the well-being of human society—whether as individuals or groups of individuals, called nations—is sought out in association, not in turning against one another in reciprocal hostilities" ("Ein neuerlicher Aufruf" 1891: 1). Indeed, from the start, the Austrian Peace Society pointed out that although there would always be struggles when dealing with conflicts or hostilities, the institution of war as such had to become an anachronism, "like feudalism, the Inquisition, and the death penalty." To succeed in our goal "to abolish it, we must spread the word" ("Österreichische Friedensgesellschaft" 1891: 5).

Austrian Member of Parliament Peter Baron Pirquet stood at Suttner's side as the political representative of the Austrian Peace Society, leading the Austrian delegations at the yearly Inter-Parliamentary Union (IPU) meetings. Both the IPU, at the legal professional level, and the international peace movement, at the ground level, worked in a supra-national capacity (not an anti-national one, as they often pointed out) to help reconcile intra-state differences and unify all peoples, to recognize the solidarity of interests among all "civilized" peoples, so as to make war truly anachronistic (Suttner 1893). By 1909, Suttner foresaw the advent of "universal peace pacts" between states (Suttner 1909b).

Suttner's call to action inspired an immediate group of followers. Later Nobel Peace Prize laureate Alfred Hermann Fried, for instance, recalled sitting in a Berlin café in early November 1891, reading about the newly founded Austrian Peace Society:

> What an experience. I began to cry, buckets—I suddenly saw that the idea, which I had cherished since childhood, was consolidating into a working organization. . . . There were others who saw war the same way as I did, as an evil, and they were meeting in international congresses. It was a revelation. I belonged with them. . . . And I wrote that very day to Bertha von Suttner, living then in Schloß Harmannsdorf, offering my collaboration.
> —Quoted in Tuider 2009: 140–1

Fried considered Suttner's positive response "the most important milestone" in his life, since "I was integrated into the cogs and wheels of the peace movement and from then on never stopped contributing to it" (Tuider 2009: 141).

Members of newly launched Peace Societies in other European countries (the German Peace Society was founded in 1892, the Hungarian Peace Society in 1895, for instance), rallied by Suttner, met regularly, discussed current affairs, wrote petitions to state politicians—delivering them by hand, if deemed appropriate—and basically served to encourage public debate and suggest new laws to lawmakers.[12] Not surprisingly, much of their early—and even later—work was met with ridicule, scorn, and antagonism.

Die Waffen nieder: a Monthly Peace Journal (1892–9)

In 1892, encouraged by Alfred Hermann Fried, Suttner agreed to become the editor-in-chief of a new monthly for peace advocacy, named *Die Waffen nieder*, which averaged forty pages a run. Its goal was to familiarize a German-speaking public (mostly residing in the Austro-Hungarian Empire, Germany, or Switzerland) with the idea of peace, and its regular readership included participants at the yearly Inter-parliamentary and Universal Peace Conferences as well as ordinary members of peace societies. It also boldly addressed controversy, often publishing statements by defenders if not promoters of militarization, which then would be debunked by pacifists. It was also educational, including tips on books, and inspired by modern democratic mores, such as by adding letters to and responses from its editors. As Suttner also explained, the point of the journal was to be combative—"because no matter how often the word peace recurs in our pages, what we are really doing is waging war—against war" (Suttner 1898: 119). Suttner herself took an active role in discussing major issues of peace in these pages, one that continued in her colleague Fried's monthly journal *Die Friedens-Warte* (1899–today), with a regular column entitled "Randglossen" (see Fried 1917). The main ideas expressed in the journal were commonsense ones, which none the less sounded revolutionary at the time.

The Austrian Peace Society was constituted as a branch of the International Peace and Arbitration Society, headquartered in England, and Suttner was nominated its first—and during her lifetime only—president (see Cohen 2005b). In one of her first lengthy diatribes in *Die Waffen nieder*, entitled "Our Platform," Bertha von Suttner highlighted her peace society's main goal: encouraging governments to obey international law and to make the system of international arbitration prevail. The only means of achieving this, according to Suttner, was to stir action from below: the Zeitgeist must be informed and encouraged to participate, and citizens should be able to rely on a strong and energetic peace society. Furthermore, this society set the absolutely pressing goal of universal peace explicitly above other valuable and related progressive causes, such as those embedded in the movements for national liberty, overcoming widespread injustices, Freemasonry, promoting a one-world language (*Volapük*), republicanism, vegetarianism, socialism, and also feminism (Suttner 1892: 52).

A feminist in her lifestyle and a solid supporter of women's emancipation, Suttner none the less placed universal peace above women's rights, including the right to suffrage. In Suttner's opinion, women, after centuries of patriarchal socialization, were not "naturally" less belligerent in their beliefs than men. As she often pointed out, women who held political power (such as Queen Victoria) had also been warmongers: "Some people assume, completely incorrectly . . . that all women inherently, by nature, are averse to war. This is wrong-headed. Only progressively minded women . . . have the fortitude to liberate themselves from the directives of century-old institutions" (Suttner 1914).

Thus she considered "votes for women" secondary to guaranteeing sustainable peace (see Cohen 2009). Indeed, once World War I started, her position was borne out. The majority of Western women's movement activists, including for instance Emmeline Pankhurst's militant "suffragettes," accepted and even supported their respective state's war efforts.[13]

Furthermore, Suttner warned pacifist followers specifically against allowing "ourselves to be sidetracked" by purportedly realist approaches expressed through principles such as "*si vis pacem, para bellum*" (if you want peace, prepare for war), when what peace activists needed to do to promote peace was to prepare for peace (*si vis pacem, para pacem*) (Suttner 1892: 53). The premise, that the key to preventing war was to increase the number of weapons, was "totally irrational and actually only promoted by a small if loud group" (Suttner 1891: 2).

She likewise criticized the national Red Cross organizations for not drawing a "line in the sand" and voicing their uncompromising opposition to war; what they instead attempted to do, according to Suttner, was to regulate the type of weapons that could be employed and the treatment for the wounded or imprisoned. If the peace movement did not distance itself from such approaches, Suttner argued, they might as well become a branch of the war ministry (Suttner 1891: 2). The peace society membership should focus on replacing the institution of war with the rule of international law.

Speeches

Apart from presiding at meetings of the Austrian Peace Society and editing the peace journal, Bertha von Suttner traveled—mostly in Europe, although she also traveled to the United States twice, once for three weeks in 1904 and once for six months in 1912 (cf. Cohen 2009)—attending annual peace congresses and giving public lectures. According to an account published in Die Friedens-Warte ("Im Briefkasten," 39) in February 1904, Suttner gave over 230 speeches between 1892 and 1904, including 165 in Germany alone. According to a biographer who knew her personally, Suttner was a soft- and slow-spoken speaker, to whom attention was drawn by the "particularly piquant expression of her eyes (which) seemingly sprang from some inner fountain of keen, quickening thought" (Playne 1936: 186). In her talks, Suttner always informed her audiences about current conflicts and suggested how the peace movement—and especially arbitration courts—could resolve them.

One of her most memorable speeches was the one she gave in Christiana (today's Oslo) in April 1906, in acceptance of her Nobel Peace Prize. She entitled it "The Evolution of the Peace Movement." Here at the turn of the century, she argued, two "philosophies" or "eras of civilization" were "wrestling with one another": one leading to annihilation (e.g., with its Dreadnoughts, submarines, dirigibles), the other to international solidarity. Indeed, the peace movement was a symptom rather than a cause of the changes taking place—if too slowly for some: "Up to the present time," she said, "the military organization of our society has been founded upon a denial of the possibility of peace, a contempt for the value of human life, and an acceptance of the urge to kill" (Suttner 1906). What was now necessary, she argued, optimistically, was that

> we must also look for the new growth pushing up from the ground below ... a vigorous new spirit is supplanting the blatant and threatening old. No longer weak and formless, this promising new life is already widely established and determined to survive.... Factors contributing to the development of this process are technical inventions, improved communications, economic interdependence, and closer international relations. The instinct of self-preservation in human society, acting almost subconsciously, as do all drives in the human mind, is rebelling against the constantly refined methods of annihilation and against the destruction of humanity.
> —Suttner 1906

Appealing to Philanthropists

Another feature of Suttner's peace work was seeking the support of international philanthropists. Right from the start, Suttner actively sought the participation of contemporary social leaders: successful businessmen and authors, whose prestige might sway the general public. In this she had quite a number of successes. First, Alfred Nobel

(1833–96); without his financial support, the Austrian Peace Society may not have kept afloat for longer than a year. Remarkably, as Edelgard Biedermann discovered, the pair only met three times, the last one being in 1892 at the occasion of the Universal Peace Congress, when Nobel began to form ideas about sponsoring a peace prize. However, Nobel believed in *"si vis pacem, para bellum."* He considered that once weapons of mass destruction were developed, their use would be too devastating and war would be forever prevented. As he wrote to Suttner: "My factories may make an end of war sooner than your congresses. The day when two army corps can annihilate each other in one second, all civilized nations, it is to be hoped, will recoil from war and discharge their troops"; and yet, he also continued to support peace associations: in his last letter to Suttner, written on November 21, 1896, about three weeks before his death, he again promoted her cause: "I am delighted to see that the peace movement is gaining ground" (quoted in Suttner 1909a: 271, 191).

Suttner also corresponded and met on a number of occasions the enormously wealthy Scottish-American steel industrialist, arms manufacturer, and anti-unionist Andrew Carnegie (1835–1919) (cf. Suttner 1910). In the last two decades of his life, Carnegie donated relatively large sums to the peace movement, which included retirement payments to select internationally renowned peace activists (e.g., Bertha von Suttner, Alfred Hermann Fried), the costs for the building of the Peace Palace (*Vredespaleis*) in The Hague (current home of the Permanent Court of Arbitration), and the running costs for the Carnegie Endowment for International Peace (in Washington, DC).

Suttner also became acquainted with Jewish-Polish-Russian banker and railroad magnate Jan Gottlieb Bloch (a.k.a. Johann de Bloch, Ivan Stanislavovich Bliokh) (1835–1901). In 1898 Bloch published in St. Petersburg a six-volume (3,271-page) empirical work entitled *Budushchaia voina v tekhnicheskom, ekonomicheskom i politicheskom otnosheniakh* (*The Future of War in Technical, Economic and Political Relations*) in which, particularly after reviewing logistics and economic impacts (such as high inflation, lack of taxes, famine) as well as the expected drop in soldiers' and civilians' morale, he foresaw the end of war. As he remarkably summarized for British journalist William T. Stead: "I maintain that war has become impossible alike from a military, economic and political point of view . . . the great war cannot be made, and any attempts to make it would result in suicide" (Stead 1899: 21). Bloch was also a key sponsor of the International Museum of War and Peace, which opened in Lucerne, Switzerland, in 1902.

The First International Peace Conference in The Hague (1899)

Strikingly, Suttner experienced her second big breakthrough ten years after the publication of *Die Waffen nieder*, this time not as a book author but as a promoter of the First International Peace Conference in The Hague (1899). The growing attraction of the aim of universal peace led to a surge in international popular support for the peace movement and for Suttner personally. The conference was initiated in August 1898, with an appeal by Tsar Nicholas II to Western leaders, to explicitly participate in a conference

> to converge in one powerful focus the efforts of all States which are sincerely seeking to make the great idea of universal peace triumph over the elements of trouble and discord. It would at the same time confirm their agreement by the solemn establishment of the principles of justice and right, upon which repose the security of States and the welfare of peoples.
>
> —"Tsar's rescript" 1909

As historian Sandi Cooper explains, this rescript, which "recognized that no real security came from perpetually increased arms expenditures and that the misuse of capital and labor would eventually destroy European culture and economies" (1991: 97), reinvigorated the peace movement. One hundred and eight delegates from twenty-six countries gathered in The Hague, and meetings took place between May 18 and July 29. By 1899, peace activists and legal scholars could count 153 successful cases of arbitration (see Cooper 1991: 91). Although concrete blueprints for moving toward an international framework to overcome war were not on the table, the negotiations did settle on conventions for the "Pacific Settlement of Disputes" and the "Laws and Customs of War on Land" ("The Hague Convention"). In particular, the then weapons of mass destruction—projectiles launched from balloons and other dirigibles as well as asphyxiating gases and dum-dum bullets—were now forbidden.

Mass public support of the conference landed in foreign diplomats' offices: e.g., as numerous resolutions of endorsement, plans or schemes, over a million women's signatures collected by German feminist-pacifist Margarethe Leonore Selenka, on behalf of the Peace and Arbitration Committee of the International Council of Women, who also co-organized over 565 peace rallies in the rescript's honor (see Cooper 1991: 69; Holl 2007: 108).

A particularly interesting reflection of the enhanced public status Suttner obtained as a promoter of the conference is evidenced by the fact that she became a prominent figure in the illustrations of the German-language satirical press, albeit from a mostly derogatory angle. One of the first of these caricatures is entitled *"Der Zar als Tenor"* (The Tsar as tenor) (*Ulk*, January 13, 1899: cover) and illustrates a singing Nicholas II, holding "Die Waffen nieder by Bertha von Suttner," surrounded by "his European band." A month later, the same journal posted an intimate bathroom scene: we find Nicholas II, as father, dressed casually and smoking a cigar, bent down to hold his dirty, crying son ("war") by the arm; Bertha, standing as a rather large matron, holds a bar of soap. The caricature is entitled "Caution is the aunt of diplomacy" (*Vorsicht ist die Tante der Diplomatie*) and the captioned dialogue tells us that Suttner wants to wash their child in the bathtub ("disarmament"), but Nicholas II objects, saying the bucket will most certainly do for a start (*Ulk*, February 10, 1899: cover). This caricature, like many others, offers a variety of possible interpretations, all generally derisive: against the peace movement, but also against self-confident women—both represented by Bertha von Suttner. Yet they honor her as well: after all, Suttner, as a woman, has not yet even been afforded suffrage, and yet acts as influential counterpart or partner to the highest authority in Russia and thus participates in Great Power politics.

The Austrian press was even less respectful. A caricature in the *Neue Glühlichter* (May 11, 1899: cover), for example, depicted a young and dainty Suttner, wearing a bright yellow dress and holding *Die Waffen nieder!* She is being kicked in the buttocks out of a door (of the conference, presumably), by an enormous brown boot (with attached spur). It is entitled *"Die Einleitung zur Friedenskonferenz in Haag, oder Die russische Friedensliebe"* (The introduction to the peace conference in The Hague, or the Russian "love of peace"). Similarly the *Humoristische Blätter* (August 13, 1899: cover) printed a caricature entitled *"Heimkehr der Friedens-Bertha"* (Peace-Bertha returns home) with the caption: "The child was dead in her arms." In a seeming homage to Johann Wolfgang von Goethe's 1782 well-known ballad entitled *Erlkönig* (The Erlking), it illustrates a night scene, with a full moon and Suttner sitting with a dying child and olive branches in her lap, on a frightened, wildly galloping horse.

In fact, Bertha von Suttner, while not allowed to attend The Hague's closed meetings, headed the peace movement activities surrounding them: hosting a variety of lectures and informal interactions between official participants and peace advocates and writing up newspaper articles. Zionist leader Theodor Herzl had engaged her to send reports for his journal *Die Welt*, and she wrote for other papers, too (see Cohen 2005b). She also published daily logs, documenting her experiences, and a collection of materials for the general public (Suttner 1901).

But the enthusiasm that emerged before and during the Hague Conference was short-lived. Armed conflicts between European states, within their colonized territories, and even between Russia and Japan, soon started, along with an increasing rush to produce ever more technologically sophisticated weaponry. All of this greatly overshadowed the small if growing use of international arbitration courts. The military always had a monopoly on state resources: weapons, money, and last but not least the media, which was especially adept at stirring up irrational mass fear and the call for "defense" (or "security"), to be obtained by an ever-escalating reliance on ever-more-sophisticated weapons. Clearly discouraged, Suttner was not however a defeatist, as she often proved in her public speeches:

> The greatest numbers, the masses, act as if they were indifferent. . . . But there are millions of people who think as we do . . . and desire from the bottom of their hearts to prevent a future war. But who say nevertheless—it would be so fine, but it can't work. [To them I say]: "It surely would work, if people just made it happen!"
> —Suttner 1900: 4, 35

To this end, Suttner and her colleagues continued right up until the start of World War I to hold congresses, write, and lecture about the dangers of the growing militarization and to highlight the legal efforts undertaken by state diplomats and the peace movement.

SUTTNER'S LEGACY

One could argue that Bertha von Suttner lived two lives. Born and raised as an aristocrat, she discovered her political calling, pacifism—or as she defined it, the abolition of military weapons and the organization of international arbitration courts—in her mid-forties, which largely went against her class interests. Suttner's novel, *Die Waffen nieder!*, clearly hit a nerve, especially in its European and North American readership. An early review compared Suttner's vivid descriptions of the horrors of war to Russian artist Vasily Vereshchagin's well-received and realistic anti-war paintings. Out of all the evils that afflict human society, war was the worst (Kulka 1890). And an early harbinger of praise also came from Lev Tolstoy,[14] who encouragingly wished on it an impact on the European peace culture analogous to the one that Harriet Beecher Stowe's *Uncle Tom's Cabin* had had on propelling the anti-slavery movement in the United States (see Braker 1991). Diplomats, too, such as US ambassador Andrew Dickson White, praised Suttner's novel as "brilliant" (1905: 260). Even Wilhelm Liebknecht had it reprinted in instalments in the German Social Democrat Party's daily *Vorwärts*, which of course played a substantial role in introducing Suttner to a working-class public. Suttner herself modestly attributed the novel's success to being a reflection of the Zeitgeist (Suttner 1900: 181). Of course, Suttner also had many detractors, well exemplified by the anonymous defaming line printed in the *Ostdeutsche Rundschau* (July 8, 1894): "Who cries 'Die Waffen nieder!'? A vainglorious, hysterical 'blue stocking'—Baroness Suttner."

FIGURE 5.3: Bertha von Suttner quoted on a protest banner in 2012. Credit: DPA/Getty Images.

Importantly, Suttner was able not only to wage a "war against war," but also to promote an alternative. Influenced by Charles Darwin and other evolutionary thinkers, she expected the prevailing war culture to "evolve" into a sustainable peace culture. Just as she denounced the devastation on the battlefields, so too did she focus on the potentials for human happiness, exemplified for instance in the clear marital bliss between Martha Althaus and Friedrich Tilling. Her independently minded, intelligent, and articulate heroine also inspired many readers, not least feminists in the international women's movement.

Suttner considered pacifism both an inevitable and an ethically imperative means of saving civilization. As she said in a 1904 speech entitled *Der Krieg und seine Bekämpfung* (War and the fight against it): "Our opponents think that the wish to get rid of war is absurd—like the wish to get rid of death. Such a thing would be truly fine, but it is impossible, they say. Yet war is not death; it is murder. And not to murder someone is not an impossibility" (Suttner 1904: 4). Or, as she wrote in *Die Waffen nieder*: "Revenge, again and again revenge? ... No reasonable person would consider cleaning spots of paint with paint or spots of oil with oil. Only blood, this should always be washed out with blood!" (Suttner [n.d.]: 203). And yet the major obstacles to the peace movement have never been the few active warmongers or preachers of racial hate, but the vast majority of citizens who sit back and are apathetic in the face of warmongering. Standing up against the purportedly "natural" human drive toward war, as Bertha von Suttner did, and trying to challenge it as a construct, an outdated norm, was an extraordinarily brave and responsible choice.

Suttner's efforts certainly had a perceptible impact during her lifetime, not least in forcefully assisting the shift in public opinion against the idea of war as something heroic.

For her efforts, she was viciously attacked and ridiculed by the mainstream ("malestream") media. In some way, this is hardly surprising, since by persistently claiming that society—and men in the first place—had to put down its weapons, Suttner was in fact attacking a hegemonic masculine ideal of her day, one that still reverberates. Clearly, a "disarmed" Western society would entirely shake up the supposedly "natural" (and not least gendered) status quo, which would have long-lasting repercussions across the social and national fabrics of today's world.

Indeed, representatives of the growing international women's movement gradually acknowledged and appreciated Suttner's progressive efforts, as exemplified by local Women's Club President, Clara Laddey of Arlington, New Jersey, who wrote to US peace activist Lucia Ames Mead in 1907 that "Baroness Bertha von Suttner . . . was one of the greatest Peace Promoters of the last thirty years."[15] The Norwegian Council of Women, in their official nomination of Suttner for the Nobel Peace Prize, wrote: "No one has more strongly than her expressed women's demand for peace" (quoted in Veseth 2000: 34). Some male lawmakers, too, recognized Suttner's success in touching, even stirring the hearts of the public so as to make grand strides toward the abolition of war, as exemplified in an editorial in *The American Journal of International Law*: "The Baroness von Suttner's book [*Die Waffen nieder!*] put [the institution of war] on the defensive. . . . This is the service which this high minded and gifted woman rendered to the cause of mankind" (1914: 614). But Suttner's achievements, along with those of innumerable others committed to a more peaceful civilization, were obviously unable to reverse the sway of those in power. As Suttner clairvoyantly predicted in April 1912: "The powers, though having a terrible fear of war, seem hopelessly drifting toward a conflagration that will set back our culture and civilization for a century" (Suttner 1912). The horrors of World War I began at the end of July 1914: Suttner was off merely by about two years.

In coming to terms with the experiences of World War I, some people voiced a superficial and defeatist criticism of Suttner, saying, for example, that "she didn't succeed in changing anything. Her life's work was in ashes even before she had the good luck to die" (Dolmetsch 1992, 182). Others, in the international peace movement, for instance, looked for individuals to blame within their own ranks. It is thus particularly eye-opening to witness future German Nobel Peace Prize laureate Carl von Ossietzky (1889–1938) slander Suttner ten years after her death as a gullible female oozing with sentimentality. As he wrote in *"Die Pazifisten"* (The Pacifists) (1924: 38):

> Suttner's pacifism amounted to little more than whingeing (*Wehleidigkeit*). She fought against canons with holy water and she adored contracts and institutions with touching childishness. She was a priestess of souls . . . How else could one encounter this mild and good lady? Like so many women, who fight for the realization of an idea out of a pure womanish soul—one which after all requires manly resilience and a crystal-clear view of the facts—she glided into the implausible, believing to have converted those who merely shed a couple of crocodile tears, all the while remaining stuck in superficiality rather than obtaining any real objectives: Lacking any incisive form, she ultimately opted for kitsch. Until a gentle aroma of ridiculousness gradually surrounded the "Peace Bertha," an aroma which unfortunately remains in the German peace movement up until today. . . . For the majority, pacifism has carried the character of exclusiveness with it, and worse still, of unmanliness.

In fact, Suttner's activism and political writings were resolutely aimed at concise and rational argumentation, even if at times she also called on women, especially, to be attuned to their emotional perception and reactions, which could also at times collude with public war-prone attitudes. In her letter to pioneering German feminist pacifists, months before she died, Suttner explained that "our thoughts should be clear and sharp, and our feelings warm and noble.... We need passion to negotiate and be effective, only passion moves us" (Suttner 1914). Although sentimentality may play strongly in many of her high-life novels (see Hierdeis 2005), her political vision of peace was not informed by sentimentality. Women have been held to a different standard. When men express similar sentiments, such as philosopher and pacifist Bertrand Russell, in his "Ethics of War," where he writes that "Opinions on such a subject as war *are the outcome of feeling rather than of thought*" (1915: 127, emphasis added), *they* are not accused of being "sentimental."

Similarly unjustified, in my view, are feminist critics and scholars who tend to credit Suttner's achievements with only "symbolic" success (see Kinnebrock 2005: 374–5, for example), or peace scholars, who reduce Suttner to a "female public relations star" (for example, Herren 2013: 46). Suttner actually contributed considerably to our notions today of a peace culture.

One who understood this particularly well was Stefan Zweig, who famously brought Suttner back to life in his memoirs, *The World of Yesterday*:

> She came up to me in great excitement, "The people have no idea what is going on!" she cried quite loudly on the street, although she usually spoke quietly and with deliberation. "The war is already upon us, and once again they have hidden and kept it from us. Why don't you do something, you young people? It is your concern most of all. Defend yourselves! Unite! Don't always let us few old women to whom no one listens do everything.
>
> — Zweig 1964: 209

Back in 1918 Zweig also appraised Suttner's impact more accurately than most then and ever since: "I'm one of those all too many people who did not appreciate Bertha von Suttner during her lifetime. And it could have been so easy. But no, it is warmongering that is easy, not pacifism. Bertha von Suttner had known about this war twenty years ago!" (Zweig 1918: 1).[16] He clearly recognized, for instance, the misogynist slant in many attacks on Suttner, which he also criticized: "One called her passionate monotony weakness of thought; her clarity—banality. Eventually she became ridiculous, the 'Peace-Bertha' of satirical journals and people called her 'a good woman' in that pitying tone, which equates goodness with stupidity" (Zweig 1918: 1). He concluded his eulogy with sentiments as powerful then, after three years of war, as they are today:

> But I ask you—and myself—am I speaking truthfully when I say that we had no idea, that we did not know about the coming world war. Yes and no. Both as an answer would not be an exaggeration, because everyone has a peculiar way of knowing, a habitual and dangerous way of knowing, and simultaneously a desire to remain ignorant, which is basically connected to our will to live. We notice quite a lot and yet do not quite see it consciously, because we do not want to see it, because we forcefully repress it and push it back into our subconscious, into the twilight of our senses, our feelings.... Thus it came to pass in peace time that we did not believe in war—out of nonchalance, flippancy, or recklessness, or out of a mental instinct of self-preservation, because we did not want to believe it, because we did not want our comfortable way of life to be in any way disturbed.
>
> — Zweig 1918: 4

FIGURE 5.4: Bertha von Suttner at her writing desk. Credit: Ullstein Bild Dtl./Getty Images.

Bertha von Suttner proved to be one of the most earnest and engaged peace activists of her time. That we still live in cultures of war means that her work continues to have relevance. As she wrote in 1914: "So . . . get to work and be unwavering! Montecuccoli said 'To wage war one needs money, money, and more money.' I will not say that our campaign couldn't use some of that. But the main thing is still: perseverance, perseverance, and more perseverance!" (Suttner 1914)

CHAPTER SIX

Peace Movements

MARTIN CEADEL

INTRODUCTION

The period in question is a meaningful one for the peace movement, running neatly as it does from the latter's institutionalization until the inauguration of the first intergovernmental body designed to prevent war. In 1815 the world's first peace associations, mooted for a quarter of a century but delayed by international conflicts, were created in the United States, their British counterparts following within months. And in 1920 the League of Nations, the first-ever international political organization, was formally established, its Covenant implementing proposals put forward by peace activists early in World War I. Between these dates the movement experienced three distinct phases. For its first half-century it was dominated by British and American associations which, after a muted beginning, found the courage to condemn their own governments. This Anglo-American-led movement reached a peak of optimism during the late 1840s and the beginning of the 1850s, when the intellectual tide seemed to be turning in its favor, but thereafter faced a decade and a half of adversity. The second phase began in 1867, as peace activism gradually revived, this time led by Europeans reacting against their continent's costly conscript armies while declining to criticize their own governments. Phase three saw World War I destroy most of the nineteenth-century movement, and create some dynamic new associations, most notably those in Britain and the United States that proposed a League of Nations.

THE PEACE MOVEMENT: CAMPAIGNING FOR *PACIFICISM* OR PACIFISM

Although the virtues of peace have been extolled since antiquity, the "peace movement" as here understood was an aspect of the political modernity that emerged during the late eighteenth century in the form of ideological contestation and grassroots mobilization. An ideological debate clarified "peace" as an ideal condition whose attainability was, however, disputed; and the revolutions in America and France and the emergence of radical and evangelical pressure politics in Britain demonstrated the possibility of a "movement" promoting such an ideal.

What distinguished peace-movement thinking was its rejection not only of the aggressive war which militarists glorified for its intrinsic worth and which crusaders believed could sometimes be a means toward justice but also—and more controversially—of the conventional wisdom that aggression could be deterred by strong defenses. I have treated this last, often summed up in the dictum "if you want peace, prepare for war," as a distinct ideology called "defencism" (Ceadel 1987: ch. 5) whereas International Relations scholars have tacitly incorporated it into their category of "realism." Defencism or realism assumed that an armed truce was the best that the international system could expect to achieve, whereas the peace movement was defined by its aspiration toward the more permanent and profound condition of peace that would result from the abolition of war. (This optimism applied primarily to relations among "civilized" states: the extent to which it also applied to the latter's relations with the colonial world was often left unclear.)

There were always two approaches to the abolition of war: absolutist and reformist. The absolutist, for which the word "pacifism" is now best reserved, was the claim that it could be achieved immediately by unconditionally renouncing military force. The boldness of this claim explained its minority status even within the peace movement. Absolutism believed, in effect, that war would be abolished by mass conscientious objection. Its intellectual origins lay in the belief of some Protestant sects that certain social practices, in this case military service, were sinful for them. From 1796, when the first tracts arguing that this was the correct reading of their faith for all Christians, and not merely for members of certain sects, were published in London, pacifism spread, albeit gradually and on a very small scale, into a number of Protestant churches and denominations (Ceadel 1996: ch. 5). Eventually, pacifism would also be inferred from minority, absolutist interpretations of socialism and utilitarianism (Ceadel 1980).

The peace movement's reformist majority followed the enlightenment tradition of dismissing certain social practices, in this case war, as irrational for all and capable of being reformed out of existence. Realizing that this process would take time, however, reformists accepted in the meantime that military force might have to be used to defend progressives against reactionaries wedded to primitive practices. Following a suggestion by A.J.P. Taylor (1957: 51) I have called this reformist position *pacificism*, because it was pacific in its aspiration to abolish war but not pacifist in the sense of immediately renouncing it. *Pacificism* assumed a natural harmony of interests among states, even if governments irrationally denied it. This harmony was inferred from utilitarian principles by Jeremy Bentham, who in 1789 made the first known suggestion of a peace association (in imitation of the Society for Effecting the Abolition of the Slave Trade, set up by British Quakers two years previously) and wrote an essay that anticipated many of the *pacificist* ideas of the next hundred years (Conway 1989). And it was inferred from a rational-Christian conception of the divine purpose by the Unitarian merchants who, a couple of years after Britain entered the French wars of 1793–1815, launched the world's first peace campaign (Cookson 1982), although they did not feel it appropriate to establish a peace association in wartime. In due course, each progressive ideology promoted its own version of *pacificism*. The radical one blamed war on élites and vested interests, and argued that only republican or democratic control of foreign policy could eradicate it. The liberal version blamed war on the cult of state sovereignty, and over the years backed a range of internationalist solutions, including free trade, arbitration, a world court, and intergovernmental organization. The socialist one indicted capitalism as the cause of war; and feminist *pacificism* accused patriarchy.

To pioneer the optimistic belief that war could ultimately be abolished required a measure of physical security; and actively to campaign for that belief required a measure of political liberty. Continental Europe had little of either, except on its northern maritime fringes. The easily crossable land frontiers of its heartland made defencism—or, for a powerful state, militarism—seem the soundest policy. In addition, both authoritarian political systems and Catholic, Lutheran, and Orthodox churches worked against pluralism, individualism, and dissent. And the continent's most influential pacifist sectarians, the Mennonites, often appeared to seek special exemption for themselves rather than to make a general case for conscientious objection.

By contrast, the United States (especially New England) and Britain both enjoyed favorable geopolitical and cultural conditions: their threat of invasion was lower; their liberal and commercial values allowed voluntary associations to operate with greater freedom and encouraged internationalism; and their Protestant churches nurtured conscientious dissent. In addition, their exposure to the Quaker variety of sectarianism gave them a better understanding of pacifism. Having declared themselves non-resistant in 1661, in response to the restoration of the British monarchy, most Quakers not only refused militia service: they also refused to hire substitutes or pay fines in lieu, suffering confiscation of property instead. By thus declining to be personally exempted while fellow citizens with lesser religious scruples fought on their behalf, Quakers implied that all Christians should follow their example. As their principled behavior acquired respect on both sides of the Atlantic, Quakers forged links with evangelicals from mainstream churches and denominations, a few of whom imitated their pacifist views.

1815–67: THE RISE AND FALL OF AN ANGLO-AMERICAN-LED MOVEMENT

The Anglo-American world's favorable geopolitical situations and political cultures explained why peace activism was first institutionalized there. Because on both sides of the Atlantic a significant minority of activists were absolutists, the thorniest early question for peace associations was whether to have a pacifist or a *pacificist* basis or some combination of the two. From the early 1850s, however, a bigger problem was posed by the temptations of crusading.

The United States led the way because it extricated itself from its War of 1812, which had been particularly unpopular in New England, before Napoleon's final defeat.[1] Yet the absolutist wing of its early peace movement became fragmented; its leading association, the American Peace Society (APS), failed to find a durable formula for securing cooperation between absolutists (of whatever kind) and reformists; and within a quarter of a century many leading activists were giving anti-slavery priority over peace.

Some of these organizational problems arose from the fact that—unlike in the British movement—the Quakers, weakened by a doctrinal controversy that split them into Orthodox and Hicksite factions, did not play a dominant role. It was a devout Presbyterian merchant, David Low Dodge, who in August 1815 established the world's first peace association, the New York Peace Society: this initially catered for pacifists only, and recruited poorly on this narrow basis. It was a Congregationalist-turned-Unitarian minister, Noah Worcester, who four months later established the Massachusetts Peace Society: although Worcester was a pacifist, he welcomed *pacificists* on an equal, diversity-of-opinions basis. And it was on the initiative of former sea captain William Ladd that in 1828 these and other local associations merged to form the APS: this began on a diversity-of-opinions basis but then somewhat incoherently modified it, in part because Ladd himself was soon converted from *pacificism* to pacifism.

Ladd's conversion was a symptom of the upsurge of Christian absolutism which took place in the 1830s on both sides of the Atlantic but was most intense in New England where a hard core of ultra-puritans viewed their own political community not as basically godly though capable of spiritual improvement but as fundamentally sinful. These ultras, led by William Lloyd Garrison, embraced an anarcho-pacifism that rejected not only war but also personal self-defense, the death penalty, and—perhaps understandably in a polity whose federal constitution, for all its liberal features, recognized slavery—participation in politics. Dodge had taken a similar view; but the abrasive Garrison far outdid him in stridency, threatening to leave the APS unless it changed policy. The society met him halfway in what turned out to be an unsatisfactory and unstable compromise: in 1837 the APS formally espoused pacifism, even though many members considered this an unwise narrowing of its appeal; but it refused to move toward anarchism, so the following year Garrison seceded to form the New England Non-Resistance Society. The pacifist commitment of 1837 had thus failed in its principal purpose of retaining Garrison's support but could not be rescinded because, despite being weakened by the Garrisonian secession, absolutists remained strong enough within the APS to block this.

However, these absolutists could not prevent the leadership passing resolutions insisting that the APS "invited the cooperation of all persons who strongly desire the extinction of war": in other words, despite its new official pacifism the society still welcomed *pacificist* members. Moreover, Ladd's main campaigning interest, which became that of the APS, was the congress and court of nations, a liberal-*pacificist* proposal for improving the prospects of international arbitration that had been originated by Bentham and developed by his disciple James Mill. (The congress would be an international assembly to fill in the many gaps in international law; and the court would be an international tribunal to apply the new legal code to particular disputes.) Thus, in respect of the absolutism-or-reformism issue, the APS had got into a damaging muddle. Its policy was *pacificist*, as was much of its membership. So too was its leadership after the conciliatory Ladd died in 1841 and the APS came under the control of George C. Beckwith, who was concerned above all to make it uncontroversial and respectable. Beckwith's strategy of moderation had the advantage of pre-empting the creation of an explicitly *pacificist* rival to the APS but the disadvantage of upsetting those who wanted the society's official absolutism to be taken seriously. One of these last, Connecticut's "learned blacksmith" Elihu Burritt, was to set up his own international pacifist association while on a visit to Britain in 1846, as will shortly be noted.

Even so, during 1846–8 activists of all persuasions, *pacificist*, pacifist, and anarcho-pacifist, came together to condemn their country's war with Mexico, which was not only aggressive but helpful to the slaveholding states (where, significantly, peace associations had no support). This united stand proved to be the American movement's nineteenth-century peak: during the 1850s the cause of peace largely surrendered to that of anti-slavery. Even Garrisonians tacitly switched from promoting their own "ultra" beliefs to arguing that all those who did not share these were morally obliged to crusade against slavery. During the civil war they even argued that only anarcho-pacifists like themselves had the moral right to be conscientious objectors to military service: everyone who voted and accepted the legitimacy under certain circumstances of military force should fight the slaveholders. For its part the APS supported the northern states on the grounds that theirs was a police action against rebels rather than a war. Such a position, which pacifism's leading historian has called "sophistical" (Brock 1991: 55–7), did much to discredit the American peace movement by 1865.

During this same half-century its British counterpart was largely untroubled by anarcho-pacifism; and it also managed the relationship between its absolutists and reformists more successfully, thanks to Quaker leadership. In the 1850s, however, many of its peace activists also became distracted by the lure of crusading, in this case against Europe's despots.[2]

The first British peace association, the Society for Abolishing War formed in March 1816 by the Unitarian publisher and radical politician Sir Richard Philipps (van der Linden 1987: 2), was for *pacificists* only. However, the Society for the Promotion of Permanent and Universal Peace—soon known locally as the Peace Society and internationally as the London Peace Society (LPS)—was set up in June 1816 by a group of Quaker-led evangelicals on a basis of top-tier pacifism. In other words, the LPS required its committee members, who set policy, to be pacifist, but invited *pacificists* to join its rank and file. Thus, though constituting a numerical majority, *pacificists* had to accept a position of ideological inferiority: they had to defer doctrinally to a pacifist leadership which condescendingly expressed the hope that they would in due course move to the "high ground" occupied by the committee and embrace its "grand principle" of rejecting defensive war too.

This two-tier structure (to which, after consultation with the LPS, the New York Peace Society moved in 1818) served the society well for half a century, during which it established itself as the leader of the international movement. Admitting a lower tier of *pacificists*—such as Bentham, who was among the 190 subscribers listed in the first annual report—enabled the LPS to acquire a critical mass of support. Requiring its committee to be pacifist was necessary to recruit and retain Quakers, whose donations enabled it avoid the financial difficulties which caused Sir Richard Phillips's organization to fade away within a few years, and who also provided a countrywide network of support that made the LPS the world's first peace association with a national reach. Indeed, the link with the Society of Friends was so close that the LPS had to be careful never to have a majority of Quakers on its committee, so that it could present itself as an ecumenical rather than a sectarian body. During its first decade and a half, when the government feared social unrest, the LPS's Christian pacifism enabled it to present itself as a pious rather than subversive organization; and it initially took care not to condemn the death penalty. In addition, its rejection of *all* wars spared it the divisive experience of having to debate which ones counted as defensive and which did not.

In Britain's more optimistic political climate of 1832–51, the LPS was able to come out as a pressure group, petitioning Parliament, hiring lecturers, and supporting secular and non-absolutist policies such as arbitration. In 1843 it took the bold step of organizing a General Peace Convention in London, the first-ever international peace congress. However, as other groups rallied to the cause of peace, it lost its virtual monopoly of British activism, a fact reflected in the coming into common English usage during the 1840s of the generic term "peace movement." Even so, the LPS's two-tier strategy enabled it to hold its own against rivals, both reformist and absolutist, who mainly emanated from Britain's cities in the midlands and north, newly empowered by the Great Reform Act of 1832 and also by industrial and commercial development, though challengers also appeared from across the Atlantic.

The LPS's welcoming of *pacificists* as ordinary members enabled it to cooperate with both radicals and liberals. It recruited several popular lecturers from the moral-force wing of Chartism, a radical mass movement which from 1838 campaigned for manhood suffrage and deployed both the radical-*pacificist* argument that wars "would seldom or scarcely ever occur" if aristocratic rule "were put down" by such a reform (Weisser 1975: 85) and the laborist argument that militia service, if it were to be revived, would bear unfairly on the working classes. The LPS also worked closely with Richard Cobden, the influential liberal activist who, after the triumph in 1846 of his Anti-Corn-Law League, took up the peace cause. Cobden did not want the British government to compensate for its loss of protectionist duties by increasing direct taxation, so he sought to lower public expenditure, and considered the armaments bill to be the easiest to cut. Consequently, to minimize the risks attached to reducing armaments, he took up the cause of arbitration. However, he rejected the congress and court of nations, and suggested instead that arbitration clauses be inserted into all diplomatic and commercial treaties with other states. Significantly, Cobden did not establish his own association to promote this liberal-*pacificist* package of free trade, reduction of armaments, and arbitration treaties; nor did he join the Peace of Nations Society, a *pacificist* organization created in 1849, which in consequence flopped. Instead, Cobden relied for extra-parliamentary support on the LPS (mediated through a front organization, the Peace Congress Committee, which spared Cobdenites the need to defer to the society's pacifism).

Meanwhile, on the absolutist front, the LPS faced three distinct rivals. The first was a "moral radical party" (Tyrell 1987) of prosperous provincial businessmen, most of them nonconformists, led by nineteenth-century Britain's greatest all-round progressive activist, the Birmingham-based Quaker corn merchant Joseph Sturge. Moral radicals believed that the London philanthropic establishment was insufficiently bold in its pursuit of its professed goals. They therefore set up their own organizations: for example, in 1842 Sturge formed a Birmingham Peace Association as an independent pacifist body, and seemingly contemplated a British Peace Association too. In the event, probably because the LPS galvanized itself to hold its General Peace Convention of 1843, Sturge decided to cooperate rather than compete.

By then, Sturgeite moral radicalism was in any case being outflanked on the absolutist front by Garrison's handful of British followers, who set up their own local Anti-War Associations in the large cities furthest from London, though, partly because the British Empire was no longer (since abolition in 1833) contaminated by slavery, these organizations never took root.

The LPS's third and most challenging pacifist rival was based more on class interest than ideological distance from the metropolis. In 1846 Elihu Burritt arrived from New England to discover his British artisan counterparts not only politicized by Chartism but alarmed by a proposed revival of militia service. He formulated an absolutist pledge against military service that became the membership basis for a League of Universal Brotherhood (LUB), which challenged the APS in his home country and the LPS in Britain. Yet these challenges soon faded out, as Burritt became distracted by his project of holding annual international peace congresses, which he did successfully in Brussels, Paris, Frankfurt, and London during 1848–51, a period of European revolutionary excitement. Neglected by its founder, the LUB lost momentum, and in Britain was smothered in a cooperative but ultimately controlling embrace by the LPS's talented new secretary, Henry Richard, whose four-decade domination of the society began in 1848. As its artisan base dwindled, the LUB's most active component came to be its Olive Leaf Circles, women's groups that sent goodwill messages to other countries—perhaps the earliest example of autonomous female peace activism.

What made the British peace movement stand out internationally was its clout and courage. During 1847, the year the LPS had become influential enough to be editorially denounced in *The Times*, its campaigning was a factor in causing the government to abandon its intended revival of compulsory militia service. The movement reached its

FIGURE 6.1: Crowds outside the Great Exhibition, 1851. Credit: Getty Images.

nineteenth-century peak of confidence at the London peace congress, which coincided with the Great Exhibition of 1851.

Thereafter, the actions of France's Napoleon III reinvigorated defencism, while progressive opinion became drawn to crusading in support of the liberties of Europe, culminating in widespread enthusiasm for the Crimean War of 1854–6 against the hated Tsar of Russia. It was a tribute to the LPS's perceived power that some defencists blamed it for having led the Tsar on and put considerable effort into denouncing its "peace at any price" policy. The LPS courageously opposed the Crimean involvement, the first pre-existing peace association to condemn from the outset a war being prosecuted with overwhelming national support. As that support ebbed in 1855, the LPS's stand was endorsed more noisily by the Stop-the-War League, an *ad hoc* body created by radical *pacificists* in London. In 1857, though the peace cause was in a post-Crimea slump, Richard Cobden boldly and skillfully brought down Palmerston's government in parliament for its gratuitous attack on China, the Arrow War, though Palmerston bounced back at the ensuing general election. Courageously, too, the LPS condemned the American Civil War of 1861–5, even though many of its followers sympathized with the northern states.

For the geographical and cultural reasons already mentioned, Europe lagged far behind during this first half-century of institutionalized activism. In France such peace sentiment as there was emanated from the Protestant minority; and the Société de la morale chrétienne, established in 1821 with the help of one of the Quaker founders of the LPS, did not even have "peace" in its title. Europe's first autonomous and explicit peace effort, the Société de la paix de Genève created in 1830 by Count Jean-Jacques de Sellon, was little more than "an entourage or sounding board" (van der Linden 1987: 122) for the Swiss Protestant nobleman who founded it, and expired with him in 1839. Moreover, the figures for delegates registered by the General Peace Convention of 1843 were revealing: only six from continental Europe, compared with twenty-six from the United States and 292 from the United Kingdom.

1867–1914: A EUROPE-LED "PATRIOTIC" MOVEMENT

During its second half-century the peace movement's center of gravity shifted toward continental Europe, particularly France; and in due course a new and cautious brand of *pacificism* emerged there, as well as a marginal but menacing far-left brand and, albeit on a minute scale, pacifism of an idiosyncratic kind.

In 1867, as Napoleon III clumsily confronted an expansionist Prussia, several *pacificist* associations were created by Frenchmen. One, which underwent several changes of name over the decades, ending up as the Société française pour l'arbitrage entre nations, was led by Frédéric Passy, a free-trade economist who admired Cobden. It was ideologically liberal in the Anglo-American tradition, and drew its main support from France's Protestant and Jewish minorities. Its principal rival, the Ligue internationale de la paix et de la liberté, was established by a journalist and follower of Saint Simon, Charles Lemonnier, at a congress in Geneva, where the delegates included many who had just come on from a meeting of Marx's First International in nearby Lausanne. It was radical in its ideology, and therefore closer to the mainstream of French republicanism, arguing that free trade and arbitration by themselves could not eliminate war: republican institutions must also be created. In its ideologically confident early years it succumbed to crusading: for example, at its 1869 congress in Lausanne the French novelist Victor Hugo, who presided, called for a "last" war to achieve "eternal" peace (Cooper 1991b: 42).

But in 1870 Napoleon III lost Alsace-Lorraine to Prussia, as a consequence of which Germany united and industrialized. The perspective of the Ligue internationale de la paix et de la liberté, and indeed of the French peace movement as a whole, gradually softened as the country's position in relation to Germany deteriorated. A strong regime of international law, requiring arbitration of disputes and enforcing arbitral awards, seemed increasingly to be in France's national interest, because it offered a possible way to regain Alsace-Lorraine, constrain Germany, and free France to concentrate on its colonies (Chickering 1975: ch. 8). A distinctively juridical approach with an emphasis on enforcement—as exemplified in the name eventually taken by one prominent peace association formed in 1887, the Association de la paix par le droit—thus came to dominate a French *pacificism* that saw itself as entirely congruent with the interests and values of the country's republican regime. In 1889, to promote their program internationally, French activists helped to found the Inter-Parliamentary Union and, more importantly, re-launched annual international (now called "universal") peace congresses, which three years later acquired their own secretariat at Berne, the International Peace Bureau. France developed a sufficiently large number of peace associations to justify bringing them together each year in National Peace Congresses. But none was pacifist, so when at the 1904 such congress a Protestant pastor, Jean Allegret, called for the recognition of conscientious objection, he was "soundly defeated" on the grounds that "the equality of all persons before the law included military service" (Cooper 1991a: 381). To almost everyone in the French peace movement, in other words, their republic itself enshrined peace principles and was therefore entitled to require all citizens to defend it.

Thus when Lemmonier's successor as leader of the Ligue internationale de la paix et de la liberté, Émile Arnaud, coined the word "pacifisme" in 1901 as a label for the French peace movement's program, he was describing what Sandi E. Cooper, in her important study of continental activism, labeled "patriotic pacifism" (Cooper 1991b). In my terminology, of course, it would be "patriotic *pacificism*." It was patriotic because it accepted the right of European states to fulfill their national and even imperial destinies. Admittedly, most continental associations formed under the stimulus of the new series of universal peace congresses could not identify as closely as French ones did with their political regimes because their own were authoritarian. It was to avoid accusations of subversion that they appeared as patriotic as they could. Thus the Austrian Peace Society, a small circle around its aristocratic founder in 1891, Bertha von Suttner, did not condemn Austria-Hungary's provocative annexation of Bosnia-Hercegovina in 1908 (Laurence 1978; Wank 1988). The even greater political marginality of the German Peace Society, formed in 1892, was symbolized by the fact that its co-founder Alfred Fried was a Jew from Vienna. The cantankerous Fried soon left the society but remained Germany's best-known

FIGURE 6.2: Alfred Hermann Fried (1864–1921), co-founder of the German Peace Movement and winner of the Nobel Peace Prize in 1911. Credit: Imagno/Getty Images.

peace activist, tirelessly expounding a "scientific" *pacifism*. To survive in a political culture in which militarism was more influential than *pacifism*, Germany's peace movement had to avoid criticism of national policy. So weak was it that, having written a doctoral thesis about it, the historian Roger Chickering reconfigured the published version in order to focus not on German activism itself, such as it was, but instead on those "features in the German political system that accounted for the fact . . . that the peace movement was significantly weaker in Germany than elsewhere" (Chickering 1975: vxi–vxii).

When Italy's best-known activist, Ernesto Moneta of the Lombard Peace Union, came out in enthusiastic support for his country's seizure of Libya in 1911 (Castelli 2010) his patriotism was obvious enough; but what of his *pacifism*? It was little more than a rejection of the social-Darwinist claim that nations and empires were locked into an inexorable struggle for supremacy and survival. Patriotic *pacificists* retained Mazzini's pre-Darwinian view that, once their legitimate national and imperial aspirations had been fulfilled, states would prove to be mutually tolerant units within a stable international system, and thus capable of arbitrating their disputes.

Unpatriotic *pacificism* did exist in continental Europe, but only on the alienated left of the political spectrum. The few who condemned Austria-Hungary's foreign policy, for example, were anarchists such as Rudolf Grossman (Laurence 1989). In more industrial and therefore trade-unionized countries, socialists affiliated to the Second International, formed in 1889, discussed the possibility of holding a general strike against any decision of their state to go to war.

Surprisingly, given political-cultural conditions that could scarcely have differed more from those of 1830s New England, pacifism of a neo-Garrisonian kind appeared in Europe. It was the brainchild of the Russian writer Leo Tolstoy, who had repented of his aristocratic, military, and hedonistic past, and expounded an ascetic, no-force Christian pacifism in books published in the 1880s and 1890s. Because of censorship these works had little impact in his own country; but they caught the imagination of a generation of young idealists around the world (Alston 2014), for which mainstream peace activism was too bland.

The American peace movement also developed a notably patriotic hue during the early years of the twentieth century that served it well until confronted by World War I. It had stagnated during the late nineteenth century, partly because of the legacy of the civil war but also because, in the absence of a foreign threat, peace was an issue of lower political salience than the domestic problems generated by the rapid industrialization of that period. Admittedly, in 1866 the vacancy for a straightforwardly pacifist association created by APS and Garrisonian support for the north was filled by the Universal Peace Union, led by Quaker wool merchant Alfred H. Love, who unlike Garrison and most of his followers had refused not only to serve militarily but also to make a payment in lieu. Yet it never had more than 400 members and, after outspokenly denouncing America's war of 1898 against Spain, became moribund, disappearing altogether after Love's death in 1913. The APS also opposed that war, albeit only "in a quiet way," its nominal pacifism being kept alive by its Quaker secretary from 1892 to 1915, Benjamin H. Trueblood, who personally believed: "No nation would think of attacking us if we had not a single warship, not one coast-defense gun" (Brock 1968a: 884; Brock 1991: 302).

The American peace movement revived in response to the widening of the country's international horizons in consequence of its economic transformation during the three decades following the civil war. Its foreign policy became more assertive; but unlike Germany the United States did not see itself as joining the great-power game of secret diplomacy and imperialism, despite its war with Spain and acquisition of the Philippines as a colony. America's principal overseas interests being trade, investment, and missionary activity, it conceived of its foreign policy in *pacificist* terms; and the organizations that its confident associational culture spawned in order to make sense of its enhanced global role—such as the Cosmopolitan Clubs formed by university students—viewed themselves as peace associations. (In the Cold War the equivalent explanatory function would be fulfilled by self-consciously "realist" academic departments of International Relations.) The country's federal Constitution, policed in the conservative interest by its authoritative Supreme Court, predisposed Republicans as well as Democrats to promote the United States as an example of successful inter-state cooperation. In one historian's words: "Most of the spokesmen for the pre-war peace movement were almost ecstatic over American political institutions and proposed them unreservedly for models abroad" (Marchand 1972: xiii). *Pacificism* of this kind was thus fully compatible with American patriotism. And the weakness of socialism and the moderation of mainstream trade unionism in the United States meant that unpatriotic *pacificism* was much weaker than in continental Europe.

In particular, America's influential legal profession was responsive not only to the idea of international arbitration but more especially to the claim that a world court would be a practicable mechanism for resolving inter-state disputes. Unlike in France, it was widely assumed that the decisions of such a court would not require enforcement other than by moral pressure, which was reassuring to Americans still fearful of military entanglement in the power politics of the old world. Not only lawyers but industrialists and businessmen believed that their particular expertise would enable the peace cause to prevail globally. In 1910–11 the steel magnate Andrew Carnegie and the publisher Edwin Ginn both endowed foundations that soon had the peace associations of the world queuing up for subsidies. In particular, money from the Carnegie Endowment for International Peace

FIGURE 6.3: Andrew Carnegie (1835–1919) at Carnegie Hall in 1907. Credit: Ullstein Bild Dtl./Getty Images.

enabled the APS to reclaim its position as leader of the movement in the United States, but only at the cost of its own subordination to its paymaster.

Britain's peace movement was during this period the least patriotic in Cooper's sense and the most independent-minded, though it surrendered its world-leadership role and the LPS lost much of its vigor during the quarter of a century preceding World War I.

After 1867, peace sentiment had partially revived in Britain, as reaction belatedly set in against the Crimean adventure. Yet from this point the LPS's two-tier structure, previously an advantage, became a handicap. While pacifism as well as *pacificism* was gaining ground, it had enabled the LPS to keep control of both wings of the movement. But Christian evangelicalism was now falling behind secular liberalism as the driving force behind peace activism. In consequence, pacifism stagnated: in particular, as Quakers prospered and became acculturated in the second half of the nineteenth century, and as the militia duties which had once prompted them to take a pacifist stand became a dead letter, an increasing number started to regard their peace testimony as formalistic rather than requiring them intellectually to justify a policy of non-resistance. At the same time *pacificism*, in the form of support for arbitration, was rapidly gaining ground, especially after William Gladstone, leader of the new Liberal Party, chose in 1872 to disguise a diplomatic concession to the United States over the *Alabama* case as an arbitral award. After 1876, moreover, Gladstone positioned his party as a liberal-*pacificist* critic of the imperialist defencism of Disraeli's Conservatives. The LPS responded to this upsurge in arbitration-driven *pacificism* by emphasizing that, just it had always admitted *pacificist* members, it had since the 1830s supported arbitration; and to reinforce this point it changed the name of its longstanding periodical, *Herald of Peace*, to *Herald of Peace and International Arbitration*. And, although the society could not renounce its top-tier pacifism without offending key Quaker donors who remained committed absolutists, it was prepared to play it down: for example, in 1879 Henry Richard, though himself an uncompromising pacifist, characterized it as merely the belief of "a small body of persons" which had "never been imported into politics."

However, mindful of the "peace at any price" jibe that defencists had so successfully pioneered during the Crimean War, many *pacificists* now wanted nothing to do with the LPS's top-tier pacifism. They therefore formed non-pacifist associations that, though financially frail in the absence of Quaker money, managed for the first time to establish themselves. The most notable was the International Arbitration and Peace Association, established in 1880 to promote arbitral solutions to the disputes of the day. In 1888 moreover the Workmen's Peace Association, an artisan organization which had been set up in 1870 by the London carpenter Randal Cremer to oppose British entry into the Franco–Prussian War and which had initially taken a pacifist position, relaunched itself on a *pacificist* basis as the International Arbitration League. The LPS's playing-down of its pacifism thus failed to pre-empt the formation of *pacificist* associations. Ironically, it also prevented the society from satisfying the appetite for rigorous absolutism being revealed by the appeal of Tolstoyanism to young idealists. By contrast, the LPS's pacifism, designed both to minimize offense to *pacificists* and to make minimal demands on its adherents, failed to excite. During its second half-century of existence the LPS's two-tier structure thus caused it to fall between two stools, satisfying neither reformists nor absolutists.

In the course of the 1880s, moreover, the LPS not only lost both its dominance of the British peace movement (when the arbitration associations were launched), and its leadership of the international movement (when the Inter-Parliamentary Union, the universal peace congresses, and the International Peace Bureau were created): it also started to lose vitality. In the early years of that decade it had shown the same willingness to suffer adversity as during the Crimean War, most notably in 1882 when for all its recent *pacificist* rhetoric Gladstone's government occupied Egypt, which soon led to its being sucked militarily into the Sudan too. The LPS protested strongly against these acts of aggression, as did Henry Richard in his capacity (since 1868) as a Liberal MP; but this proved to be its final act of political courage. Richard retired from the secretaryship in 1884, becoming honorary secretary: this event, and more definitively his death in 1888, ended the society's confident period; and it even discussed merging with the arbitration associations, which had a financial incentive to agree to this. In the end the LPS soldiered on, appointing Evans Darby as its secretary (1888–1915), under whom its pacifism became increasingly formalistic, being interpreted as requiring no action on its members' part. The society thus not only stayed silent at the outbreak of the Boer War in 1899, claiming that its views were already so well known as not to need restating, but even criticized those condemning the conflict. However, other activists stepped into the breach, despite extreme public hostility toward "pro-Boers." In particular, the maverick journalist W.T. Stead and the Methodist-minister-turned-novelist Silas Hocking launched a Stop-the-War League, an *ad hoc* organization that received support from the arbitration associations.

The Boer War coincided with the first Hague Conference and the launching of Germany's naval challenge, these three events prompting a creative debate in Britain about the causes of international conflict during which the ideological differences between the radical, liberal, and socialist strands of *pacificism*—as expounded respectively by J.A. Hobson, Norman Angell, and Keir Hardie—became better understood. They also stimulated claims from the woman's suffrage movement that their cause would also help that of peace, though feminist *pacificism* was not fully articulated at this time. The established peace associations contributed little to this debate, the vigor of which suggested that, as the peace cause was made more salient by a deteriorating European situation, it had much more underlying support than they had the organizational capacity to mobilize.

1914–20: A MOVEMENT RECONSTRUCTED BY WORLD WAR

After a century of institutionalized activism, the peace movement was almost wholly rebuilt as a result of the 1914–18 war, with British and American associations regaining positions of prominence, particularly through their campaign for a League of Nations. Novel features of this phase were the roles played by neutral countries, women, and the far left. Neutral states could stage international peace meetings and shelter activists who had fled belligerent states. Female activists, being exempt from military service, could campaign against the war without being thought cowardly or weak, and could also fill vacancies in peace associations caused by the conscripting or imprisoning of male activists. The far left, alienated from their country's values and structures, had little to lose politically by opposing the war; but where they managed to harm the war effort it was less by winning intellectual converts to their socialist-*pacificist* critique of international relations than by opportunistically harnessing the material discontents of soldiers and civilians.

The widespread initial belief in every belligerent country that its own cause was defensive meant that most *pacificists*—even the socialist parties of the Second

International—rallied to the flag in 1914. Their problem, if they wished still to be considered part of the peace movement (rather than defectors to defencism) was to show themselves still working to abolish war as well as to achieve victory. Pro-war *pacificists* managed this best in Britain. But the idea of a continuing peace movement would have been hard to sustain during wartime had there not also been some activists who stood out against their national war effort. In this respect too Britain stood out: it had influential radical *pacificists* who maintained a critical detachment from the war without losing touch with the political mainstream in the way the far left did; and it also had a vocal pacifist minority.

The transformation of the British peace movement was rapid and dramatic. The LPS repeated its supine behavior of the Boer War, and by the end of 1914 had been effectively superseded by a No-Conscription Fellowship (NCF) created by socialists who interpreted their creed as forbidding the taking of human life (Kennedy 1981), and by a Fellowship of Reconciliation (FoR) created by spiritually intense Christian pacifists (Wallis 1991; Barrett 2014). When conscription was introduced in 1916, Britain's Liberal-led government made generous legislative provision for conscientious objection that in principle allowed claims from those without religious beliefs and (after brief uncertainty) offered exemption even from civilian service. Assessing conscience was inevitably problematical; and in practice the tribunals tasked with applying the law often applied civil society's rather less advanced notions of fairness instead. By contrast, the only other conscripting states recognizing conscientious objection (the United States, which followed its Civil War practice, and two British Dominions, Canada and New Zealand) allowed claims only from members of historic peace sects only—an easier criterion to apply—and offered exemption only from combatant service, so that even recognized sectarian objectors faced induction into the army to perform other duties. At least 16,500 Britons, perhaps as many as 20,000, declared themselves objectors.[3] Among the most courageously "absolute" of these were members of a new millennial sect, the International Bible Students Association, known after 1931 as Jehovah's Witnesses (Perkins 2016). But it was the suffering of well-connected absolutists such as Clifford Allen, Fenner Brockway, and Stephen Hobhouse, and the supportive work of the NCF (which had no counterpart in any other country) that did most to raise the profile of pacifism.

On the *pacificist* wing of the British movement, the arbitration associations, which both supported the war, were superseded by new organizations with more up-to-date policies that in due course became highly influential: the Union of Democratic Control (UDC) and the League of Nations Society (LNS).

The UDC was established within ten days of the outbreak of war by radical neutralists who blamed British military intervention on secret diplomats and arms traders and were therefore widely assumed to oppose the war. Formally, however, it claimed merely to be working to ensure that the eventual peace settlement, whenever it came, respected democratic wishes and in particular avoided annexations and indemnities (Swartz 1971; Harris 1996). In 1917 the UDC's policy was adopted not only by Britain's emerging Labour Party but also by the Petrograd Soviet.

The LNS was formed in May 1915 by liberal-*pacificist* supporters of British intervention who took seriously the aspiration to make it the war to end war, arguing that in future arbitration had to be organized and enforced by an international political organization. Its program had been devised by a group of liberal intellectuals chaired by Britain's former ambassador in Washington, Viscount Bryce, which at its chairman's insistence concentrated on producing a moderate League scheme that governments could accept: this practicality is what fundamentally distinguished it from the utopian schemes of French and American legalists. Essentially, Bryce settled for a cooling-off period during which states submitted disputes to a third party: except in cases agreed to be purely legal, states were not required to accept the resulting third-party recommendations, though if they did not respect the cooling-off period they would be subjected to forcible sanctions. The close fit between the Bryce group's proposals of early 1915 and the core of the League of Nations Covenant of 1919 made Britain's LNS, in tandem with its American counterpart, the League to Enforce Peace (LEP), arguably the most influential pressure group in the modern history of international relations (Winkler 1952; Ceadel 2013).

The American peace movement was shocked by the European conflict, and eventually split between those supporting military "preparedness" on the part of the United States and those urging it and other neutral states to offer "mediation." The established associations took the former position, either out of patriotic instinct or—as in the case of the APS, which had initially favored mediation but changed tack in 1915—because of its financial dependence upon the peace foundations, whose trustees feared being thought pacifist. A new organization which was created in New York to promote a non-legalistic internationalism and soon adopted the Bryce group's approach, the LEP, even made clear on its letterhead that it did "not seek to end the present war" (Marchand 1972: 157). American advocates of a world court criticized the LEP; but it was at the latter's first-anniversary meeting in May 1916 that President Wilson, himself no fan of the legalist approach, famously espoused the League idea.

Mediation was preferred by some longstanding activists, such as Louis P. Lochner, a former Cosmopolitan Clubs organizer active in Chicago, where in December 1914 he became secretary of an Emergency Peace Federation. It also brought new elements into the peace movement, notably social activists, Protestant ministers, and socialists. Jane Addams, the hugely admired Chicago social worker who at this time was a near-pacifist, helped to create a Woman's Peace Party in January 1915 on the grounds that peace was necessary to achieve female suffrage in the United States as well as that female suffrage would help the peace cause (Marchand 1972: 201–2). Jessie Wallace Hughan, a socialist schoolteacher, formed an Anti-Enlistment League in May 1915, which in due course collected 3,500 pacifist pledges. She also joined the American version of Britain's FoR that was established November 1915; so too did Norman Thomas (a Presbyterian pastor who later led the Socialist Party), A.J. Muste (a Congregationalist minister who later became the country's best-known pacifist and labor activist), and John Nevin Sayre (a theology lecturer and Episcopalian rector), all of whom parted company with their congregations on account of their views on war (Johnpoll 1970; Robinson 1973; Howlett 1990; Bennett 2003). However, not all converts to the cause went as far as pacifism: the socialist leaders of the Anti-Preparedness Committee that was established in New York in December 1915 and re-branded as the American Union against Militarism in April 1916—for example, Crystal Eastman—were *pacificists* (Chatfield 1971: 22–7).

When the United States entered the war in April 1917, virtually all advocates of preparedness supported this decision, including not only the LEP but the APS which thereby finally abandoned its nominal pacifism. Most previous opponents of intervention, such as the founding president of Stanford University, David Starr Jordan, a liberal *pacificist*, now bowed to the inevitable. Intolerance of dissent was far greater than in Britain, as Norman Angell, one of the founders of the UDC who spent half the 1914–18 period in Britain and half in the United States, was alarmed to discover when he was suddenly arrested in New York (Ceadel 2009: 222). In total 64,693 Americans claimed conscientious objection—proportionately more than in Britain because of the profusion of Protestant sects—of whom seven-eighths had their eligibility for non-combatant service accepted by local draft broads. About half were then exempted on medical or other grounds, so that only 20,873 were inducted (as non-combatants) into the army. Of these, such was the pressure placed on them, four-fifths agreed to combatant service, leaving "only 3,989 who refused to accept any kind of military duty" (Peterson and Fite 1957: 126), which is why the number of American conscientious objectors has sometimes been put as low as "4,000" (Chatfield 1992: 45). Pacifists outside historic peace sects were ineligible for any kind of exemption: thus the social worker and civil-liberties campaigner Roger Baldwin, who as a socialist was "opposed" both "to the use of force to accomplish any end, however good" and to "any service whatsoever designed to help prosecute the war," refused his army medical and was sentenced to a year's imprisonment (Cottrell 2000: 86). Such pacifists attracted considerably less public sympathy than their British counterparts, however. Only the far-left fringe of American politics, which came together on May 30, 1917, to create the socialist-*pacificist* People's Council for Democracy and Peace, attempted to campaign against the war. The American peace movement had thus become polarized between embattled, war-opposing socialists, who linked peace to fundamental social and political change of a kind that seemed to be occurring in Russia, and serene, war-supporting liberals, who pointed out how President Wilson's military intervention was dramatically improving the prospects for a League of Nations.

Taking advantage of its country's neutrality, the Dutch Anti-War Council held an international meeting in The Hague on April 7–10, 1915, and created the Central Organization for a Durable Peace, which, like the UDC whose ideas influenced it, looked merely to influence the eventual post-war settlement. It was, however, overshadowed by the International Congress of Women held in the same city three weeks later. This was not the first international women's peace meeting: twenty-eight female socialist *pacificists* had gathered in Berne in neutral Switzerland on March 25, 1915, six months before their male counterparts held their better-known conference in Zimmerwald. But the congress at The Hague drew on the international suffragist network, an assertive minority within which dissented from the war, and attracted 1,136 delegates, with Jane Addams in the chair, though no French or Russian woman came. It was careful to make clear it was not a "peace at any price" demonstration but a call for mediation by neutrals and for a female say in the terms of any settlement. It sent envoys to European leaders, a strategy advocated by Rosika Schwimmer, a multilingual, charismatic, yet contentious Hungarian pacifist who had lectured in the United States and later helped to persuade the industrialist Henry Ford to fund a "peace ship." This last sailed in December 1915 from New Jersey to neutral Scandinavia to promote mediation, a voyage that, however, incurred ridicule from the outset and ended in acrimony (Patterson 2008; Wernitznig 2015). A more enduring legacy of the congress was the creation of national groups, such as Britain's Women's International League: at Zurich in 1919, these came together as the Women's International League for Peace and Freedom, the first major female peace association.

In the belligerent states of continental Europe *pacificists*, other than those on the extreme left, endorsed the national cause; and pacifism was almost non-existent. In France, for example, Émile Arnaud joined up at the age of fifty and won a *Croix de guerre*. However, the word he had coined was becoming identified internationally with a refusal to bear arms, so Theodore Ruyssen of the Association de la paix par le droit started to promote "juripacifisme" instead, so as to emphasize the law-and-order approach long adopted by French peace associations. This approach was by 1918 adapted into support for the Anglo-American idea of a League of Nations, albeit in an over-ambitious French version equipped with its own military forces (Clinton 2011: 141–6). The SFIO also rallied to a political *Union sacrée*, so dissent was mainly confined to anarcho-syndicalists. France produced only a handful who took a pacifist stand. Its most famous literary expression of detachment from the war effort was "Au-dessus de la mêlée" by the novelist Romain Rolland, who sheltered in Switzerland throughout the conflict. But this essay merely criticized the war's propaganda excesses and the view that Germany was solely responsible: Rolland was not to discover nonviolence until the 1920s.

The German Peace Society did its best not to offend its government. Alfred Fried fled to Switzerland at the end of 1914. However, in Munich the outspoken feminist couple Anita Augspurg and Lida Gustava Heymann denounced a "men's war" fought between "men's states," and, slipping through the cracks of Germany's decentralized structure of military rule, attended the women's congress at The Hague, though they were soon banned from public agitation (Evans 1976: 218–22).

In the summer of 1915, moreover, a new organization of liberal intellectuals, the *Bund Neues Vaterland*, began to criticize annexationists, but was suppressed within months (Shand 1975: 96–8). Germany's main dissent came from the far left that emerged within the Social Democrats and eventually split away. The first deputy to break ranks, in December 1914, was Karl Liebknecht, who in February 1915 was drafted into the army, albeit in a works battalion rather than a combatant one, in an attempt to silence him. It was indicative of how legitimate compulsory military service then was in Germany that Liebknecht compliantly served three short tours of military duty, though he sent a defiant

FIGURE 6.4: Karl Liebknecht (1871–1919) addresses a crowd on November 9, 1918. Credit: Photo 12/Getty Images.

message to the Zimmerwald conference in September 1915 urging an "international class war for peace," and was arrested in May 1916 for telling demonstrators in Berlin: "Down with the War! Down with the government!" (Chickering 1998: 156). Food shortages damaged German morale, contributing to the government's eventual acceptance of an armistice, which enabled it to contain the growing threat from the far left.

Russia had virtually no peace activism other than socialist *pacificism*. Like the Trudoviks, the Social Democrats as a whole had in August 1914 abstained in the vote for war credits. The leader of their Bolshevik faction, Lenin, retreated to Switzerland, where he pushed the Zimmerwald movement beyond its original, UDC-influenced policy of demanding a peace without annexations and indemnities toward an insistence on socialist revolution. In Russia the Bolsheviks skillfully exploited the peasantry's social grievances with their slogan "peace, land, and bread," and on seizing power took their country out of the war. Austria-Hungary lost the support of its ethnic minorities, and disintegrated even before the armistice. A paradox of World War I was thus that the states with the weakest peace associations were also the least able to maintain public support for the war effort.

The League of Nations Covenant, which was agreed by the Paris Peace Conference in 1919 and came into effect the following year, imposed the first-ever restriction on a state's sovereign right to go to war. Originally devised and promoted by Anglo-American liberal *pacificists*, as already noted, it constituted the crowning achievement of institutionalized peace activism's first century.

CHAPTER SEVEN

Peace, Security, and Deterrence: "The greatest work of civilization"

The Hague Conferences of 1899, 1907, and 1915

MAARTJE ABBENHUIS

Where the nineteenth century witnessed the rise of organized peace activism in the Anglo-European world, the early twentieth century confirmed a shift to internationalism among these activists. Sandi Cooper defines the turn as one reflecting a change in purpose: where the ambitions of peace organizations shifted from the advance of peace in a broad sense to a pragmatic strategy for improving international relations in a specific sense (1976). By 1900, many peace groups—including the London Peace Society, the American Peace Society, the International Arbitration and Peace Association, and the majority of the organizations associated with the International Peace Bureau—embraced the general principles promoted by so-called "liberal internationalists"[1] who advocated for the advance of international arbitration, the limitation of war through the regulation of international law, and the gradual demilitarization of armed force. Most of these activists promoted the concept of "peace through law," that is, the regulation of international affairs through treaty law and multilateral agreement. Most of them were progressivists convinced that every small step taken in aid of peaceful diplomatic relations and the avoidance of war was a worthwhile and significant one. While radical pacifists existed in all Western societies at the *fin de siècle*, they represented a minority voice, even among peace activists themselves. By 1900, most internationalists did not support the idea that peace had to be achieved at any cost. Rather, they looked for achievement in managing state behavior through rational and realistic steps, keeping the regulation of international law, the limitation of arms, and the creation of international conciliation mechanisms as foremost priorities. For them, peace and security were to be secured through international agreement.

The two Hague peace conferences of 1899 and 1907 offered these internationalists a key focal point for their activism. Like other historians of peace, Cooper argues for the seminal importance of the Hague conferences to expanding the agenda of peace activists and the prominence of peace topics in public affairs (1991b). Historians of internationalism and world governance, including Inis L. Claude (1956), Warren F. Kuehl (1969), Ian Clark (2007), Glenda Sluga (2013), and Mark Mazower (2013), also contend that the Hague conferences mattered in setting the tone of twentieth-century NGO (non-government organization) activism and the concept of internationalism more broadly. International legal historians acknowledge that the Hague conferences brought into existence some of the most significant developments in the growth of a global judicial order (Best 1983, 1991; Rosenne 2001; Hueck 2004). Madeleine Herren-Oesch and Cornelia Knab, furthermore, suggest that the Hague conferences presented break-through moments for thinking internationally (2007).

The Hague conferences marked, as Warren Kuehl argues, both a beginning and an end (1969: 48). They functioned as the hinge linking the nineteenth-century world of localized peace activism to the twentieth-century world of global internationalist activism. Certainly, the Hague conferences birthed key changes in international relations, even if some of them came into the world, as Barbara Tuchman suggests, "by forceps and barely breathing" (1966: 266). As an example: the 1899 conference established the Permanent Court of Arbitration (PCA), offering a conciliation mechanism for all signatory powers. The 1899 Hague Conventions also created a universally applicable code of military conduct, the first of its kind, and confirmed the significance of Geneva law (Wylie 2017). Embedded in the conventions were several declarations and *voeux* ("wishes") that set the tone for international treaty law for decades to come, including the Martens Clause, which still forms the basis of much humanitarian and human rights law today (Cassese 2000; Meron 2000; Schmircks n.d.; Sarkin 2007). The 1899 Hague declarations ensured that arms limitation became a legitimate topic for diplomatic negotiation (Webster 2017; cf. Tate 1942). The declarations banning dum-dum bullets, the lobbing of gas canisters, and aerial bombardment also had a long-lasting effect on the expectation that military restraint should be a feature of "civilized" warfare (Dorsey 2017). The subsequent 1907 Hague Conference delineated the law of neutrality, confirming that states could declare their non-belligerency when others went to war and protecting their sovereignty and economic rights when that happened (Abbenhuis 2013, 2014). The 1907 Hague Conventions also regulated maritime warfare, aiming to overcome centuries of contested practice and conflicting customary rights (Abbenhuis 2013, 2014).

It is a rather easy argument to make that the Hague conferences mattered. They offer a convincing (if somewhat simplistic) "point of origin" story for all manner of twentieth- and twenty-first-century developments in international affairs (cf. Lesaffer 2013). But presenting The Hague as an origins argument alone undercuts the internationalist agency that abounded in the Western world before 1899. It also wrongly implies that there were few restraints placed on the conduct of war before 1899 and suggests that The Hague's primary relevance relates to its longer-term legacies.[2] Most historians tend to argue that the age of internationalism, the judicial ordering of the world, the limitation of armaments, and the regulation of warfare, human rights, and humanitarianism did not make tangible progress until after World War I. They suggest that the twentieth century was the "age of internationalism" (as opposed to the nineteenth-century "age of nationalism") and posit that this internationalist age began in 1918, not 1899 (cf. Sluga 2013).

Such arguments have obvious merit. The Hague mattered to a whole range of twentieth-century shifts in international politics, including to the rise of the League of Nations and the United Nations, the concept of collective security, and the establishment of the Permanent Court of International Justice in 1919 (later the International Court of Justice). However, the Hague conferences also mattered to contemporaries. The conferences held in The Hague in 1899 and 1907 and the cultural productions that evolved around them had a significant bearing on contemporary international affairs. They helped to shape perceptions of the rights and wrongs of state behavior, the waging of war, and the principles

FIGURE 7.1: Peace Conference at The Hague, 1899. Credit: Library of Congress/Getty Images.

that underwrote the concept of "civilization" in international relations more broadly. The Hague mattered to people from the moment the Russian Tsar Nicholas II recommended the idea of a disarmament conference in August 1898. The relevance of the conferences should not be presented as an origins story alone.

This chapter argues that the two Hague conferences of 1899 and 1907, and the 1915 Hague conference that was never held, spoke to a globalized public audience fearful of war and hopeful for change in international affairs. It argues that peace was a powerful contemporary idea represented in the world's newspaper media.[3] It connects this peace reporting to the activism of key internationalists, including by organizations like the Inter-Parliamentary Union (IPU), the Institute of International Law (Institut de droit international), and the International Council of Women (ICW). Above all, the chapter argues that The Hague mattered to contemporary assessments of war, peace, and international affairs. In so doing, it builds on Glenda Sluga's contention that the early twentieth century witnessed a global internationalist turn and "cultivated an international sociability and a specifically internationally minded public opinion" (2013: 16, 19, 21; cf. Cooper 1976: 249). It thereby disputes the historiography that suggests that the subject of peace was of little concern to Anglo-Europeans before 1914 (cf. Winter 2006). According to Roger Chickering, for example, peace advocacy was an irrelevant idea in Wilhelmine Germany: it failed to permeate the mainstream press, and the German peace movement only registered 10,000 members out of a population of nearly 70 million in 1914 (Chickering 1988; cf. Riesenberger 1999). Sandi Cooper admits that while peace "pricked at the public conscience" of Europeans, nationalism overwhelmed pacifist sentiment in that same period (1976: 11). Martin Ceadel, meanwhile, makes a persuasive case for the ideal of peace making slow progress across the "long" nineteenth century that stretched from 1815 to 1914 (2000; cf. Clark 2007: 64). In the United States, furthermore, Progressive Era Americans may have happily embraced internationalism as an all-American notion but, as Patterson suggests, the American organized peace movement nevertheless remained largely ineffective before the outbreak of global war in 1914 (1976: vii–viii: cf. Kuehl 1969: 75–6; cf. Marchan 1972: 5, 10, 23).

Such arguments are further supported by the work of international historians, who present the two Hague conferences as distractions from the "real business" of great power politics. The origins of World War I were the product of ethnic nationalism, heightened militarism, and aggressive imperialism after all. As a result, many historians—Richard Langhorne (1981: 65), Margaret MacMillan (2013: 284), Sondra Herman (1969: 18), Calvin DeArmond Davis (1962: cf. 1975), N.J. Brailey (2002), and Daniel Hucker (2015: 406) among them—consider the conferences largely as failures. Historians of the early twentieth century's arms race, furthermore, tend to dismiss the attempts made in 1899 and 1907 to limit arms and weapons development as meager at best (Keefer 2006). Historians of humanitarianism attach some contemporary relevance to the Hague events, but it is only recently that Neville Wylie suggested that the 1899 Hague conference was essential to the development of Geneva law (2017). Even historians of international law in the early twentieth century tend to prefer the argument that the Hague conventions enabled state violence, be it genocide, warfare, or imperialism (Bourke 2015; Hull 2003, 2008; cf. Best 1983: 177).

Relegating The Hague to the margins of the history of international relations and peace activism to the margins of social history in the pre-1914 era robs the Hague conferences of much of their contemporary color and relevance. In contrast, this chapter argues that the history of The Hague is more than an origins story. It suggests that The Hague permeated global media representations of war and international crisis from 1899 on and that, by 1914, the term "The Hague" signified what was considered as "civilized" behavior by states. An analysis of the public meanings attached to the term "The Hague" after 1899 illustrates that this age of rising nationalism and excessive militarism was also characterized by a media critique of those same developments. Military power had many detractors before 1914 and peace mattered to many people, who feared the prospect of industrial warfare. Furthermore, organized peace activism after 1899 was defined by attempts to advance and promote the Hague conventions and the Hague conferences as forums for advancing international diplomacy. If the *fin de siècle* confirmed the turn from peace activism to internationalism, as Cooper rightly contends, then it was The Hague which defined the terms of that internationalist agency.

The first Hague conference was called at the insistence of Russia's emperor, Nicholas II, whose rescript released in August 1898 called for an international conference to "put an end to . . . incessant armaments" and "seek the means of warding off the calamities which are threatening the whole world."[4] The rescript astounded the diplomats who received it at the Romanov court in St. Petersburg as much as it dismayed their home governments. None of the great powers had any desire to discuss, let alone commit to, the limitation of their armies and armaments. Military leaders and most diplomats were scathing of the Tsar's suggestion even if they lauded it in their official responses.[5]

The world's newspaper reading publics, who encountered the rescript in their local dailies, were equally astonished. As the clergyman, J. Guinness Rogers, noted in a

FIGURE 7.2: This contemporary cartoon entitled "The peace oracle" presented the first Hague peace conference of 1899 as a ruse: more a conference of war and militarists than an event aimed at promoting global peace. Credit: *De vredes-conferentie. Prentenboek voor oud en jong.* Amsterdam, H. Gerlings, 1899, p. 29.

remarkably insightful editorial: "It came upon the world as a surprise—it would not be too much to describe it as a sensation" (1898: 707). Across the world, editorials reflected on the rescript and commented on its relevance. This commentary presented an array of opinions, some of which were cynical, others approving and hopeful. For example, the editor of the *Friend of India & Statesman*, India's oldest liberal newspaper, proclaimed that the most "striking feature of this remarkable document" was "the fact that the head of the greatest army in the world has invited all the nations to lay down their arms" (September

29, 1898: 4). It beggared belief, so the editorial continued, that any power would take the initiative seriously. Yet numerous other newspaper editors in Africa, Asia, the Americas, and Europe praised the Tsar's initiative. The *Australasian*, a Melbourne newspaper, enthused in March 1899 that, thanks to the Tsar, statesmen everywhere "had grown eloquent on the advantages of peace" (March 11, 1899: 537). The *Gazette Algerienne* feared that if the Tsar's conference failed then the earth would be struck by a "*formidable tremblement*" (formidable trembling) when the industrial powers launched their monstrous military arsenals at each other (April 12, 1899: 1). Several Austro-Hungarian newspapers considered the rescript as the Tsar's olive branch to stabilize international affairs, while the pacifist-inspired *Indépendence Belge* hailed the announcement as the "first step to a peace union between all the peoples of earth" (*Surinamer*, September 22, 1898: n.p.). Across the Atlantic Ocean, the *New York Times* went so far as to claim that the Tsar's conference might spell "the beginning of the most momentous and beneficent movement in modern history, indeed, of all history" (*Chicago Daily Tribune* August 31, 1898: 6). In general, and regardless of their national or imperial affiliations, militarists and conservatives everywhere tended to dismiss the Tsar's conference as a farcical development, not worthy of serious deliberation (Chomé 1899; Low 1899: 689; Stengel 1899). Liberals, for their part, hedged their bets, hopeful for the promise of the regulation of the international law of war and the potential to advance arbitration at the conference. Most socialists and anarchists, however, were cynical and dismissed the idea as quickly and easily as their conservative counterparts (Gustavo 1899: 2). Yet numerous trade union groups nevertheless proclaimed their favor for the Tsar's proposals (*Australasian* September 3, 1898: 542; Stengel 1899: 29; Suttner 1910, vol. 2: 198; Newton 1985: 64; Dülffer 1988: 28; Hamann 1996: 142).

Most importantly, the rescript inspired a wide-ranging and globalized public movement in its support. In Britain, hundreds of public meetings, some of which were organized by W.T. Stead's International Peace Crusade, were held from September 1898 on in church halls, trade union quarters, the meeting rooms of the Society of Friends, town squares, and the parlors of women's organizations. More than 1400 petitions landed on Lord Salisbury's desk in the Foreign Office urging the British government to do all it could to support the Tsar's peace cause (Higgins 2016, 2017; PRO).[6] In Germany, Margarethe Lenore Selenka mobilized the International Council of Women to organize celebrations around the world on May 15, 1899 to acclaim the conference and to send resolutions to The Hague promoting the principles of peace, arbitration, and disarmament. More than 585 meetings across 18 countries were held that day throughout the Americas, Europe, Japan, Russia, and the British Empire. These meetings, representing as many as three million women in total, celebrated the message of peace and applauded The Hague's conference (International Council of Women 1899: 232; Selenka 1900: VII). But these women were not alone. Across Europe, petitions signed by hundreds of thousands of individuals were collected urging their governments to make history at The Hague.[7] A "monster petition" representing the opinions of eight million Christians from 145 American churches was handed to President McKinnon late in December 1898 (*Evening Post* 57 (1) January 3, 1899: 5). According to Rybachenok, thousands of letters, resolutions, and proposals were also sent to St. Petersburg from around the world (2005: 135). Even though most of the diplomats who went to The Hague were pessimistic about the event and believed little would be achieved there, the "will of the people" as expressed by this global activism as well as by an extensive media coverage ensured that the Tsar's conference had to succeed, even if only as a public relations stunt (cf. Cooper 1972: 13). As the French Foreign Minister,

FIGURE 7.3: Peace envoys at The Hague, 1899. Credit: Hulton Archive/Getty Images.

Théophile Delcassé, exasperatedly exclaimed at the time: the conference must bear fruit if Europe's governments were to "spare the public opinion of Europe, since this has been aroused by the senseless step of the Russians" (in Porter 1936: 210).

In the end, the Hague conference opened on May 18, 1899 amid widespread public aplomb. Twenty-six governments sent representatives to discuss disarmament, arbitration, and the regulation of the laws of war on land. At least thirty-seven newspapers sent special correspondents (Eyffinger 1999: 346; Gestrich 2001: 233). No newspaper left the conference off their publication agenda, however. Their readers were attentive to the event and to its results. The world's leading peace activists were also in The Hague during the conference, including Baroness Bertha von Suttner, W.T. Stead, Ivan Bloch, Felix Moscheles, Charles Richet, Jacques Novicov, Alfred Fried, William Evans Darby, Benjamin Trueblood, and Lady Ishbel Aberdeen. They came, as Darby noted, to influence the negotiators, to keep the press focused on the issues that mattered and to witness history being made (in *Herald of Peace* 599, July 1, 1899: 245; Hamann 1996: 148).

The extraordinary achievements of the conference—including the establishment of the PCA, the extension of Geneva law to warfare at sea, the invention of the Martens Clause and the creation of a military code of conduct—heartened most internationalist activists. These achievements came in part due to the willingness of key delegates and their governments to support these developments (Lammasch 1922: 14–15). Despite their pessimism about the likelihood of any success, they took the process and the negotiations seriously (Scott 1909, vol. 1; Davis 1962; Dülffer 1980; Eyffinger 1999). To that end, it mattered that several prominent delegates were members of the internationalist Inter-Parliamentary Union and

FIGURE 7.4: This cartoon, originally printed in the German magazine *Ulk* in 1899, with the title "A new tenor in the European concert", depicted Tsar Nicholas II singing from a new song sheet, namely that of Baroness Bertha von Suttner's famous pacifist novel *Die Waffen Nieder* (Lay Down Your Arms). In the cartoon the Tsar's voice is drowned out by the loud militarist music made by the European powers playing instruments around him. The original caption of the cartoon read: "The voice may be sympathetic but it is a little weak for the orchestra". Credit: *De vredes-conferentie. Prentenboek voor oud en jong*. Amsterdam, H. Gerlings, 1899, p. 13.

others of the Institut de droit international (Lammasch 1922: 13; Quidde 1939; Wehberg 1939). Both organizations dedicated their advocacy to advancing international arbitration and the regulation of international law. But it also mattered that the conference made headline news. As Tuchman suggests, the "delegates were uncomfortably aware of the conscience of the world over their shoulder" (1962: 257).[8] There is ample evidence in the official transcript of the conference to recognize that many delegates (and thus their governments) took President Baron de Staal's reminder—that their "deliberations must lead to a tangible result which the whole human race confidently expects"—to heart (in Scott 1909, vol. 1: 17).

Despite claims that not much attention was given to the Hague conference in the media, a study of contemporary newspaper reports suggests otherwise (Suttner 1901: 88–9; Perris 1911: 29; Eyffinger 1999: 347). Between May 18 and July 29, 1899, The Hague featured prominently in the world's news. As the *Friend of India* suggested: "nothing strikes the newspaper reader more at the present moment than the progress of measures taken to promote international peace" (July 6, 1899: 6). The editor of the *Los Angeles Times* agreed and noted that The Hague presented a "prolific theme for the paragraphers and editorial writers of the world" (June 23, 1899: 8). As an example, the *Los Angeles Times* referred to the event 118 times between May 18 and August 1, 1898, including in several pointed editorials. The Parisian daily *Le Matin* made 201 references to "La Haye" in that same period, while sixty-four out of a total of seventy-four issues of the *Wiener Zeitung* in Vienna discussed the conference, often at great length.[9] Even in Australia, Sydney's *Children's Newspaper* reported on The Hague's events on at least three occasions in 1899 (April 28, 1899: 6; May 30, 1899: 4; June 27, 1899: 6). Many newspaper editors also voiced their fury when the conference secretariat declared that the conference negotiations would happen behind closed doors (*Los Angeles Times* May 21, 1899: A4; NA 2.21.018: 314; *Algemeen Handelsblad* May 28, 1899: n.p.; *Children's Newspaper* June 27, 1899: 6; Rybachenok 2005: 133–4, 251). Only after noting the high level of public backlash to the announcement did the secretariat establish a press office—the first of its kind—which relayed a daily account of agenda items and decisions made. But the compromise was unsatisfactory: the briefings were short and lent no color or depth to what occurred (Scott 1909, vol. 1: 54; 1920, vol. 1: 20; R.P. Maxwell to British Foreign Office May 30, 1899: PROFO83/1700). As a result, journalists had to find their own conference "news" by courting and interviewing official delegates and peace activists alike, hoping for leaks. Bertha von Suttner, for example, was considered the most interviewed person in The Hague (Hamann 1996: 150). Between May and July 1899, peace topics infused the press.

Thus, it is particularly significant that when the German delegation purposely stalled the negotiations regarding the establishment of the Permanent Court of Arbitration, newspapers around the world reported that two envoys from The Hague traveled to Berlin to negotiate directly with Kaiser Wilhelm II on the matter (*Neue Hamburger Zeitung* June 19, 1899: 1; White 1912: 61–77). Many of the English-language newspapers condemned the German emperor for his hardline position on international arbitration (e.g., *Los Angeles Times* June 13, 1899: 8). In turn, the German government quickly realized that if the negotiations stalled, Germany would be held to account. Altogether, it was a public relations disaster that the Kaiser and his government could ill afford (Campbell 1957: 158; Dülffer 1980: 131–7). In the end, the Germans accepted the establishment of the PCA, albeit on a voluntary basis. Wilhelm II also undertook damage control by speaking directly on the subject at a Wiesbaden dinner, proclaiming his favor for The Hague (in private he despised the conference for undermining Germany's sovereign authority: Dülffer 1988: 23). The *Berlin Post* judiciously reported the Kaiser's speech, ensuring its circulation around the world's major newspapers (*Friend of India & Statesman* June 22, 1899: 20–1). But the damage was done. If any state came out looking bad at The Hague in 1899, it was Germany (Basily 1973: 12; Hamilton 2008: 19).

For most delegates, the 1899 Hague conference was a success: they made tangible progress on a range of incredibly complex and difficult concepts. For most internationalists, The Hague's achievements were also welcome developments that made possible a future where warfare would be a state's last act, not its first, as Ludwig Quidde explained (D'Estournelles 1899: 127). The world's media was altogether less complimentary. Across the globe, editorials assessed the conference's achievements as bleak, "woe-begone," and failed (*Los Angeles Times* June 29, 1899: 8; *Blackwood's Edinburgh Magazine* July 1899: 139–42; *Wahre Jacob* 338, July 4, 1899: 3019; *Friend of India & Statesman* August 3, 1899: 1; *Anglo-Saxon Review* September 1899: 260; *Japan Times* September 9, 1899: 2). It certainly did not help that Britain engaged in a war in South Africa within weeks of the closing of the conference and refused to send the Boers' claims to the PCA for arbitration. The outbreak and repression of the Boxer rebellion in China soon after did little to help alleviate these doleful perspectives. The world's peace seemed as far off as ever. If the

Tsar's rescript had spoken of the potential of a new world order then these crises reinforced the general understanding that military power still ruled supreme.

Yet it would be a mistake to suggest that contemporaries considered the first Hague peace conference only in negative terms. Many newspapers published thoughtful editorials reflecting on the significance of The Hague's achievements and on the conference's importance as a turning point in international affairs. The *Japan Times*, for example, described the event both as a failure and a new beginning (August 31, 1899: 4). The *Cologne Gazette* in Germany talked of the conference acting as an effective "barrier" to the outbreak of war, while the *Berlin Tageblatt* considered the establishment of the PCA as "an important step to securing the peace of the world" (both in *Los Angeles Times* 16, July 1899: A2; July 30, 1899: 2). In an incisive editorial in that same paper, Arthur Levysohn exclaimed that the conference had ensured a more "peaceful attitude" (*friedfertige Haltung*) among Germans (*Berliner Tageblatt* July 23: 1). In Britain, the *Economist*'s editors wrote "in no mood of cynicism": "we do not doubt that the conference will have useful results, and that everyone will discover that is so" (July 15, 1899: 1007). The Anglican *Church Times* echoed a similar sentiment, suggesting that "the establishment of a permanent Court of Arbitration is an admission by the civilised world that reason and justice ought to prevail" (August 8, 1899: 129). In the Netherlands, the *Leeuwarder Courant* intimated that arbitration was the most important legacy of the conference and that the "softening of war" was a "priceless legacy" given by "this century to the next" (August 8, 1899: n.p.). In Russia, the *Peterburgskija Vledeomosti* also editorialized that the "meeting at The Hague will exercise an important and beneficent [*sic*] effect. . . . Every new idea requires time to mature" (in *Herald of Peace* August 1, 1899: 258).

These same newspapers also embraced The Hague as a lens through which to gauge the conduct of the Anglo–Boer War, the Boxer crisis, and the Russo–Japanese War. Whether the belligerents breached the Hague conventions was a topic of discussion in many newspapers, as was the understanding that armed forces should behave in prescribed ways. Assessments of the rights and wrongs of these wars were filtered through the terms of the Hague rules and the expectation that warfare should only occur if the avenue of mediation or arbitration was exhausted. Such conceptualizations of the legitimate limits of "civilized" warfare continued well into World War I and were conducted by the neutral and belligerent press, with obvious exceptions (Munro 2017). After 1899, in fact, The Hague underpinned the moral framing of conflict in the media across the globe. With The Hague also came expectations that the peace and security of the world depended on successful international agreements.

The first Hague conference was extraordinarily inspirational. After 1899, internationalists everywhere embraced the success of the conference's messages and mobilized behind them, as did a number of the official delegates. They aimed at promoting understanding of The Hague's achievements and advocated for future Hague conferences and the gradual advance of international law as a way of improving international relations more generally. The Inter-Parliamentary Union, for example, announced its intentions of perfecting the Hague conventions, especially those relating to international arbitration, at its annual conference in August 1899 (*Advocate of Peace* 61 (9) October 1899: 220). From this point on, it used The Hague as a platform for much of its internationalist advocacy and set up several committees to advance key internationalist ideas associated with the Hague conventions (Inter-Parliamentary Union 1902). In turn, the International Council of Women not only reiterated its commitment to arbitration at its 1899 quinquennial meeting, it also set up committees to promote the work of the Hague conference more

FIGURE 7.5: This cartoon from the Dutch newspaper *De Amsterdammer* comments on the first Hague peace conference by suggesting that it would leave Death with nothing to do. Entitled, "War against War", the caption had Death lamenting: "Must I lose my best harvest?" Credit: "Kruistocht tegen den Oorlog", cartoonist unknown, *De Amsterdammer* 8 April 1899, np.

generally (International Council for Women 1899: 48). By 1914, the ICW's Peace and Arbitration Committee promoted peace-friendly school curricula, held an annual celebration of the Hague peace conferences on May 18 "Peace Day," distributed peace and arbitration literature around the world and promoted key changes to the Hague conventions for governments to consider at the forthcoming third Hague conference (International Council for Women 1914). The members of the Institut de droit international, for their part, made careful study of the conventions and initiated research projects around their extension and improvement, which they published and circulated among the world's governments (Scott 1916). Alfred Fried, the Austrian peace activist and editor of the German-language *Friedens-Warte* journal, presented all these internationalists' actions as holy writ, as the "*grössten Kulturwerke aller Zeiten*" ("the greatest work of civilization of all time": in *Die Friedens-Warte* September 1899: 75).

That a second Hague peace conference was held was almost entirely the outcome of public diplomacy. In 1904, the Inter-Parliamentary Union met for the first time on American soil in the city of St. Louis. The conference sent a resolution to President Roosevelt urging him to call the world back to The Hague to improve the PCA, to advance the disarmament agenda and to rework the laws of war and neutrality. Roosevelt saw the potential public appeal of the move and sent out a missive to the world's governments. This act helped to solidify his nomination for the Nobel Peace Prize, which he won later that year, the first world leader to do so. Roosevelt's Hague initiative, however, fizzled when the diplomacy of hosting a conference proved too complicated for the United States State Department and his own resolve slackened (Tuchman 1962: 275). At any rate, Russia and Japan were not about to attend to a peace conference while they were at war.

At the conclusion of the conflict, however, Nicholas II took up the initiative, in part to regain public favor after Russia's devastating military demise and to offset public resentment at the revolutionary developments in his empire's heartland.

The second Hague peace conference, held between June 15 and October 18, 1907, was as publicly appealing as its predecessor. Peace petitions, manifestos, resolutions, letters, and grand schemes for the betterment of the world were forwarded to St. Petersburg, The Hague, and home governments everywhere.[10] The Hague's conference secretariat included twenty-six secretaries who worked at collating and responding to the material received (Beresteyn 1907: 1). The global press was equally attentive, again reflecting a wide array of opinions about the likely success of the event. Whereas cynicism abounded in some publications, others were hopeful of the potential of advancing the regulation of international affairs (Choate 1913: 55–6). They recognized that this second Hague conference built on the work of the first and, much like many liberal internationalists, saw potential in progressing the laws of war and neutrality, the PCA, and international arbitration more generally.

Unlike the 1899 conference, however, the governments that met in The Hague in 1907 were better prepared. Not only were there more of them: forty-four delegations participated, globalizing the reach of the negotiations substantially. These governments were also more aware of the need to manage the public relations of the event. The conference secretariat carefully prepared for the media attention, issuing passes and credentials to key correspondents for plenary sessions, writing press releases, and fielding enquiries (Beresteyn 1907). Delegations had clearer strategies for courting the press, too. The Germans were particularly judicious to the press attention, advancing a public image of conciliation and support for positive change to maritime and neutrality law. At any rate, the German government had prepared their public relations field well in advance (Obkircher 1939: 80–1). Disarmament had been purposely kept off the agenda, at Germany's insistence, in order to avoid the negative ramifications of that particular political hot potato.

Altogether the second Hague conference was more global, more contested and lasted longer than its predecessor. After four months of deliberations, the 1907 Hague Conventions made substantial improvements to the PCA, established a comprehensive law of neutrality, recommended the creation of an International Prize Court (IPC), and made substantial improvements to the maritime law of war (Scott 1909, vol. 2; Davis 1975; Dülffer 1980; Eyffinger 2007). At the insistence of Great Britain, a follow-up conference involving the world's maritime powers was held in London in 1909, which made extraordinary advances to the laws governing warfare at sea. In the end, it was Britain's inability to ratify the Declaration of London that prevented the establishment of the IPC. Though internationalists and peace activists were disappointed, they were not despondent. As the prominent international lawyer T.J. Lawrence declared in 1912, the rejection by the House of Lords of the Declaration of London and with it the establishment of the IPC was not reflective of "the opinion of the people." All that was needed was "a serious effort" by the public to promote the IPC at the next Hague conference, which "would generate the force required, and make it clear that the British public will tolerate no further failure" (1912: 7).

As with the 1899 event, the second Hague peace conference received concerted and global attention in the press. The new states in attendance not only signed up to the 1899 Conventions, thereby expanding their global reach, but also made much of their involvement in the 1907 conference. The Latin American delegates were particularly attentive to their public profile, holding protracted speeches during the deliberations, which they hoped would be widely reported, thereby promoting the importance of their country's voice on this global diplomatic stage. The world's internationalists and peace activists also came to The Hague in 1907 to promote their causes, in greater numbers and with more impressive agendas than they had in 1899. The Koreans, who did not have an official delegation at the conference, nevertheless sent a secret mission to The Hague to protest against Japan's occupation of their country. They attained widespread media attention, even if most governments would not receive them (Ceuster 2008; Moon 2013).

Perhaps the most significant achievement of the second Hague conference was the decision to regularize the event. Delegates agreed that a third Hague conference should be held in 1913 or 1914 (in the end, it was postponed until 1915). The Dutch government was appointed to take care of the administrative process in consultation with a committee of key states (NA 2.05.03: 560). Their ambition was to establish an ongoing working agenda focused on key international laws and international developments. For internationalists, the declaration to regularize the Hague conferences confirmed their faith in the progressive promise of international law. It also inspired them to professionalize their Hague advocacy even further. There was real reason to do so, as The Hague was now a permanent feature of the international environment. As the American peace journal *Arbitrator* exclaimed in 1908: "The Palace of Peace which Mr Carnegie is building is not likely to want tenants" for the "representatives of the nations . . . do not consider their work completed" (April: 139).

By this stage, the city of The Hague had also become a key site for ongoing internationalist activism. Enterprising individuals sought to physically rebuild The Hague as the center of the world. For example, Peter Horrix and P.H. Eijkman's Fondation international aimed at turning the city into a "world capital," replete with a world library, world university, world newspaper, and office space for all the world's international organizations (Somsen 2012: 45–64; 2013: 201–20). All these developments received widespread media attention. It was the building of a Peace Palace funded by a generous grant from the American philanthropist Andrew Carnegie, however, that solidified The Hague's internationalist status (Eyffinger 1988; Leeuwin 2000; Joor 2013). The palace, which housed the PCA, a law academy, and a library, took years to appear. Its design was commissioned by international competition, won (rather controversially) by the French architect Louis Cordonnier. The first stone was laid down in an elaborate ceremony held during the second Hague conference. The finished building was officially opened in 1913 amid much pomp and circumstance. The ostentatious building was lauded and hated in equal part by locals and visitors alike. Yet it also offered a focal point for the idea of The Hague to foment.

The outbreak of World War I disrupted these Hague developments. Most importantly, the third Hague peace conference was never held. The outbreak of war ended the hopes and dreams many internationalists had for The Hague's mechanisms. The outbreak of the war also solidified the opinion that the Hague conferences had failed. Where in 1908 James Brown Scott proudly declared that the second Hague conference was an enormous achievement for international relations (Scott 1908: 12) and Raymond L. Bridgman called the conference "a success so conspicuous its failures combined were merely an insignificant incident" (1908: 29), in 1923 A.W. Ward and G.P. Gooch remarked on the conference's "slender harvest" in their seminal study of British foreign politics (354). Other academic studies in the interwar years also decimated The Hague's reputation (Junk 1928; Langer 1935; Beazly 1936).

But The Hague's legacies nevertheless abounded after 1914. Throughout the war, the media invoked the Hague conventions to assess the morality of the belligerents' war conduct. Internationalists and governments alike also planned for a post-war world order by assessing which of The Hague's developments they would keep and which they wanted to adapt or jettison (Macdonnell 1915: xxiv). In 1915, an international congress of women was held in The Hague amid a wave of controversy. The congress involved women from around the world, who collectively professed the need for the belligerent governments to negotiate an end to the war (Patterson 2008). The congress received concerted attention in the world's media (Munro 2018). If anything, it confirmed that the city of The Hague remained a powerful site of peace activism and judicial development. That legacy continues to this day.

CHAPTER EIGHT

Peace as Integration

Tolstoy on Peace and the End of History

JEFF LOVE

Lev Nikolaevich (Leo) Tolstoy (1828–1910) is widely acclaimed as a giant of world literature, but he also became an ardent activist for peace whose notion of nonviolent resistance played a major role in the decolonization of India and the civil rights movement in the United States led by Martin Luther King, Jr. In Russia itself Tolstoy was both admired and attacked for his increasing pacifism. His major rival—and, for some, cultural antipode, Fyodor Mikhailovich Dostoevsky (1821–81)—complained bitterly about Tolstoy's lack of support for the Russian volunteers who went to aid Serbia in its fight for independence in 1877 and 1888, as evidenced in the final book of *Anna Karenina* (1877).

Tolstoy's pacifism is often associated with the period following his so-called crisis and conversion, which took place after he finished *Anna Karenina*. The notable essays and treatises of this later period, especially his famous work *The Kingdom of God Is Within You* (1894), provide rich evidence of Tolstoy's association of peace with the extinguishment of self-interest, a point reflected expansively in Tolstoy's final major novel, *Resurrection* (1899). While these works are no doubt of considerable importance in and of themselves, I wish to orient this chapter to another work, arguably Tolstoy's most daring, compendious and far-reaching—*War and Peace* (1869), the great novel that continues to be at the center of the Tolstoyan canon. Indeed, one can argue that *War and Peace* contains Tolstoy's most profound meditation on peace, a meditation all the more powerful because of the sharp contrast it draws with war and the impulse to war Tolstoy identifies in the novel with Napoleon. The concept of wise passivity, the questioning of Napoleon's monstrous ambition as pitted against Russian self-abnegation, have become tropes of Russian culture whose influence proceeds and complements the more overt pacifism of Tolstoy's later works, a pacifism that draws on these tropes as it expands them. Nonviolent resistance, the most innovative aspect of Tolstoy's later pacifism, has significant philosophical roots in *War and Peace*.

As a consequence, in the following I present a detailed account of the central attitude to peace expressed in *War and Peace* and suggest that this view played and continues to play an important role in Russian thought.

CALCULUS

For Tolstoy peace demands an end to history. We suffer from history because we suffer from time. If we come to an end of history, we also come to an end of time. Peace is

FIGURE 8.1: Leo Tolstoy (1828–1910). Credit: The Image Bank/Getty Images.

precisely this end of time, and any other notion of peace is illusory. The famous phrase from *The Book of Revelations* Fyodor Dostoevsky so admired, that there will be "time no more," applies with equal, if not more, force to Tolstoy. In his hugely ambitious and, some would say, imbalanced creative work *War and Peace*, Tolstoy addresses the overcoming of history and time extensively by reference to mathematics and, in particular, to one of the culminating inventions of modern mathematics, calculus. The key underlying concept in Tolstoy's treatment of calculus is integration. The aim of integration is to ascertain the totality of patterns constituting history through an art of combination that reveals the laws of human interaction once and for all. Tolstoy's enterprise in *War and Peace* is to write the book that embodies and illustrates these laws, identifying all possibilities of historical action. History becomes thenceforth the unlimited or infinite repetition of a finite series of possibilities. In this sense, history comes to an end—and final peace is achieved—since all historical possibilities have been exhausted. Struggle, the initiation of violence, makes no sense since nothing can be initiated that has not already been done before.

With calculus, Tolstoy seeks to show us that the laws by which we live are binding such that history is nothing more than repetition. Linear, open history is an illusion we retain to justify our sense of independent agency. The reality is, however, quite different. We are

FIGURE 8.2: Tolstoy as an officer of the Imperial Russian Army in Crimea. Credit: Bettmann/Getty Images.

literally pawns of history, and peace can be brought to human affairs the moment we accept that nothing more need be done, that no new step can be taken. If all is cliché, if we are nothing but more or less aware actors in a play we did not and could not write, then our only recourse is to go on without attempting to change history because change can bring only further repetition. If we no longer strive to change history, having learned the futility of doing so, we shall have brought about peace in effect, the final termination of conflict.

The key assumptions here are twofold: that conflict initiates in the desire to change, and that change can be achieved only through conflict. Peace results, then, essentially from the frustration or elimination of change, and nothing eliminates change more forcefully and with greater simplicity than to assert that nothing new can emerge from action, that all that can ensue is the repetition of actions taken in the past. The past is the present and the present is the past—time comes to an end because the difference between divisions of time (into past, present, and future) dissolves into what amounts to a continuous present resulting from a point of view in which all possibilities of human action are already at hand.

Tolstoy articulates this concept of history in different ways in *War and Peace*, though it remains open to debate whether the grand fictional world of the text is an attempt to achieve a complete view of history to rival Hegel's *Phenomenology of the Spirit* in scope and audacity, if not in execution, or whether, as Sir Isaiah Berlin argued, persuasively for many, the fictional text refutes that very possibility, openly undermining any concept of history (Berlin 1978: 48–9). In terms of our investigation, these alternatives amount to an evaluation of the prospects for attaining peace.

Putting this question of prospects aside for the moment, in what follows I want first to provide a more detailed account of Tolstoy's concept of integration as it is set out by the narrator in Book III of *War and Peace* and as it might apply to explain certain aspects of the fictional text. I then want to return to the issue of prospects by considering the now venerable question first raised by Sir Isaiah Berlin as to the relation between theoretical construct and fictional execution in *War and Peace* precisely as offering a commentary on both the desirability and the possibility of attaining peace (Berlin 1978: 24).

INTEGRATION

Nowhere is the essentially egalitarian aspect of *War and Peace* more in evidence than in the discussion of calculus the narrator introduces at the beginning of the Third Part of Book III. The narrator begins this discussion with a problem: "Absolute continuity of motion is not comprehensible to the human mind. Laws of motion of any kind only become comprehensible to man when he examines arbitrarily selected elements of that motion; but at the same time, a large proportion of human error comes from the arbitrary division of continuous motion into discontinuous elements" (Tolstoy 2010: 881). He proceeds then to a solution:

> A modern branch of mathematics, having achieved the art of dealing with the infinitely small, can now yield solutions in other more complex problems of motion, which used to appear insoluble. This modern branch of mathematics, unknown to the ancients, when dealing with problems of motion, admits the conception of the infinitely small, and so conforms to the chief condition of motion (absolute continuity) and thereby corrects the inevitable error which the human mind cannot avoid when dealing with separate elements of motion instead of examining continuous motion. In seeking the laws of historical movement just the same thing happens. The movement of humanity, arising as it does from innumerable arbitrary human wills, is continuous. To understand the laws of this continuous movement is the aim of history. But to arrive at these laws, resulting from the sum of all those human wills, man's mind postulates arbitrary and disconnected units. The first method of history is to take an arbitrarily selected series of continuous events and examine it apart from others, though there is and can be no beginning to any event, for one event always flows uninterruptedly from another. The second method is to consider the actions of some one man—a king or a commander—as equivalent to the sum of many individual wills; whereas the sum of individual wills is never expressed by the activity of a single historic personage. Historical science in its endeavor to draw nearer to truth continually takes smaller and smaller units for examination. But however small the units it takes, we feel that to take any unit disconnected from others, or to assume a beginning of any phenomenon, or to say that the will of many men is expressed by the actions of any one historic personage, is in itself false. It needs no critical exertion to reduce utterly to dust any deductions drawn from history. It is merely necessary to select some larger or smaller unit as the subject of observation—as criticism has every right to do, seeing that whatever unit history

observes must always be arbitrarily selected. Only by taking an infinitesimally small unit for observation (the differential of history, that is, the individual tendencies of men) and attaining to the art of integrating them (that is, finding the sum of these infinitesimals) can we hope to arrive at the laws of history.

—Tolstoy 2010: 881–2

Few have found this solution convincing. Sir Isaiah Berlin simply dismissed Tolstoy's discussion of calculus out of hand as evidence of a thin attempt at holistic theorizing contradicted by the fictional text itself (Berlin 1978: 48). Like the majority of critics of the novel, Berlin interpreted Tolstoy's polemical engagement with historians not as an attempt to develop a new, more holistic, way of narrating history, but as a firm rejection of historical narratives as falsifying the past or, worse, as being essentially incapable of providing an accurate or true account of the past. Berlin considered Tolstoy to be a kind of modern nominalist fundamentally incapable of asserting a stable system of identities; to the contrary, for Berlin Tolstoy saw mainly differences, what distinguished one thing from another (Berlin 1978: 51). Other critics of *War and Peace* make similar claims while emphasizing Tolstoy's skepticism or, in the memorable phrase of Gary Saul Morson, his "epistemic nihilism" (Morson 1987: 109).

Yet, if one takes Tolstoy's calculus argument seriously, quite a different picture of the novel and Tolstoy's thinking emerges. While one cannot deny the polemical aspect of Tolstoy's engagement with what he saw as the norms of historical narrative, it is indeed surprising to what extent the positive counterargument, derived from calculus, has been ignored or neglected. By doing so, the critical reception of Tolstoy's novel has not only put aside his arguments against historical narratives but critics have also missed one of the overriding aspects of Tolstoy's theorizing in *War and Peace*; namely, to investigate whether a final narrative might be possible that would satisfy and end all conflict. For, if nothing else, *War and Peace* is itself an immense narrative of conflicts; aside from the most obvious one at its center, there are numerous subsidiary narratives that reflect what one of the main characters in the novel says after having given an important speech to his brothers in the Masonic Lodge—the endless or infinite variety (*beskonechnoe raznoobrazie*) of points of view (Tolstoy 2010: 466).

The calculus argument aims to reconcile these points of view by showing how each can only be partial and thus limited. Tolstoy aims to develop the largely hidden Newtonian aspect of modern historical writing—he seeks to develop a science of history that might match Newton's science of nature. Tolstoy lays the foundation for this argument by referring to history as a kind of continuum or a continuity of motion. In other words, Tolstoy defines the foundation of history as a continuum of change—the foundation of identity is accordingly never identical with itself or always at variance with itself. If this is so, we may simply assert that history as such can never congeal into an identity or series of identities—the identity of history is not to have an identity. The fault of the ancients is that they were unable to conceive of motion in any other way than to be resistant to our understanding—rest, not motion, is what mattered for the ancients, and they were able to grasp motion only as a series of fixed segments rather like those that Zeno imagines in his attempt to refute the reality of motion (Lee 1936: 52–78). It is no surprise that Tolstoy refers to another of Zeno's arguments, the race of Achilles and the tortoise, in his discussion of calculus because that argument likewise imposes the assumption that motion consists of a series of discrete segments or parts. The paradoxical aspect of this way of thinking is that motion is in itself outside of our capacity to understand—indeed, we can argue that the ancient view seeks to transform motion into static segments in order to grasp what motion itself is, an inherently fraught way of approaching the matter.

The underlying conflict here is of considerable significance. It is the conflict between motion and rest. As one commentator puts it, the conflict between motion and rest may be understood as a conflict between war and peace. For those, like Heraclitus, who claim that "war is the father of all things," motion is primary, and rest is merely a form of motion (Kahn 1981: 67). For those who claim that rest is primary, motion is a problem or can be understood only as a type of rest. There seems to be no way of resolving this conflict—until calculus, until Newton. Although Tolstoy uses language developed by Leibniz to describe those infinitesimally small units of motion,[1] it seems clear that Tolstoy is referring to a Newtonian model of nature as the foundation for his conception of an attitude to history that can transform history from its status as narratives reflecting various points of view, to a radically egalitarian narrative of all, absolutely all, as Tolstoy writes in the Second Part of the Epilogue (Tolstoy 2010: 1278).

I have stressed the egalitarian quality of Tolstoy's approach to history in order to emphasize its most radical underlying aspect—the elimination of narratives directed by particular views that have no ground other than a kind of collective self-interest. Throughout *War and Peace*, and far prior to the explicit discussions of history that begin in Book III of the novel, Tolstoy criticizes points of view that are obviously partial or based in some form of self-interest; indeed, the most obvious and domineering point of view is that of Napoleon himself. For, one might say, Napoleon is the very incarnation of self-interest, of naked self-assertion. While I shall have a good deal to say about this aspect of Napoleon later on, suffice to say for the moment that Tolstoy's advocacy of a Newtonian model of history makes all patterns of movement, regardless of their intent or specific identity, equal by virtue of the fact that they are patterns of motion first and foremost. In other words, the advantage to be gained by applying a Newtonian model of nature to history is that all patterns of motion are made up of equal and infinitesimally small "units" regardless of the identities (otherwise arbitrary in Tolstoy's mind) that we may conventionally apply to them.

To grasp what Tolstoy is after here, I think it is helpful to view the Newtonian model within the greater context of the mathematization of nature that begins with Descartes. By declaring external reality to be *res extensa* capable of being grasped quantitatively, i.e., through mathematics, Descartes creates a mathematical system of equivalences that transforms everything external into a point on a grid. All "natural" objects may be transformed into points on a grid regardless of their "natural" identity, thereby allowing one to place them into an "abstract" mathematical space that allows one to grasp the external world as a system of equivalences governed by consistent mathematical laws, whether they be algebraic or those of calculus. In such a manner, one may transform the understanding of the world from one based on a necessarily partial apprehension of things, or on an apprehension of things that differs in accord with its object, to one that grasps everything based on the reduction of everything to one common measure. To be sure, the diversity of objects as traditionally understood may be impeded or undermined by this holistic conception of the world, but what is lost in particularity is gained in the possibility of promulgating general laws applying to all things in so far as they are mathematized objects.

Hence, Tolstoy, by reducing all historical phenomena to units of motion, seeks to develop the same hegemonic approach to history with the promulgation of laws that are indisputable. In so doing, Tolstoy fundamentally changes history. Gone are the differing

FIGURE 8.3: French Emperor Napoleon (1769–1821) in defeat, March 31, 1814. Credit: Corbis Historical/Getty Images.

accounts of things that make for conflict; rather, the differing accounts emerge as essentially linked, despite their differences, by a common underlying conception of motion and thus of history as well. There are at least two basic ways to view these differing accounts, both eliminated by Tolstoy's calculus proposal. On the one hand, difference appears to describe a variation that hews to an underlying commonality as a condition of difference. According to this well-worn idea of difference, one can recognize difference only where there is an underlying similarity that allows one to declare something different coherently—difference is thus a variation of a deeper commonality. On the other hand, there is a far more radical notion of difference that considers difference to be an almost absolute otherness. Within these terms, the different is perceived as being essentially incomprehensible within the framework that is attempting to understand it: difference becomes a word for a failure of or limit to understanding. The first kind of difference appears as a variation within an already comprehensible framework, whereas the second appears as an "X" that can be grasped only within a given framework as the limit of that network.

This distinction is fundamental. One kind of difference emerges within, the other outside or as the outside of a given framework. To address this distinction within the terms I have been using so far, the first understanding of difference relies on an underlying equivalence, whereas the second asserts the impossibility of such equivalence. Conflict seldom emerges from the first understanding of difference because the framework asserts a procedure of some kind for adjudicating difference based on the framework within which the difference emerges—that is, a difference that is not acceptable is recognized as error. But the second case is far more complicated because the framework itself is not secure, so that a difference cannot be decided within it. The most significant aspect of historical conflict has to derive from the second case where the only effective resolution of a dispute is through conflict or conquest whereby the differing view is simply abolished or assimilated—translated—into the terms of the triumphant view.

Calculus completely undermines the possibility of this latter kind of conflict because calculus creates a system of equivalences that govern every motion, or historical action, no matter what its original identity might be—calculus is universal because it transforms all motion into measurable units the rules governing which are produced from within the system of calculus itself. Calculus is in this sense a self-policing system that applies to every kind of motion. The imposingly egalitarian aspect of calculus resides in this aspect. There are no ducks flying, no men walking, no bullets whizzing through the air. There are simply kinds of motion differentiated quantitatively by speed, distance, and time. All that is is in motion and it is measurable as such—every action can be transformed into the system of equivalences—relations—that is calculus. Leibniz is arguably more blunt than Newton in this respect:

> Mathematics or the art of measuring can elucidate such things very nicely, for everything in nature is, as it were, set out in number, measure and weight or force. If, for example, one sphere meets another sphere in free space and if one knows their sizes and their paths and directions before collision, one can then foretell and calculate how they will rebound and what course they will take after the impact. Such splendid laws also apply, no matter how many spheres are taken or whether objects are taken other than spheres. From this one sees then that everything proceeds mathematically—that is, infallibly—in the whole wide world, so that if someone could have sufficient insight into the inner parts of things, and in addition had remembrance and intelligence enough to consider all the circumstances and to take them into account, he would be a prophet and would see the future in the present as in a mirror.
> —Cassirer 1956: 11–12

As I noted earlier, the mathematical impulse described by Leibniz in this passage aims at transforming all activities into a system in which there is no longer any past, present, or future—all is present in a fully articulated or articulable present. No surprises are possible, no novelty, and thus no conflict either since the future is already latent in the present—it is present—in a completely reliable, or, to use Leibniz's words, "infallible" manner. The complete mathematization of nature eliminates error. If one extends this mathematization of nature to history, as Tolstoy wishes to do, then all error in human activity must also be eliminated; and, if all error is eliminated, there is no further possibility for conflict since the truth is fully and finally present and inevitable.

The only possible deviation would be the voluntary insistence on error. Yet, this sense of volition would have to be deluded as well. For if all human behavior is governed by laws that are equivalent to the laws of nature, no error is possible. To insist on the possibility of error is itself an error or delusion: one imagines that one is free and this imagination can only be delusion. All disagreement becomes delusion—madness.

One consequence of applying this remarkable model of nature to human action is to confirm the implication that history, to the extent it consists of conflict, arises from errors or delusions that our predecessors have been unable to overcome. With the advent of the Newtonian model, conflict or error may finally be shown to be exactly what it is such that those who persist in error clearly have nothing but pure resistance to the truth left to them. They cannot assert their own truth against the mathematical view, they cannot gainsay that view other than by rejecting the truth so as to persist in error, which emerges as *freedom*.

The Newtonian turn in history Tolstoy advocates is not only an attempt to grasp history as such but also to consider all human activity as reflecting the equilibrium of a mathematical or natural system. What is at stake is precisely the interpretation of the human being as an essentially natural being subject to natural laws. The human being who seeks to ignore these natural laws can do so only by affirming a conception of freedom that is both false and incoherent—freedom is incoherence itself. For Tolstoy equilibrium imposes a structure on human beings in their social lives (and is there any other?) that effectively eliminates any freedom. Tolstoy thus exposes the insistence on freedom as the most problematic insistence. The kind of openness identified by the critics of *War and Peace* I have mentioned, those who view the novel as expressing a profound skepticism about history as an accurate record of the past, proves to be fraught with violence since freedom—at least for Tolstoy—arises only when there is no system, no overarching set of laws or rules that govern all things understood primarily as collocations or "products" of action. In the final account, Tolstoy questions the insistence on freedom as itself violent and pernicious.

FIGURE 8.4: *War and Peace* illustration, 1912 edition. Credit: De Agostini Picture Library/Getty Images.

FREEDOM AND SELF-ASSERTION

The equation of error with freedom is not especially novel. Nor is it especially novel to interpret freedom as the source of violence and conflict. By advancing a model of natural law that is total and infallible, Tolstoy expresses in other terms a vision of the world that has a great deal in common with any theological worldview that asserts, as Christianity does, an omniscient and omnipotent God. Tolstoy even goes so far as to suggest that those who have not discovered the natural laws governing all things but who sense that they exist are more astute, that, indeed, the intimation of divinity is closer to the natural order of things than the worst of all errors: the stubborn insistence on human freedom. The insistence on freedom, on the capacity for radical self-assertion, that has to be at the same time an assertion that we are not subject to immutable natural laws, is also by extension a denial of any divinity.

In terms of the novel, what character could be a better representative of this tendency than Napoleon himself, the initiator and "master" of war? As Tolstoy knew well, Napoleon was much more than a remarkably successful general and politician; he was the incarnation of the self-creating human being who by force of will and genius managed to transform the world—a worthy successor to Alexander and Caesar—in a word, a god. Unlike the God representing the world as equilibrium, however, the human god asserts itself by violence and has no possibility of self-assertion other than by violence, by negation of nature as a system that governs all things. To the contrary, the human being declaring freedom must do so by refuting the notion of equilibrium and therewith any system of nature.

War and Peace as a narrative is generated by Napoleonic aggression—the ostensibly free acts of Napoleon or, rather, Napoleon's insistence on his own freedom can lead only to violence—this insistence being, as we have noted, the very root of violence. Hence, as in the Christian tradition, the origin of violence is disobedience, the refusal to accept God's law or, indeed, any law.[2] Naked self-assertion transforms the world into something to be negated to the extent it does not lend itself to human freedom; of course, the ultimate and perhaps most disturbing form of this self-assertion is the ambition to conquer death itself. Arguably the most radical self-assertion is war, the war against death or the nature that insists that we must die.

Freedom, self-assertion, and violence find their counterpart in the novel in what has been called the "wise passivity" of the Russian commanders, above all, that of Kutuzov. Indeed, in the broader allegorical structure of the novel, the bald and ferocious self-assertion of Napoleon is opposed by the humility and self-abnegation of Kutuzov and the Russian commanders, like Prince Bagration, who evince a totally different attitude to war. This contrast emerges initially and most forcefully in an important episode that comes relatively early in the novel—the battle of Schön Grabern—and in which Prince Bagration plays a prominent role (Tolstoy 2010: 193–4). Since this episode brings out an important issue regarding the status of theorizing in the novel as well, I think it is worth pausing for a moment to consider the questions the episode raises in more detail.

The contrast revolves around the differing comportments of Prince Andrei Bolkonsky, one of the novel's central heroes, and Prince Bagration. Prince Andrei is a zealous acolyte of Napoleon and believes ardently in Napoleon's genius as a commander capable of deciding battles in his favor due to his superior knowledge. The battle unfolds as a complete refutation of Prince Andrei's conception of Napoleon with the astonishing figure of Prince Bagration who presides over the battle like a statue, not giving commands but seeming to assent to whatever is taking place. Prince Bagration's unusual reticence to

FIGURE 8.5: Field Marshal Kutuzov (1745–1813). Credit: Print Collector/Getty Images.

take command, his apparent passivity, has led to many conjectures. The most prevalent has been to rely on this episode as evidence of Tolstoy's skepticism or suspicions of historical writing, in particular, in regard to the notion that certain individuals may exert a decisive impact on a battle, on history itself (see McPeak and Orwin 2012: 85–97). But that is not all. One might argue that there is a contradiction latent in the text between the apparently fallacious notion that there can be a science of war—a science of human action—and the Newtonion turn Tolstoy finally advocates in the latter half of the novel culminating in the extended discussion in the Second Part of the Epilogue at the very end of the novel.

This contradiction is only superficial. And the reason is highly significant. There is a basic difference between the military science that so attracts Prince Andrei and the Newtonian turn that ends the novel. The difference is this: military science is predicated upon a notion of agency and, thus, freedom that is wholly inimical to the Newtonian turn Tolstoy later takes—indeed, the notion of freedom that is essential to military science undermines the possibility of any science since science demands complete regularity and repeatability of result (at least for Tolstoy). What appears to be a science is little more than the expression of a fantasy of agency and authority, a point that Tolstoy makes with increasing urgency and parodic delight as the narrative progresses. Tolstoy's depiction of Napoleon as somewhat of a fool has been frequently criticized;[3] yet, from the point of view of the Newtonian turn Napoleon *is* a fool, not to mention a deluded and dangerous dreamer, whose fundamental error is to refuse to recognize his own limitations. As Tolstoy writes at one point, Napoleon, who most thought most free, turns out to have been most necessitated. Of course, the latter part of this statement is exaggerated. In the Newtonian universe Tolstoy imagines, no one can be more (or less) necessitated than anyone else.

FREEDOM AND SELF-PRESERVATION

Freedom is criminal. Napoleon is a criminal. He is punished by the stunning defeat inflicted upon the Grande Armée in Russia. Freedom is criminal precisely because the free actor has to contravene norms in order to prove that she is indeed free. If she simply follows norms, like all others, how can she ever know herself to be free? Freedom requires conflict. This way of thinking about freedom must appear abhorrent at first glance. Freedom cannot be wholly negative, a refusal to obey. To the contrary, freedom must have a positive aspect: in so far as we are free to disobey, we are then free to obey as well. Freedom is not merely self-assertion. Freedom can also show itself in self-abnegation. Some might insist in fact that the freest act is suicide since the actor is free of the underlying and debilitating fear of death that is expressed in the imperative to self-preservation (Kojève 1999: 162). The issue becomes still more complicated since self-assertion, to the extent it is a reflection of the urge to prevail over others, is a characteristic expression of the imperative to self-preservation, radicalized (or purified) to be self-preservation at any cost. In this respect, Tolstoy may have a point when he claims that Napoleon is the most necessitated of all since his illusion of freedom emerges from the necessity of self-preservation (Tolstoy 2010: 650).

What am I getting at here? Let me take an example: How might we reconcile self-preservation with the Newtonian view whereby actions are essentially expressed by laws that bind all human beings? The Newtonian view would seem to ignore the imperative to self-preservation in so far as the laws it imposes have no concern for human self-preservation or liberation from restrictive laws themselves to the extent they restrict self-assertion: the Newtonian laws apply to all beings in motion *as* motion regardless of any other identity or desire or intention. The consequence of the Newtonian approach to the world is that no one thing has a privilege over any other: the law applies equally to all, and those who seek to overturn or contravene the law cannot succeed. To the extent they believe in their capacity to shape the laws, they are profoundly and irremediably *deceived*.

Hence, Napoleon is deceived, and doubly so. On the one hand, he believes in his power to shape events decisively according to his own wishes. Foremost among these must be the wish to overcome death through the immortality to be gained from his glorious military victories. On the other hand, he seems to be utterly unaware of the extent to which his desire to be immortal (or infinitely powerful) arises from the overweening imperative to self-preservation—immortality as a goal makes sense only to those who are driven by the desire to self-preservation without any reservation at all. Though many have criticized Tolstoy for his tendentious portrait of Napoleon, from the premises Tolstoy establishes, such a portrait has to seem virtually inevitable. And it extends to all the many other characters in the novel who show Napoleonic traits, from Prince Andrei to Dolokhov.

Again it is Kutuzov who provides the primary contrast with so-called "wise passivity." If Tolstoy's portrait of Napoleon has been criticized as creating a sort of straw man, so has his portrait of Kutuzov been criticized as overly laudatory, if not downright strange. For Kutuzov appears almost as a "mystic" general who grasps events "intuitively" rather than by careful planning and forethought (Tolstoy 2010: 799):

> Prince Andrei could not have explained how or why it was, but after that interview with Kutuzov he went back to his regiment reassured as to the general course of affairs and as to the man to whom it had been entrusted. The more he realized the absence of all personal motive in that old man—in whom there seemed to remain only the habit of passions, and in place of an intellect (grouping events and drawing conclusions) only the capacity calmly to contemplate the course of events—the more reassured he was that everything would be as it should. "He will not bring in any plan of his own. He will not devise or undertake anything," thought Prince Andrei, "but he will hear everything, remember everything, and put everything in its place. He will not hinder anything useful nor allow anything harmful."

The chief quality evinced by Kutuzov is respect for the complexity of events and the possibilities that emerge in them. Far from attempting to determine events, Kutuzov attempts to work with them, to engage with what is going on around him as dynamically as possible in the realization that he cannot hope to make history *ex nihilo* like a god but to operate in accordance with the event as it is happening. Kutuzov shows contempt for the theoreticians of war precisely because he does not think that one can impose one's will on a battle. Kutuzov seems intuitively convinced of the complexity of events and the limited purview of human freedom, which, for him, seems to be largely restricted to seeing and accepting the laws that impose themselves on us in our active lives.

While Kutuzov certainly does not give expression to his reticent approach to battles this way, his respect for the overwhelming power of events, their capacity to overcome human wishes of any kind, is in accord with the Newtonian view. Kutuzov uses all his experience of war to identify and evaluate the various segments of the battles in which he is involved in order to see them better. Likewise, the characters that resemble Kutuzov in their reticence to seize control of events, from Bagration to Platon Karataev, show both remarkable patience and remarkable attention to the context as they attempt to take advantage of the way an event is turning—like good empirical scientists, they attempt to interpret a new situation by carefully attending to it rather than attempting to force it to fit their preconceptions.

In the end, Kutuzov and his various epigones in the novel are not masters of war or violence. Indeed, their mastery arises from a belief that war can have no masters, that war ultimately must bring about the failure of the urge for freedom Tolstoy attributes to the modern aggressive soldier of the Napoleonic armies. For these reasons—and many others—Kutuzov remains reticent, not eager to show his hand: he often dawdles rather than acting decisively, and the only notion of action he advocates is carefully keyed to dealing with what is given before him in the battle. His acting is reactive not transformational and creative—Kutuzov is resolutely incapable of creative action. Unlike Napoleon, Kutuzov resists the temptation to view his power over men as evidence of power over nature as a whole. Unlike Napoleon, Kutuzov is essentially a man of peace forced into the awkward position of military engagement by Napoleonic aggression, which is fueled by illusion and fear.

Joseph Conrad once wrote: "Action is consolatory. It is the enemy of thought and the friend of flattering illusions. Only in the conduct of our action can we find the sense of mastery over the Fates" (Conrad 2009: 50). Tolstoy's view of freedom in *War and Peace* allows a subtler reading of this famous line from *Nostromo*. For Tolstoy allows a kind of action that respects limitation without turning into pessimism or the sort of violence advocated by the Napoleonic man. When Conrad refers to action, he seems to refer precisely to the Napoleonic—and modern—human being that has transformed freedom from a vice into the highest virtue—one is most virtuous when one is free. While this transformation may have a lot to do with Machiavelli's transformation of *virtù* into a term denoting the possession of power, it also gives perhaps the best insight into how Tolstoy conceives of Napoleon and why that conception seems perverse to so many. Napoleon from this perspective is the incarnation of the Machiavellian man devoted to the acquisition of power so as to force fate (Machievallian *fortuna*) to bend to his will. Napoleon is not merely a criminal, he is the greatest criminal, the epitome of the modern striving to maximize power at any cost, a line that seems to extend from Machiavelli to Nietzsche. If Napoleon, then, is truly after power "at any cost," he can only be a source of violence until supreme power, whatever that might be, is achieved (Machiavelli 1998: 98–101).

This pursuit of freedom cannot bring peace other than through a kind of self-immolation or negation of the world as it is (a view perceptible in Adolf Hitler in the twentieth century). It is perhaps the most profound and seductive enemy of peace one can imagine. As Conrad suggests, action is seductive precisely because it promises a release from our fate, a release from death. The darkest counter to the hope promised by action is the kind of fatalism one finds in *War and Peace* in the image of General Bagration, the almost "oriental" fatalism that is also a very controversial aspect of the novel. But this fatalism is only fatal if one refuses to accept its simplest message—that human beings are all mortal—or to accept that message as a condemnation so unbearable that any action that might oppose the passive acceptance of death would be preferable.

Conrad seems to insist on action, and, as I have noted, appears to interpret *all* action as necessarily oriented to combating death. Tolstoy provides a striking alternative—action that does not resist death but *affirms* its hold over us. This kind of action, the reticence one finds in Bagration and Kutuzov and Platon Karataev, is indeed action yet its orientation is not to war but to peace, to establishing an equilibrium that may govern action in the future and ensure that peace may be not only achieved but sustained to the farthest extent possible.

OVERCOMING FREEDOM

We return here to the Newtonian view and the various levels on which it appears in the novel. By this I mean the ways that the novel distributes a view of the world and action that abets equilibrium and an acknowledgment that the actions that have seemed to make history, wars and conquest first of all, cannot achieve what they intend. Moreover—and perhaps most harshly—the novel condemns the stubborn insistence on action as an exercise of sovereign freedom. Action pretending to self-assertion or, indeed, to self-creation, arises from profound self-deception and an unwillingness to look at things as they are in themselves but only as they are for us, for our utility and triumph over others and nature itself.

Bagration, Kutuzov, and Platon Karataev are the signal representatives of a striving for peace in the novel. One might bring peace about almost instantaneously, it may seem, if one were only ready to exercise the very limited freedom one has for the only non-criminal end to which freedom is suited: the acceptance of necessity. Those who believe they are free in the most aggressive sense, like Napoleon, have no freedom because they have forsaken the only kind of freedom that can be meaningful in the novel—the freedom to accept necessity and thus reject the chimeras of self-deception that lead only to violence and misery without end.

Of course the novel is hardly so clear cut. One can make many arguments about the Napoleonic characters; yet, their prevalence itself suggests that deception is much more than a temptation of the great conquerors. Tolstoy struggles at length in the novel and, especially, in the Second Part of the Epilogue, to explain why freedom, understood as sovereign freedom, is so difficult to overcome. The question itself may seem silly to some. Freedom is with little doubt the highest aim of our modern consumer capitalist culture—one, of course, that differs considerably from Tolstoy's world—and it may seem to some disingenuous to regard freedom in any other way. Tolstoy's challenge in this respect lies rooted in his distrust of this notion of freedom, a distrust that in turn arises from a seemingly traditional adherence to negative considerations of freedom as being essentially hostile, harmful, and evil.

Tolstoy grounds this distrust in one of the most peculiar arguments in the novel that assumes the fundamental importance of time in the process of understanding. Simply put, we come to understand events more fully as they recede from us in time, a cliché to be sure, but one deployed to interesting effect in *War and Peace*. One of the novel's most famous effects is what one may call the "confusion effect." The great battles the novel depicts are confusing; during them no one seems to know exactly what is going on, and most characters make guesses based on their experience and inclination. Whether one is with Bagration at Schön Grabern or Pierre at Borodino, the cumulative effect of the battle narratives is to show clearly how confusing the battles are for those participating in them. This clear representation of confusion may seem ironic or contradictory except that it makes perfect sense if one accepts the underlying logic; namely, that the confusion belongs to the time of the battle itself. Thenceforth, as more and more views are gathered and assimilated, the nature of the battle becomes clearer.

An analogy may be helpful. If one took a single paragraph and cut it up according to the individual sentences, how would one put it back together? If the paragraph were relatively simple, one might be able to put it back together fairly quickly but one would be forced to do so by reading each sentence and setting them in the proper order that could only be secured when all the sentences had been put together. If the paragraph were quite or very complicated, it might take a great deal more time; if it were of immense or infinite complication, it might never be clear how to restore the paragraph to its original structure.

To apply the metaphor to the case at hand, a battle is like a paragraph except that one cannot know its original structure because it is not given. Moreover, the battle is so complicated that it might take many different shapes once historians try to put it back together (which is invariably what they try to do) without ever knowing what its final outcome will be since they are still within an unfinished historical record themselves. Still, they can make sufficient surmises to imagine that a certain disposition of the sentences is superior to others (may be clearer, seem more logical). The final structure should elude them, however, unless they have a model that ensures or guarantees a certain structure and that model is reflected fairly exactly in the historical event. Tolstoy's advocacy of calculus and the Newtonian view pushes in this final direction.

All of this is to make the following point: for Tolstoy the present is as a series of scattered sentences. One does not know the order that may apply to them and one feels free on account of that cognitive limitation. While Tolstoy may claim that there is finally nothing new under the sun, he also suggests that in the present we are simply unable to make this claim successfully. The temptation, then, is to feel free, to feel that events can arise and be shaped by one's own will rather than by laws that seem to curtail the feeling of openness and immediacy that belongs to the present. As time moves on, however, this feeling must be challenged as more and more pieces come together in accordance with a structure that does not suggest that the event happened "just so" but that it was shaped by numerous interventions.

Even in the face of these proofs, such as they are, that the spontaneous notion of the present may be based on a lie encouraged by a largely illusory sense of openness, there is no doubt strong motivation to embrace spontaneity since, as Tolstoy remarks:

> However often experiment and reasoning may show a man that under the same conditions and with the same character he will do the same thing as before, yet when, under the same conditions and with the same character, he approaches for the thousandth time the action that always ends in the same way, he feels as certainly convinced as before the experiment that he can act as he pleases. Every man, savage or sage, however incontestably reason and experiment may prove to him that it is impossible to imagine two different courses of action in precisely the same conditions, feels that without this irrational conception (which constitutes the essence of freedom) he cannot imagine life.
> —Tolstoy 2010: 1294

Tolstoy blames the lack of acceptance of a Newtonian model of history squarely on an irrational desire for freedom without which human beings would find it impossible to live. As he remarks at another point in the Second Part of the Epilogue, a "man having no freedom cannot be conceived of except as deprived of life" (Tolstoy 2010: 1295). This is the clearest equation of life and freedom. It is a momentous claim if we consider the various arguments I have brought forth so far to suggest that the novel promotes a notion of peace that equates the latter with an acknowledgment both of the abnegation of the striving for freedom and an acceptance of a Newtonian view of history that imposes itself equally on all.

Tolstoy's claim that life without a sense of freedom is impossible turns the entire argument of the novel on its head. Peace is possible but not desirable! Peace robs us of life. Criminal freedom is irresistible and ineradicable. As long as there is life there is war or, as Friedrich Schelling remarked in his famous long essay on the nature of human freedom, "where there is no struggle, there is no life" (Schelling 2006: 63). Heraclitus' saying seems to prevail with peace seen as the dull acceptance of a life of routine, a life without violence, to be sure, but also without excitement or challenge, a life that one cannot "live dangerously" as Nietzsche put it (Nietzsche 2001: 161).

SELF-ABNEGATION

Tolstoy's equation of freedom with life may not fail to convince those who prize freedom, but it must appear as strangely contradictory in the context of his argument against freedom as the wellspring of conflict and violence. Or it may simply appear to be an indication that the problem of freedom is a tragic one—we are unable to free ourselves of an illusion that, though pernicious and violent, grants our lives a significance they could not otherwise possess. The obvious corollary is that the life of self-abnegation or affirmation of the restrictions applicable to our lives is lacking significance—it is literally not a meaningful life.

Tolstoy thus suggests that, notwithstanding the creation of a writing of history that complies with the Newtonian turn, there is little to no chance that this view of history may be accepted because it signals the end of freedom. In a way that is much more redolent of Dostoevsky, Tolstoy argues that we cannot embrace the truth. We are offended by the truth that compels us to give up any notion of freedom. We must have a sense of our own ability to challenge nature and death. Otherwise, we are left or burdened with the impossibility of changing what ails us, a meager prospect.

The novel ends on this curious note with Pierre Bezukhov. One of the leading characters in the novel, Pierre's trajectory in the novel is a complex one, punctuated by moments of crisis where he finds he is unable to move forward because his attempts at self-assertion continually (and comically) fail. Finally, he encounters Platon Karataev and liberates himself by liberating himself from seeking meaning in his life through self-assertion. He seems to accept without reserve the example of Platon Karataev. Yet, at the very end of the novel, we find Pierre in a moment of radical transformation where he begins to take part in events in an attempt to bring forth change in the Russian state; evidently Pierre is on his way to becoming a Decembrist—a revolutionary in the most disastrously failed coup in Russian history.

Pierre fails to heed the teaching of self-abnegation. This failure leads to what we can only imagine as a tragic destiny. The implication is obvious: no matter how strong the lure of peace may be for those tired of war and violence, the rule of peace is likely not sustainable—the lure of freedom, violence, transgression cannot be overcome. Tolstoy ends the novel with a most unsettling perspective on the possibility and desirability of peace. He links both possibility and desirability when he stresses the fundamental importance of freedom, even if freedom proves to be an illusion, and one that is at the origin of the most terrible and violent aspects of human history. The horror of violence, according to Tolstoy, is preferable to the muffled oblivion of peace.

VII.

The view presented in this chapter strives to locate the origins of Tolstoy's later pacifism in what I consider Tolstoy's most comprehensive examination of the relation of war to peace. This is arguably an unusual stance since most treatments of Tolstoy's pacifism concentrate on what is referred to as the "later" or "post-conversion" Tolstoy who, from 1878 until his death in 1910, increasingly assumed the mantle of the prophet launching critique after critique of Russian society and what we might call liberalism (Gustafson 1986: xi–xiii; but McKeough 2009: 35–56). This is the Tolstoy who insisted that all government is violence, the Tolstoy who created his own version of Christianity in a series of works that emerged in the 1880s and 1890s. What these works miss, however, is the

FIGURE 8.6: Leo Tolstoy. Credit: Mansell/Getty Images.

comprehensive vision of *War and Peace*. They tend to be more polemical and, indeed, more violent in their call for a new kind of society without war, without masters and servants, without property. At their core, however, is the very same fundamental position that I have outlined in this chapter, a position whose essence is to emphasize that radical self-abnegation is the only way to achieve peace, that peace without the extirpation of self-interest is impossible. In doing so, Tolstoy gave expression to one of the deepest currents in Russian thought, both in the largely implicit Christian mode of *War and Peace* and in the explicit, if wholly idiosyncratic, Christianity of his later writings. Moreover, Tolstoy's later writings would spread these Russian ideas to Mahatma Gandhi in India and Martin Luther King, Jr. in the United States in the form of nonviolent resistance, the very epitome of self-abnegation, and one of the most influential forms of politics in the twentieth century.

NOTES

Introduction

1. For a comprehensive overview of the major events and developments during the "long nineteenth century," see especially Hobsbawm 1963, 1975, 1987; Evans 2017; Osterhammel 2014.
2. This was paid for by US industrialist Andrew Carnegie's Endowment for International Peace (1910), which also supported European peace societies.
3. With Germany at Versailles, 1919; with Hungary at Trianon, 1920; with the Ottoman Empire at Sèvres, 1920; with Austria at St Germain-en-Laye, 1919; with Bulgaria at Neuilly, 1919—see MacMillan 2001).

Chapter 1

1. I am grateful to Laurent Franceschetti, David Armitage, Jennifer Pitts, William Graham, Patricia Herlihy, and Aurelian Craiutu for having kindly reviewed and commented on this chapter.
2. De Staël 1795: 31. All translations are mine, unless otherwise indicated.
3. "L'état d'un peuple qui n'est point en guerre": see "Paix," in *Dictionnaire de l'Académie française*, 5th ed., vol. 2 (Paris: Smits, 1798), p. 213.
4. "Situation tranquille d'un État, d'un peuple, d'un royaume qui n'a point d'ennemis à combattre": "Paix," in *Dictionnaire de l'Académie française*, 6th ed., vol. 2 (Paris: Didot, 1835), p. 329.
5. Randall Lesaffer, "The Congress of Vienna (1814–1815)," *Oxford Public International Law*, http://opil.ouplaw.com/page/congress-vienna-1814-1815 (accessed January 12, 2019).
6. *Acte du Congrès de Vienne du 9 juin 1815, avec ses annexes* (Vienna: Imprimérie impériale et royale, 1815), Art. 53 to 64, pp. 45–52.
7. *Acte du Congrès de Vienne du 9 juin 1815*, Art. 74 to 84, pp. 59–66.
8. "Tenir au même état, en état de consistence". See also the definition of "consistence" as "état de stabilité, de permanence," in *Dictionnaire de l'Académie française*, 5th ed. (1798), vol. 1, p. 296.
9. Signed in Paris on September 26, 1815. "Traité de la sainte Alliance entre les Empereurs de Russie et d'Autriche et le Roi de Prusse, signé à Paris le 14/26 septembre 1815," in *Le Congrès de Vienne et les traités de 1815*, ed. Comte d'Angeberg (Léonard Chodźko) (Paris: Amyot, 1863–4), vol. 4 (1864), pp. 1547–9.
10. As for the Quakers, not unlike the German mystics, they invested great hopes in Alexander I, considering him a man elected by God. See Pypin 2000: 398–416.
11. Noah Webster, *American Dictionary of the English Language* (1828), s.v. "peace" (emphasis added).
12. See, for example, Eberl 2015, Ravlo *et al.* 2003.

13. On some of the legal aspects of this debate, see Pitts 2018, notably pp. 6–15; 92–117.
14. Though for revisions to this standard view, see Belmessous 2014.
15. *Johnson v. M'Intosh*, 21 U.S. 543 (1823). This is a subject that has raised interest from historians, particularly since the 1990s: see Miller 2005: 1; Newcomb 1992: 18–20.
16. *Johnson v. M'Intosh*, 21 U.S. 543 (1823): 21 U.S. 574.
17. James Monroe, "Seventh annual message to Congress," December 2, 1823 ("Monroe Doctrine").
18. Speech of Benjamin Disraeli to the Parliament in Disraeli 1882: 231–9.
19. For a vibrant critique of that paradox, see Kroll 2015: 238–49.
20. "Les hommes naissent et demeurent libres et égaux en droits. Les distinctions sociales ne peuvent être fondées que sur l'utilité commune" (*Déclaration des Droits de l'Homme et du Citoyen*, 1789).
21. Treaty of Portsmouth (September 5, 1905), in Tyler 1905: 564–8.
22. See, notably, Recchia and Urbinati 2009.
23. "World Alliance for International Friendship Through the Churches Collected Records, 1914–1947": Swarthmore College Peace Collection, https://www.swarthmore.edu/library/peace/CDGA.S-Z/worldalliance.htm
24. See on this concept Bew 2016.
25. First Hague Convention, July 29, 1899: "Concerning the Pacific Settlement of International Disputes," Title IV: The Avalon Project, Yale Law School, http://avalon.law.yale.edu/19th_century/hague01.asp (accessed August 2, 2018).
26. "Peace Treaty of Vereeniging," signed on May 31, 1902, at Melrose House, Pretoria.
27. The Pious Fund Case (United States of America v. Mexico), October 14, 1902, in *Reports of International Arbitral Awards*, vol. 9, pp. 1–14.
28. On the architecture of the Peace Palace, see Duranti 2017: 30–6.
29. Napoleon III, "Discours à Bordeaux du 9 octobre 1852," *Le Moniteur* (October 11, 1852).
30. "The German Imperial Proclamation," January 18, 1871. See Robinson 1904–5, vol. 2: 594–6.
31. The Covenant of the League of Nations (June 28, 1919), The Avalon Project, Yale Law School, http://avalon.law.yale.edu/20th_century/leagcov.asp
32. The Covenant of the League of Nations, Preamble.
33. The Covenant of the League of Nations, Preamble.
34. The Covenant of the League of Nations, Art. 22.

Chapter 2

1. On separate spheres see, for example, Cott 1979; Hausen 1981; Davidoff and Hall 1987; Evans 1979; Frevert 1989; Kingsley Kent 1990.
2. There is a large body of international scholarship devoted to this issue, but see, for example, Tylee 1988; Fell and Sharp 2007; Wilmers 2008; Hämmerle *et al.* 2014; Grayzel and Proctor 2017.
3. On separate sphere ideology, see Hausen 1981; Davidoff and Hall 1987; Frevert 1989.
4. The phrase "maternal thinking" comes from Sara Ruddick's seminal book of 1989.
5. On The Hague see, for example, Bussey and Tims 1965; Wiltsher 1985; Cooper 1987; Braker 1995; Rupp 1997; Vellacott 2001; Wilmers 2008; Gwinn 2011.
6. See, for example, Fischer and Whipps 2003; Alonso 2004; Fischer 2006; Knight 2010; Sheplar and Mattina 2012; Agnew 2017.

Chapter 3

1. Peter Brock 1968a, 1968b, 1970, 1972 are standard studies of faith-based pacifism in which women's role is largely uncovered. See also Curti 1929; Phelps 1930; Cookson 1982; van der Linden 1987; and Ceadel 2000, ch. 1.
2. A summary of their contribution is in Cooper 1991, ch. 1.
3. Niboyet's work is featured in Goldberg Moses 1984, esp. chs. 3–4. See also Anderson 2000, esp. chs. 6–7; Albistur *et al.* 1977: 291–303.
4. In her first issue (February 15, 1844: 1–2) Niboyet made it clear that peace was not the result of total non-resistance nor was it "at any price."
5. Wendy Chmielewski (2007) has pointed to a series of "Friendly Addresses", exchanges by British and American women (largely from Exeter and Philadelphia) in an effort to defuse tensions over a Canadian border dispute. See also Anderson 2000.
6. A summary of the meeting is in Cooper 1991: 36–44. See also Bortolotti 1985: 26–36; Petricioli et al. 2004, esp. Part I.
7. Her 1872 proposal to women of the world to protest against war each year on June 2 did not produce a permanent result. The text is now widely available on the internet; see, for instance, the site of the Nuclear Age Peace Foundation: https://www.wagingpeace.org/mothers-day-proclamation/ (accessed July 2018).
8. For details of their organization, see Cooper 1991, ch. 3. These groups still exist.
9. A brief biography of von Suttner by Irwin Abrams is in Josephson 1985: 921–4; see also Hamann 1996; Kempf 1973; Braker 1991; and Laurie Cohen in this volume, Chapter 5.
10. See Norgren 2007. Lockwood, a teacher and attorney, a lower-class American woman who raised herself through education, became a leading representative of the American Peace Society. She was the first attorney allowed to practice before the US Supreme Court.
11. An unpublished essay Rémy Fabre shared with me in 2016 shows that the anti-pacifist campaign in the prestigious *Revue des Deux Mondes* attacked the French peace leadership in 1905 as inviting weakness against the German enemy (Fabre n.d.).
12. For a survey of Augspurg's life see Kinnebrock 2005.
13. For a brief summary of Selenka's work see Lischewski 1995, 51–4. In Russia, the first public meetings of women convened for a political agenda were organized in 1899 to support the convocation of The Hague conference. The organizer was Dr. Anna Shabanova, a doctor and activist, who circulated a petition that garnered about 40,000 signatures, including those of peasant women. This event was reported some years later in *Peace News* (Moscow, 1913), December 5, 1913. I am grateful to the late Manuela Dobos of the College of Staten Island for her translation.
14. For a brief biography of Wiszniewska see Josephson 1985, 1021–3.
15. Note in her handwriting in folder, Ligue du désarmement moral par les femmes in Bibliothèque Marguerite Durand, Paris, Dossier 327 Com.
16. For a fuller discussion see Cooper 2011, 5–33.
17. Her analysis was published before Jean de Bloch's four-volume analysis of the probable consequences of a major war among the European powers.
18. For a brief biography by Michael Lutzker see Josephson 1985, 875–6. For a personal account see Sewell 1901.
19. *La Fronde,* issues in August, September, and December 1901, especially Laguerre, 1901.
20. The main Italian peace society in Milan, led by the Nobel Prize winner E.T. Moneta, insisted that Italy needed overseas territory as the French and British had. His position split the national movement but he was supported by Rosalia Gwis-Adami, a leading woman pacifist in Milan.

21. The Code de la Paix was presented by Emile Arnaud. See Sandi E. Cooper 1991, 111–13.
22. The French demographer, Jacques Bertillon, exacerbated nationalist fears in his *La Dépopulation de la France* (Paris, 1911). See a full discussion of the issue in Offen 1984.
23. Rankin had the distinction of voting against entry into both World Wars I and II.

Chapter 4

1. "Pugnare mihi non licet" was Martin's response when offered the emperor's money to fight in the Roman army; recorded in *Vita Martini* by Sulpicius Severus (*c.* 360–*c.* 420); for Chelčický, see Brock 1991: 19–24.
2. One Catholic voice in 1870 identified "our Lord's announcements . . . [that] Christianity was to prevail . . . not as other victorious powers had done . . . by force of arms . . . but by the novel expedient of sanctity and suffering." John Henry Newman cited Tertullian's *Apologia*, that "In what war . . . should we not be sufficient and ready . . . if it were not in this Religion of ours more lawful to be slain than to slay?" (Newman 1903: 456, 475).
3. Collectively, the Fireside Poets were damned by faint praise, e.g., "theirs is a poetry which still has its redemptions, minor though they may be . . ." (Lee 1985: 10). One commentator describes Lowell, Longfellow, and Holmes as Boston's "Brahmin literati" (Duberman 1966: 1). Biographies and bibliographies include: Gibian (2001); Wagenknecht (1966); Mordell (1969).
4. For Tolstoy, see "Letter to Eugen Heinrich Schmitt," October 12, 1896, in which Tolstoy refers to "a little-known, but very remarkable American author, Thoreau"; also Tolstoy, *Resurrection*, 2.29. For a critical comparison of the two men, see Manning (1943). Gandhi was influenced by Thoreau's *Walden* in Johannesburg in 1906 and he named his movement after Thoreau's essay *Civil Disobedience*; see Hendrick (1956).
5. *The Biglow Papers* was one of the Grolier Club's 1903 list of "100 Books Famous in English Literature," at number 86. A full list is available online: http://www.indiana.edu/~liblilly/etexts/grolier/ (accessed February 16, 2017).
6. Pyne resigned from the Peace Society in 1842 when one campaigner, George Pilkington, criticized the Society for including on its strictly pacifist committee someone (i.e., Pyne) who was bound by Article XXXVII of the Church of England which allows for the legal possibility of just war.
7. Two years later the Archbishops of Canterbury and York refused to sign a similar petition at all; see Peace Society 1896a: 46–7.
8. The Archbishop of Canterbury was President and the Archbishop of York a Vice-President (National Peace Council 1911: 91).
9. Letters and statements of that time are detailed in den Boggende (1986): 55–6. For an example of the foundation myth, see the History section of the International Fellowship of Reconciliation (IFOR) website, http://www.ifor.org/highlighted-history#ifor-history-1910-1930 (accessed March 15, 2017). A group of Christian leaders, including Hodgkin and Siegmund-Schültze, did meet in Berne in August 1915; however, the Movement Towards a Christian International, the body which later became IFOR, was not formed until 1919 (Barrett 2014: 190–1). For a critical account of the context within which Siegmund-Schültze was operating, see Moses (2009): 53–5.
10. See also National Archives reference MH 47/142/1_1. "We doubted whether the proposed Tribunals would prove capable of judging consciences" (Stanton n.d.: 5). For an overview of the work of the tribunals see Gregory 2008: 101–8.
11. For IBSA objectors see Perkins 2016. For Churches of Christ objectors, see Barker 1921, which ends with verses by Lowell, available at http://www.oldpaths.com/Archive/Biographies/hisnamessake.html (accessed March 15, 2017).

12. The earliest list of conscientious objector deaths was in 1919, see ([1919] 1940), *Troublesome People,* London, Central Board for Conscientious Objectors: 32–3. See also Graham ([1922] 1969): 323–4; and Boulton (1967): ch. 10. For details of all known COs, see the online Pearce Register, https://search.livesofthefirstworldwar.org/search/world-records/conscientious-objectors-register-1914-1918, accessed March 15, 2017.
13. A copy is in the collection of the Peace Museum, Bradford; BRFPM:2000.2.
14. For the story of the men sent to France, see Peet (1940): 26–31: Barrett (2016): 290–4; for Brocklesby, see Ellsworth-Jones (2007); copies of personal diaries of "Frenchmen," including Norman Gaudie, Howard Marten, and Harry Stanton, are available in the Liddle Collection, Leeds University.

Chapter 5

1. Bertha von Suttner to Alfred Nobel, n.d. [February 10, 1893], in Biedermann 2001: 126 (English in original).
2. For more on the 1907 Hague Conference, see Maartije Abbenhuis's Chapter 7 in this volume.
3. Rudolf Großmann (alias Pierre Ramus) (1882–1942), a colleague of Johann Most and Emma Goldman, was one of Austria's leading theoretical voices of anarchism. He was arrested during World War I for espionage (never proven) and died during his flight from Austria in 1942.
4. All translations from the German into English are the author's, unless otherwise noted.
5. The (undated) version used in this chapter is entitled *Die Waffen nieder: Roman,* with an Introduction by Friedrich Heer. Vienna: H. Javorsky.
6. M.A. Lerei is a wordplay in German (*Malerei*), which means the art of painting.
7. B. Oulot is a double wordplay: in French, *boulot* means "work" ("work" also being the title of an essay of Suttner's published in January 1881), whereas *boulotte* means a "chubby female," which was one of Arthur von Suttner's nicknames for his spouse.
8. Suttner uses Dotzky as a representative of one of the 30,000 or more soldiers who died or were seriously wounded in those fifteen hours of battle. As most of Suttner's initial readers probably knew, the Battle of Solferino involved approximately 300,000 soldiers along a ten-mile front, and the casualties were more or less evenly divided among the rivals. Compounding the tragedy of the battle, there were neither medical personnel nor facilities to treat the thousands of wounded and suffering. It was so destructive that it prompted the signing of an armistice within two weeks. A witness to its aftermath, a young Swiss Calvinist banker named Henry Dunant (1828–1910), was so profoundly moved by what he saw that he published his memoirs, *Un Souvenir de Solferino* (A Memory of Solferino), and shortly thereafter initiated the founding of the First Geneva Convention (for the Amelioration of the Condition of the Wounded and Sick in Armed Forces in the Field) and the International Committee of the Red Cross.
9. Suttner seems here to be taking a leaf out of Prussian General Field Marshal Helmuth Graf von Moltke's (1800–91) infamous statement: "Perpetual peace is a dream, and not even a beautiful one: and war is an inherent part of God's world order; without war, the world would get bogged down" (quoted in Helbig 1882: 434).
10. Unlike her previous novels, this one was based, according to Suttner, on empirical research: archival reports held at the Ministry of War, secondary literature by historians of recent European wars, and personal conversations with soldiers (oral history) (Suttner 1965: 180).
11. Suttner published its third edition (in 1899) under her real name, in part to put to rest the idea that Max Nordau was its author.

12. In 1910 the Austrian Peace Society collected 120,000 signatures on a petition supporting compulsory arbitration (see "Österreichische Friedensgesellschaft" 1910: 60).
13. For more on the women's movement and World War I, see Hämmerle *et al.* 2014; Wilmers 2008; Fell and Sharp 2007.
14. Although Suttner makes no mention of having read Tolstoy's *War and Peace* (first translated into German in 1892), the two began to correspond in 1891 (see Cohen 2005a). For more on Tolstoy and his peace work, see Jeff Love's Chapter 8 in this volume.
15. United Nations of Geneva, Library and Archives, Collection Suttner-Fried, folder 286, letter 2.6, dated April 17, 1907.
16. Cf. Sir Henry Maine's well-known saying: "War appears old as mankind, but peace is a modern invention" (1888: 8).

Chapter 6

1. My account of the early American peace movement is based mainly on Brock 1968a, 1991, and Ziegler 1992.
2. Unless otherwise stated, the sources for this account of the British peace movement are Ceadel 1996 and Ceadel 2000.
3. This higher figure is suggested by Cyril Pearce of Leeds University on the basis of his impressive continuing research into local newspaper accounts of previously unnoticed objectors who accepted alternative service, sometimes in their existing occupations. The Pearce Register also treats all members of the Friends Ambulance Unit as conscientious objectors. A version of the register is available on the website of London's Imperial War Museum: https://search.livesofthefirstworldwar.org/search/world-records/conscientious-objectors-register-1914-1918 (accessed November 29, 2016).

Chapter 7

1. For a history of the term see Kuehl 1986: 1–10.
2. With thanks to Randall Lesaffer.
3. For more on the "world news order" see Barth 2013: 36.
4. While the word "rescript" may not be the most technically accurate term, it is the name contemporaries attached to the Tsar's memorandum. The text of the rescript is available in all manner of published forms, in the original French and in translation. For an English translation see Scott 1909, vol. 1: 41–2. For more on the reasons why the Tsar released the rescript see Ford 1936: 354–82; Morrill 1974: 296–313.
5. There is some evidence to suggest that after the rescript's release, even Nicholas II became increasingly reluctant to hold the event (Morrill 1974: 308; Rybachenok 2005).
6. The petitions can be found in: PRO FO83/1699, 1734, 1735, 1736, 1737, 1738, 1739.
7. Many of these petitions are available in: NA 2.05.03: 524–8.
8. Tuchman may have channeled Belgian delegate Auguste Beernaert's claim in 1907 that "to-day there is no assembly which must not sit with the windows opened, listening to the voices from outside" (Eyffinger 1999: 342).
9. In searching for the term "La Haye," "vredesconferentie," "The Hague," and "Den Haag" across thirty different newspaper databases, none of the newspapers selected here were extraordinary in terms of the quantity of their references to the conference or in the quality of their editorial content.
10. Many of them can be found in NA2.05.03: 534, 542, 543, 544, 545.

Chapter 8

1. Tolstoy avoids Newton's preferred term for the infinitesimal, the "fluxion."
2. Of course, the problem here is that if laws truly do apply to all human behavior then war must be mandated by nature and peace is thus unattainable. It seems to me much more likely that Tolstoy employs the Newtonian example as an "as if": i.e., that we should act as if we were all subject to natural or divine laws. For, indeed, obedience to laws suggests an excess of freedom over those laws.
3. Nevertheless, for all its crude distortions, the Soviet-era official interpretation of the Napoleonic Wars still in many ways remained true to the spirit of Leo Tolstoy, who was by far the most important nineteenth-century mythmaker as regards his impact on Russian (and foreign) understanding of Russia's role in the Napoleonic era. Tolstoy depicts elemental Russian patriotism as uniting in defense of national soil. He paints Kutuzov as the embodiment of Russian patriotism and wisdom, contrasting him with the idiocy of so-called professional military experts, whom he sees as Germans and pedants (Lieven 2010: 10).

BIBLIOGRAPHY

Abbenhuis, Maartje (2013), "A Most Useful Tool for Diplomacy and Statecraft: Neutrality and Europe in the 'Long' Nineteenth Century," *International History Review*, 35 (1): 1–22.
Abbenhuis, Maartje (2014), *Age of Neutrals. Great Power Politics 1815–1914*, Cambridge: Cambridge University Press.
Accampo, Elinor (2006), *Blessed Motherhood: Bitter Fruit: Nelly Roussel and the Politics of Female Pain in Third Republic France*, Baltimore: Johns Hopkins University Press.
Acte du Congrès de Vienne du 9 juin 1815, avec ses annexes (1815), Vienna: Imprimérie impériale et royale, Art. 53 to 64: 45–52.
Addams, Jane ([1907] 2007), *Newer Ideals of Peace*, Urbana: University of Illinois Press.
Addams, Jane ([1922] 2010), *Peace and Bread in Time of War*, Memphis: General Books.
Addams, Jane, Emily G. Balch, and Alice Hamilton ([1915] 2003), *Women at The Hague: The International Congress of Women and Its Results*, Urbana: University of Illinois Press.
Adolf, Antony (2009), *Peace, a World History*, Cambridge: Polity Press.
Agnew, Elizabeth (2017), "A Will to Peace: Jane Addams, World War I, and 'Pacifism in Practice,'" *Peace & Change* (42) 1: https://doi.org/10.1111/pech.12216 (accessed July 27, 2018).
Albistur, Maïte and Daniel Armogathe (1977), *Histoire du feminisme français du moyen âge à nos jours*, Paris: des femmes.
Aleramo, Sibilla (1911), "L'ora virile," *Il Marzococco*, 47, November 19.
Alexandrowicz, C.H. (1967), *An Introduction to the History of the Law of Nations in the East Indies*, Oxford: Clarendon Press.
Alexandrowicz, C.H. (2017), *The Law of Nations in Global History*, ed. David Armitage and Jennifer Pitts, Oxford: Oxford University Press.
Allen, Mark (2012), "Winchester, the Clergy and the Boer War," in S.G. Parker and Tom Lawson (eds.), *God and War*, Farnham: Ashgate.
Alonso, Harriet Hyman (2004), "Jane Addams: Thinking and Acting Globally and Locally," *Journal of Women's History* (16) 1: 148–64.
Alston, Charlotte (2014), *Tolstoy and his Disciples: The History of a Radical International Movement*, London: I.B. Tauris.
Anderson, Bonnie (2000), *Joyous Greetings: The First International Women's Movement*, Oxford: Oxford University Press.
Angell, Norman ([1910] 2012), *The Great Illusion: A Study of the Relation of Military Power to National Advantage*, Gutenberg Project Ebook, http://gutenberg.org/ebooks/38535.mobile (accessed August 24, 2017).
Barker, W., ed. (1921), *For His Name's Sake*, Heanor.
Barrett, Clive (2014), *Subversive Peacemakers: War Resistance 1914–1918: An Anglican Perspective*, Cambridge: Lutterworth Press.
Barrett, Clive (2016), "Conscription, Courage and Conscience," in Peter Liddle (ed.), *Britain and the Widening War, 1915–1916*, Barnsley: Pen & Sword.
"The Baronness Bertha von Suttner (1843–1914)" (1914), *American Journal of International Law* 8/3 (July); 613–14.

Barth, Volker (2013), "The Formation of Global News Agencies, 1859–1914," in W. Boyd Rayward (ed.), *Information Beyond Borders: International Cultural and Intellectual Exchange in the Belle Époque*. London: Taylor & Francis.

Basily, Nicholas de (1973), *Memoirs: Diplomat of Imperial Russia 1903–1917*, Stanford: Hoover Institution Press.

Beazly, R. (1936), "Campbell Bannerman and Peace Opportunities in 1905–1907," *Berliner Monatshefte* 14 (April): n.p.

Belloc, Hilaire (1898), *The Modern Traveller*.

Belmessous, Saliha, ed. (2014), *Empire by Treaty: Negotiating European Expansion, 1600–1900*, Oxford: Oxford University Press.

Bennett, Scott H. (2003), *Radical Pacifism: The War Resisters League and Gandhian Nonviolence in America. 1915–1963*, Syracuse: Syracuse University Press.

Beresteyn, Olpher J.B. van (1907), "De Curiositeiten-Kamer," *Nieuws van de Dag*, October 26: 1.

Berlin, Sir Isaiah (1978), *Russian Thinkers*, Harmondsworth: Penguin.

Bertillon, Jacques (1911), *La Dépopulation de la France*, Paris.

Best, Geoffrey (1983), *Humanity in Warfare: The Modern History of the International Law of Armed Conflict*, London: Methuen.

Best, Geoffrey (1991), "The Restraint in War in Historical and Philosophical Perspective," in A.J.M. Delissen and G.J. Tanja (eds.), *Humanitarian Law of Armed Conflict Challenges Ahead: Essays in Honour of Frits Kalshoven*, 3–26, Dordrecht: Martinus Nijhoff.

Bew, John (2016), *Realpolitik: A History*, Oxford: Oxford University Press.

Bibbings, Lois (2009), *Telling Tales about Men: Conceptions of Conscientious Objectors to Military Service during the First World War*, Manchester: Manchester University Press.

Biedermann, Edelgard, ed. (2001), *Chère Baronne et Amie—Cher monsieur et ami: Der Briefwechsel zwischen Alfred Nobel und Bertha von Suttner*, Hildesheim: Olms.

Blackburn, Robin (2011), *An Unfinished Revolution: Karl Marx and Abraham Lincoln*, London: Verso.

Bortolotti, Franca Pieroni (1985), *La Donna, la pace, l'Europa: L'Associazione internazionale delle donne dalle origini alla prima guerra mondiale*, Milan: Franco Angeli.

Bosch, Mineke with Annemarie Klostermann (1990), *Politics and Friendship: Letters from the International Women's Suffrage Alliance 1902–1942*, Columbus: Ohio State University Press.

Bostridge, Mark (1998), *Florence Nightingale the Women and Legend*, London: Viking.

Boulding, Elise (2000), *Cultures of Peace: The Hidden Side of History*, Syracuse: Syracuse University Press.

Boulton, David (1967), *Objection Overruled*, London: MacGibbon & Key.

Bourke, Joanna (1999), *An Intimate History of Killing: Face-to-Face Killing in Twentieth-Century Warfare*, London: Granta.

Bourke, Joanna (2015), *Deep Violence: Military Violence, War Play and the Social Life of Weapons*, Berkeley: Counterpoint.

Brailey, Nigel J. (2002), "Sir Ernest Satow and the 1907 Second Hague Peace Conference," *Diplomacy & Statecraft* 13 (2): 201–28.

Braker, Regina (1991), "Bertha von Suttner as Author: The Harriet Beecher Stowe of the Peace Movement," *Peace and Change* 16/1 (January): 74–96.

Bremer, Frederika (1854), "Invitation to a Peace Alliance," *The Times*, August 28, 1854.

Bremer, Frederika ([Swedish, 1854] English 1856), *Hertha* [Stockholm: Adolf Bonniers Förlag], London: A. Hall, Virtue & Co.

Bridgman, Raymond L. (1908), "Success at The Hague," *Inter-Nation: A Journal of Economic Affairs* January: 29.

Brittain, Vera (1964), *Rebel Passion*, London: Allen & Unwin.
Brock, Peter (1968a), *Pacifism in the United States from the Colonial Era to the First World War*, Princeton: Princeton University Press.
Brock, Peter (1968b), *Pioneers of a Peaceable Kingdom: The Quaker Peace Testimony from the Colonial Era to the First World War*, Princeton: Princeton University Press.
Brock, Peter (1970), *Twentieth-Century Pacifism*, New York: Van Nostrand Reinhold.
Brock, Peter (1972), *Pacifism in Europe to 1914*, Princeton: Princeton University Press.
Brock, Peter (1991a), *Freedom from Violence*, Toronto: University of Toronto Press.
Brock, Peter (1991b), *Freedom from War: Nonsectarian Pacifism, 1814–1914*, Toronto: University of Toronto Press.
Brower, Benjamin Claude (2009), *A Desert Named Peace: The Violence of France's Empire in the Algerian Sahara, 1844–1902*, New York: Columbia University Press.
Brown, Heloise (1913), *The Truest Form of Patriotism: Pacifism Feminism in Britain, 1870–1902*, Manchester.
Burt, Stephen (2008), "When Poets Ruled the School," *American Literary History* (20) 3: 508–20.
Bussey, Gertrud and Margaret Tims ([1965] 1980), *Pioneers for Peace: Women's International League for Peace and Freedom 1915–1965*, Oxford: Alden Press.
Campbell Jnr, Charles. S. (1957), *Anglo-American Understanding 1898–1903*, Baltimore: Johns Hopkins University Press.
Carroll, Berenice and Clinton Fink ([1906] 2007), "Introduction," *Newer Ideals of Peace*, xiii–lxxvii, Urbana: University of Illinois Press.
Cassel, Pär Kristoffer (2012), *Grounds of Judgment: Extraterritoriality and Imperial Power in Nineteenth-Century China and Japan*, Oxford: Oxford University Press.
Cassese, Antonio (2000), "The Martens Clause. Half a Loaf or Simply Pie in the Sky?" *European Journal of International Law* 11 (1): 187–216.
Cassirer, Ernst (1956), *Determinism and Indeterminism in Modern Physics*, New Haven: Yale University Press.
Castelli, Alberto A. (2010), "Between Patriotism and Pacifism: Ernesto Teodore Moneta and the Italian conquest of Libya," *History of European Ideas* 36: 324–9.
Ceadel, Martin (1980), *Pacifism in Britain 1914–1945: The Defining of a Faith*, Oxford: Clarendon Press.
Ceadel, Martin (1987), *Thinking about Peace and War*, Oxford: Oxford University Press.
Ceadel, Martin (1996), *The Origins of War Prevention: The British Peace Movement and International Relations, 1730–1854*, Oxford: Clarendon Press.
Ceadel, Martin (2000), *Semi-Detached Idealists: The British Peace Movement and International Relations, 1854–1945*, Oxford: Oxford University Press.
Ceadel, Martin (2009), *Living the Great Illusion: Sir Norman Angell, 1872–1967*, Oxford: Oxford University Press.
Ceadel, Martin (2013), "Enforced Pacific Settlement or Guaranteed Mutual Defence? British and US Approaches to Collective Security in the Eclectic Covenant of the League of Nations," *International History Review* 35 (5): 993–1008.
Ceuster, Kees de (2008), "Success and Failure of the Korean Delegation at the Second Hague Peace Conference" (in Korean), *Han'guksa hakpo* 30: 309–54.
Chase, Malcom (2016), "The Chartist Petition of 1842," www.parliament.uk (accessed February 28, 2018).
Chatfield, Charles (1971), *For Peace and Justice: Pacifism in America 1914–1941*, Knoxville: University of Tennessee Press.

Chatfield, Charles (1992), *The American Peace Movement: Ideals and Activism*, New York: Twayne.

Chickering, Roger (1975), *Imperial Germany and a World without War*, Princeton: Princeton University Press.

Chickering, Roger (1988), "War, Peace, and Social Mobilization in Imperial Germany: Patriotic Societies, the Peace Movement and Socialist Labor," in Charles Chatfield and Peter van den Dungen (eds.), *Voices Prophesying War 1763–1984*. Knoxville: University of Tennessee Press.

Chickering, Roger (1998), *Imperial Germany and the Great War, 1914–1918*, Cambridge: Cambridge University Press.

Choate, Joseph (1913), *The Two Hague Conferences*, Princeton: Princeton University Press.

Chomé, Léon (1899), *Désarmer, C'est Déchoir: La Conference de La Haye*. Brussels: Imprimerie Gustave Deprez.

Clark, Ian (2007), *International Legitimacy and World Society*, Oxford: Oxford University Press.

Claude Jnr, Inis. L. (1956), *Swords into Plowshares. The Problems and Progress of International Organization*, New York: Random House.

Clinton, Michael (1998), *The French Peace Movement, 1821–1919*, PhD dissertation, University of Notre Dame.

Clinton, Michael (2011), "Coming to Terms with 'Pacifism': The French Case, 1901–1918," *Peace and Change* 26 (1): 1–30.

Cobden, Richard (1903), *The Political Writings of Richard Cobden*, vol. 2, London: T. Fisher Unwin.

Cohen, Laurie (2005a), "Looking in from the Outside: Bertha and Arthur von Suttner in the Caucasus, 1876–1885," *Ab Imperio* 3: 257–84.

Cohen, Laurie R. (2005b), "Seite an Seite, gegen den Strom: Die frühen Jahre der österreichischen Friedensbewegung und der Vereinigung gegen Judendiskriminierung," in Laurie R. Cohen (ed.), *"Gerade weil Sie eine Frau sind . . .". Erkundungen über Bertha von Suttner, die unbekannte Friedensnobelpreisträgerin*, 55–94, Vienna: Braumüller.

Cohen, Laurie R. (2009), "Across a Feminist–Pacifist Divide: Baroness Bertha von Suttner's Tour of the United States in 1912," *L'homme: Europäische Zeitschrift für Feministische Geschichtswissenschaft*, Special Issue Gender & 1968, 20 (2): 85–104.

Cohrs, Patrick O. (2006), *The Unfinished Peace after World War I: America, Britain and the Stabilisation of Europe, 1919–1932*, Cambridge: Cambridge University Press.

Connell, R.W. (1987), *Gender and Power: Society, the Person and Sexual Politics*, Cambridge: Polity.

Connell, R.W. (1995), *Masculinities*, Cambridge: Polity.

Conrad, Joseph ([1904] 2009), *Nostromo*, Oxford: Oxford University Press.

Constant, Benjamin (1814), *De l'Esprit de conquête et de l'usurpation dans leurs rapports avec la civilisation européenne*, 3rd ed., Paris: Le Normant.

Conway, Stephen (1989), "Bentham on Peace and War," *Utilitas* 1(1): 82–101.

Cookson, J.E. (1982), *The Friends of Peace: Anti-War Liberalism in England 1792–1815*, Cambridge: Cambridge University Press.

Cooper, Sandi E., ed. (1972), *Arbitration or War? Contemporary Reactions to the Hague Peace Conference of 1899*, New York: Garland.

Cooper, Sandi E., ed. (1976), *Internationalism in Nineteenth-Century Europe: The Crisis of Ideas and Purpose*, New York: Garland Publishing.

Cooper, Sandi (1987), "Women's Participation in European Peace Movements: The Struggle to Prevent WWI," in R. Pierson (ed.), *Women and Peace: Theoretical, Historical and Practical Perspectives*, 51–75, London: Croom Helm.

Cooper, Sandi E. (1991a), "Pacifism in France 1889–1914: International Peace as a Human Right," *French Historical Studies* 27 (2): 359–86.

Cooper, Sandi (1991b), *Patriotic Pacifism: Waging War on War in Europe 1815–1914*, New York and Oxford: Oxford University Press.

Cooper, Sandi (2011), "French Feminists and Pacifism, 1889–1914: The Evolution of New Visions," *Peace & Change* 36 (1): https://doi.org/10.1111/j.1468-0130.2010.00669.x (accessed July 27 2018).

Cott, Nancy (1979), "Passionlessness: An Interpretation of Victorian Sexual Ideology, 1790–1850," *Signs* 4 (2): 219–36.

Cottrell, Robert (2000), *Roger Nash Baldwin and the American Civil Liberties Union*, New York: Columbia University Press.

Covenant of the League of Nations (June 28, 1919), The Avalon Project, Yale Law School, http://avalon.law.yale.edu/20th_century/leagcov.asp (accessed August 2, 2018).

Crook, Paul (1994), *Darwinism, War and History*, Cambridge: Cambridge University Press.

Curti, Merle (1929), *The American Peace Crusade, 1815–1860*, Chapel Hill: University of North Carolina Press.

Czartoryski, Adam (1830), *Essai sur la diplomatie, manuscrit d'un philhellene*, ed. N. Toulouzan, Paris: Didot.

Darby, W. Evans (1908) *The Political Machinery of Peace during the Past Year*, London.

Das, Santanu (2007) "'Indian Sisters! . . . Send your husbands, brothers, sons': India, Women and the First World War," in A.S. Fell and I.E. Sharp (eds.), *The Women's Movement in Wartime: International Perspectives 1914–1919*, 18–37, Basingstoke: Palgrave Macmillan.

Davidoff, Leonore and Catherine Hall (1987), *Family Fortunes: Men and Women of the English Working Class, 1780–1950*, London: Routledge.

Davis, Calvin D. (1962), *The United States and the First Hague Peace Conference*, Ithaca: Cornell University Press.

Davis, Calvin D. (1975), *The United States and the Second Hague Peace Conference: American Diplomacy and International Organization 1899–1914*, Durham: Duke University Press.

Deegan, Mary Jo (1990), *Jane Addams and the Men of the Chicago School 1892–1918*, New Brunswick: Transaction Books.

den Boggende, Gijsbert Gerrit Jacob (1986), "The Fellowship of Reconciliation, 1914–1945," PhD thesis, McMaster University, Hamilton, Ontario.

Disraeli, Benjamin (1882), "Royal Titles Bill, 9 March 1876," in *Selected Speeches of the Late Right Honourable Earl of Beaconsfield*, ed. T.E. Kebbel, 2 vols., London: Longmans, Green, & Co., vol. 2: 231–9.

Dolmetsch, Carl (1992), *Our Favorite Guest: Mark Twain in Vienna*, Athens: University of Georgia Press.

Dorsey, M. Girard (2017), "More than Just a Taboo: The Legacy of the Chemical Warfare Prohibitions of the 1899 and 1907 Hague Conferences," in Maartje Abbenhuis, Christopher Ernest Barber, and Annalise R. Higgins (eds.), *War, Peace and International Order? The Legacies of the Hague Conferences of 1899 and 1907*, New York: Routledge.

Doyle, Michael W. (1997), *Ways of War and Peace: Realism, Liberalism, and Socialism*, New York: W.W. Norton.

Duberman, Martin (1966), *James Russell Lowell*, Boston: Houghton Mifflin.

Dudink, Stefan, Karen Hagemann, and John Tosh, eds. (2004), *Masculinities in Politics and War: Gendering Modern History*, Manchester: Manchester University Press.

Dülffer, Jost (1980), *Regeln gegen den Krieg: Die Haager Friedens-Konferenzen 1899 und 1907 in der internationalen Politik*, Berlin: Ulstein.

Eberl, Oliver (2015), "The Paradox of Peace with 'Savage' and 'Barbarian' Peoples," in Thomas Hippler and Miloš Vec (eds.), *Paradoxes of Peace in Nineteenth Century Europe*, 220–37, Oxford: Oxford University Press.

Ellsworth-Jones, Will (2007), *We Will Not Fight*, London: Aurum.
Estournelles, Baron Constant de (1899), "Die Haager Konferenz und der Transvaalkrieg," *Die Friedens-Warte* 1 (20, November): 125–8.
Evans, Alfred Bowen (1855), *War: Its Theology; Its Anomalies; Its Incidents and Its Humiliations.*, London: Peace Society.
Evans, G.R. (2014), *Edward Hicks: Pacifist Bishop at War*, Oxford: Lion Hudson.
Evans, Richard J. (1976), *The Feminist Movement in Germany 1894–1933*, London: Sage.
Evans, Richard J. (2017), *The Pursuit of Power Europe 1815–1914*, London: Penguin.
Eyffinger, Arthur (1988), *The Peace Palace. Residence for Justice—Domicile of Learning*, The Hague: n.p.
Eyffinger, Arthur (1999), *The 1899 Hague Peace Conference: The Parliament of Man, the Federation of the World*, The Hague: Kluwer Law International.
Eyffinger, Arthur (2007), *The 1907 Hague Peace Conference: The Conscience of the Civilized World*, The Hague: JudiCap.
Fabre, Rémy (n.d.), "L'Antipacifisme dans le débat culturel et politique autour de La Revue des Deux Mondes," unpublished essay, shared by the author in 2016.
Faries, John C. (1915), *The Rise of Internationalism*, New York: n.p.
Fell, Alison and Ingrid Sharp, eds. (2007), *The Women's Movement in Wartime: International Perspectives, 1914–1919*, Basingstoke: Palgrave Macmillan.
Ferguson, Niall (1998), *The Pity of War*, London: Penguin.
First Hague Convention (July 29, 1899), "Pacific Settlement of International Disputes," Title IV: The Avalon Project, Yale Law School, http://avalon.law.yale.edu/19th_century/hague01.asp (accessed August 2, 2018).
Fischer, Marilyn (2006), "Addams's International Pacifism and the Rhetoric of Maternalism," *Feminist Formations* 18 (3): 1–19.
Fischer, Marilyn and Judy D. Whipps, eds. (2003), *Addams's Essays and Speeches on Peace (1899–1935)*, Bristol: Thoemmes Press.
Fisher, David (2014), "Just War and the First World War: Where Was the Just War Tradition When It Was Needed?" in *Crucible*, Norwich: Hymns Ancient and Modern, April–June: 27–34.
Fletcher, Sheila (1989), *Maude Royden: A Life*, Oxford: Blackwell.
Ford, Thomas K. (1936), "The Genesis of the First Hague Peace Conference," *Political Science Quarterly* 51 (3): 354–82.
Freud, Sigmund ([1915] 1957), "Thoughts for the Times on War and Death," in James Strachey (ed.), *The Complete Psychological Works of Sigmund Freud Volume XIV (1914–1916)*, 274–300, London: The Hogarth Press.
Frevert, Ute (1989), *Women in German History from Bourgeois Emancipation to Sexual Liberation*, Oxford: Berg.
Frevert, Ute (2001), *Die kasernierte Nation: Militärdienst und Zivilgesellschaft in Deutschland*, Munich: Ch Beck.
Fried, Alfred Herrmann, ed. (1917), *Der Kampf um die Vermeidung des Weltkrieges. Randglossen aus zwei Jahrzehnten*, 2 vols, Orell Füssli: Zurich.
Fried, Alfred Hermann (1925), *Jugenderinnerungen*. Berlin Publ.
Fry, Ruth (1919), *Emily Hobhouse*, London: Cape.
Fuchs, Albert (1949), *Geistige Strömungen in Österreich*, Vienna.
Galtung, Johan (1964), "An Editorial," in *Journal of Peace Research* 1 (1): 1–4.
Galtung, Johan (1990), "'Cultural Violence' Responses," in *Journal of Peace Research* 22 (2): 291–305, www.jstor.org/stable/423472 (accessed August 24, 2017).

Gaudie, Norman (n.d.), unpublished manuscript diary, Leeds University, Liddle Collection WW1/CO/038.
Gentz, Friedrich von ([1818] 1876), "Considérations sur le système politique actuellement établi en Europe," in A. Prokesch von Osten (ed.), *Dépêches inédites du chevalier de Gentz aux hospodars de Valachie*, 3 vols., 354–7, Paris: Plon.
Gestrich, Andreas (2001), "Die Haager Friedenskonferenzen und die deutsche Presse," in Christof Dipper, Andreas Gestrich, and Lutz Raphael (eds.), *Krieg, Frieden und Demokratie: Festschrift für Martin Vogt zum 65 Geburtstag*, Frankfurt: Peter Lang.
Geva, Dorit (2014), "Of Bellicists and Feminists: French Conscription, Total War, and the Gender Contradictions of the State," *Politics & Society* 42 (2): 135–65.
Ghervas, Stella (2008), *Réinventer la tradition: Alexandre Stourdza et l'Europe de la Sainte-Alliance*, Paris: Honoré Champion.
Ghervas, Stella (2014a), "Antidotes to Empire: From the Congress System to the European Union," in John W. Boyer and Berthold Molden (eds.), *EUtROPEs: The Paradox of European Empire*, Chicago: University of Chicago Press (*Parisian Notebooks* 7: 49–81).
Ghervas, Stella (2014b), "La paix par le droit, ciment de la civilisation en Europe? La perspective du siècle des Lumières," in Antoine Lilti and Céline Spector (eds.), *Penser l'Europe au XVIIIe siècle: Commerce, Civilisation, Empire*, 47–69, Oxford: Voltaire Foundation.
Ghervas, Stella (2015a) "The Long Shadow of the Congress of Vienna: From International Peace to Domestic Disorders," *Journal of Modern European History* 15 (4): 458–64.
Ghervas, Stella (2015b), "La Sainte-Alliance: un pacte pacifique européen comme antydote à l'Empire," in Sylvie Aprile *et al.* (eds.), *Europe de papier: Projets européens au XIXe siècle*, 47–64, Lille: Presses Universitaires du Septentrion.
Ghervas, Stella (2019), "From the Balance of Power to a Balance of Diplomacy? Peace and Security in the Vienna Settlement," in Beatrice de Graaf, Ido de Haan, and Brian Vick (eds.), *Securing Europe: 1815 and the New European Security Culture*, 95–113, Cambridge: Cambridge University Press.
Ghervas, Stella (2020), *Conquering Peace: From the Enlightenment to the European Union*, Cambridge, MA: Harvard University Press.
Ghervas, Stella and David Armitage, eds. (2020), *A Cultural History of Peace in the Age of Enlightenment 1648–1815*, London: Bloomsbury Academic.
Gibian, Peter (2001), *Oliver Wendell Holmes and the Culture of Conversation*, Cambridge: Cambridge University Press.
Gittings, John (2012), *The Glorious Art of Peace: from the Iliad to Iraq*, Oxford: Oxford University Press.
Goegg, Marie (1878), *Deux Discours*, reprint of 1868 speeches: 4–5.
Goldberg Moses, Claire (1984), *French Feminism in the 19th Century*, Albany: SUNY.
Graham, John W. ([1922] 1969), *Conscription and Conscience*, New York: Augustus M. Kelley.
Grane, W.L. (1912), *The Passing of War*, London: Macmillan.
Grayzel, Susan and Tammy Proctor, eds. (2017), *Gender and the Great War*, Oxford: Oxford University Press.
Gregory, Adrian (2008), *The Last Great War*, Cambridge: Cambridge University Press.
Gustafson, Richard (1986), *Leo Tolstoy: Resident and Stranger*, Princeton: Princeton University Press.
Hagemann, Karenn (2004), "German Heroes: The Cult of Death for the Fatherland in Nineteenth-Century Germany," in Stefan Dudink, Karen Hagemann, and John Tosh (eds.), *Masculinities in Politics and War: Gendering Modern History*, 116–34, Manchester: Manchester University Press.

Hamann, Brigitte ([1986] 1996), *Bertha von Suttner: Ein Leben für den Frieden*, Munich: Piper; *Bertha von Suttner: A Life for Peace*, trans. Ann Dubsky, Syracuse: Syracuse University Press.

Hamilton, Keith (2008), "Britain and the Hague Peace Conference of 1899," in Keith Hamilton and Edward Johnson (eds.), *Arms and Disarmament in Diplomacy*, London: Vallentine Mitchell.

Hämmerle, Christa, Oswald Überegger, and Birgitta Bader Zaar, eds. (2014), *Gender and the First World War*, New York: Palgrave Macmillan.

Harris, Sally (1996), *Out of Control: British Foreign Policy and the Union of Democratic Control, 1914–1918*, Hull: Hull University Press.

Hausen, Karin (1981), "Family and Role Division: The Polarisation of Sexual Stereotypes in the Nineteenth Century—An Aspect of the Dissociation of Work and Family Life," in Richard Evans and W.R. Lee (eds.), *The German Family*, 51–83, London: Croom Helm.

Helbig, Friedrich (1882). "Der 'ewige Friede'—ein Menschheitsideal," *Die Gartenlaube*, 26: 431–4.

Hendrick, George (1956), "The Influence of Thoreau's 'Civil Disobedience' on Gandhi's Satyagraha," *The New England Quarterly* 29 (4): 462–71.

Herman, Sondra (1969), *Eleven Against War: Studies in American Internationalist Thought, 1898–1921*, Stanford: Hoover Institution Press.

Herren, Madeleine (2013), "'They Already Exist': Don't They? Conjuring Global Networks along the Flow of Money," in I. Löhr and R. Wenzlhuemer (eds.), *The Nation State and Beyond*, 43–61, Berlin: Springer.

Herren-Oesch, Madeleine and Cornelia Knab (2007), "Die Zweite Haager Freidenskonferenz und die Liberalisierung des politischen Informationsmarktes," *Die Friedens-Warte* 82 (4): 51–64.

Hertrampf, Susanne (2006), *"Zum Wohle der Menschheit": Feministisches Denken und Engagement internationaler Aktivistinnen, 1945–1975*, Herbolzheim: Centaurus.

Heymann, L.G. and Augspurg, A. (1919) "Was will 'Die Frau im Staat'?" *Die Frau im Staat*, 1: 1.

Heymann, L.G. ([1917/22] 1980) "Weiblicher Pazifismus," in Gisela Brinker-Gabler (ed.), *Frauen gegen den Krieg*, 65–70, Frankfurt am Main: Fischer.

Hierdeis, Irmgard (2005), "Gefühle und Ahnungen. Eine persönliche Revue der Tendenzromane von Bertha von Suttner," in Laurie R. Cohen (ed.), *"Gerade weil Sie eine Frau sind . . .". Erkundungen über Bertha von Suttner, die unbekannte Friedensnobelpreisträgerin*, 124–41, Vienna: Braumüller.

Higgins, Annalise (2016), "Petitioning for Peace: the British Public Movement in Support of the Proposed First Hague Peace Conference, 1898–1899," MA thesis, University of Auckland.

Higgins, Annalise (2017), "Writing for Peace. Reconsidering the British Public Petitioning Movement's Historical Legacies after 1898," in Maartje Abbenhuis, Christopher Ernest Barber, and Annalise R. Higgins (eds.), *War, Peace and International Order? The Legacies of the Hague Conferences of 1899 and 1907*, New York: Routledge.

Higonnet, Margaret Randolph, Jane Jenson, Sonya Michel, and Margaret Collins Weitz (eds.) (1987), *Behind the Lines: Gender and the Two World Wars*, New Haven: Yale University Press.

Hippler, Thomas and Miloš Vec, eds. (2015a), *Paradoxes of Peace in Nineteenth Century Europe*, Oxford: Oxford University Press.

Hippler, Thomas and Miloš Vec (2015b), "Peace as a Polemic Concept: Writing the History of Peace in Nineteenth Century Europe," in Thomas Hippler and Miloš Vec (eds.), *Paradoxes of Peace in Nineteenth Century Europe*, 3–16, Oxford: Oxford University Press.

Hirst, Margaret E. (1923), *The Quakers in Peace and War*, London: Swarthmore.
Hobhouse, Emily (1902), *The Brunt of War and Where It Fell*, London: Methuen & Co.
Hobhouse Balme, Jennifer (1998), *To Love One's Enemies: The Work and Life of Emily Hobhouse Compiled from Letters and Writings, Newspaper Cuttings and Official Documents*, Cobble Hill, British Columbia: Hobhouse Trust.
Hobsbawm, Eric (1963), *The Age of Revolution 1789–1848*, London: Weidenfeld & Nicolson.
Hobsbawm, Eric (1975), *The Age of Capital 1848–1875*, London: Weidenfeld & Nicolson.
Hobsbawm, Eric (1987), *The Age of Empire 1875–1914*, London: Weidenfeld & Nicolson.
Hochschild, Adam (1998), *King Leopold's Ghost: A Story of Greed, Terror, and Heroism in Colonial Africa*, London: Pan Macmillan.
Hochschild, Adam (2011), *To End all Wars: A Story of Protest and Patriotism in the First World War*, London: Pan Macmillan.
Holl, Karl (2007), *Ludwig Quidde (1848–1941). Eine Biographie*, Düsseldorf: Droste Verlag.
Howe, Julia Ward (1870), "A Mother's Day Proclamation" https://www.wagingpeace.org/mothers-day-proclamation/ (accessed July 31, 2018).
Howlett, Charles F. (n.d), "The American School Peace League and the First Peace Studies Curriculum", in *Encyclopedia of Peace Studies*, Columbia University Teachers College. Available online: https://www.tc.columbia.edu/epe/epe-entries/ (accessed July 24, 2018).
Howlett, Charles F. (1990), "John Nevin Sayre and the International Fellowship of Reconciliation," *Peace and Change* 15 (4): 123–49.
Hucker, Daniel (2015), "British Peace Activism and 'New' Diplomacy: Revisiting the 1899 Hague Peace Conference," *Diplomacy & Statecraft* 26: 405–23.
Hueck, I. (2004), "Peace, Security and International Organisations: The German International Lawyers and the Hague Conferences," in Randall Lesaffer (ed.), *Peace Treaties and International Law in European History: From the Late Middle Ages to World War One*, Cambridge: Cambridge University Press.
Hugo, Victor (1851), "Congrès de la Paix à Paris. Discours d'ouverture, 21 août 1849," in Victor Hugo, *Quatorze Discours*, Paris: La Librairie nouvelle.
Hull, Isabel V. (2003), "Military Culture and the Production of 'Final Solutions' in the Colonies: the Example of Wilhelmine Germany," in Robert Gellately and Ben Kiernan (eds.), *The Spectre of Genocide: Mass Murder in Historical Perspective*, Cambridge: Cambridge University Press.
Hull, Isabel V. (2008), "'Military Necessity' and the Laws of War in Imperial Germany," in Stathis N. Kalyva, Ian Shapiro, and Tarek E. Masoud (eds.), *Order, Conflict and Violence*, Cambridge: Cambridge University Press.
International Council for Women (1899, 1914), *International Council for Women. Reports*, n.p.
Inter-Parliamentary Union (1902), *Actes Essentiels Premier Supplements des 'Resolutions Votes par les Huit Premières Conferences Interparliamentaires'*, Berne: Imprimerie K.J. Wyss.
Jacques-Chaquin, Nicole (2001), "Illuminism," in *Encyclopedia of the Enlightenment*, ed. Michel Delon, 2 vols., vol. 1: 683–6, London: Routledge.
Jarrett, Mark (2013), *The Congress of Vienna and Its Legacy: War and Great Power Diplomacy after Napoleon*, London: I.B. Tauris.
Jasper, Ronald C.D. (1967), *George Bell*, Oxford: Oxford University Press.
Johnpoll, Bernard K. (1970), *Pacifist's Progress: Norman Thomas and the Decline of American Socialism*, Chicago: Quadrangle Books.
Jonas, Raymond (2015), *The Battle of Adwa: African Victory in the Age of Empire*, Cambridge, MA: Harvard University Press.
Jones, Edgar (2006), "The Psychology of Killing: The Combat Experience of British Soldiers during the First World War," *Journal of Contemporary History* 41 (2): 229–46.

Joor, Johan (2013), *The Building of Peace: A Hundred Years of Work on Peace through Law. The Peace Palace 1913–2013*, The Hague: Eleven.

Jordan, Jane and Ingrid Sharp, eds. (2003), *Diseases of the Body Politic: Josephine Butler and the Prostitution Campaigns*, Abirgdon: Routledge.

Josephson, Harold, ed. (1985), *Biographical Dictionary of Modern Peace Leaders*, Westport: Greenwood Press.

Junk, August (1928), *Die Mächte auf der ersten Haager Friedenskonferenz (1899). Inaugural-Dissertation zur Erlangung der Doktorwürde der Philosophischen Fakultät der Universität Frankfurt a. M.*, Borna-Leipzig: Universitätsverlag Robert Noske.

Kahn, Charles H., ed. (1981), *The Art and Thought of Heraclitus: An Edition of the Fragments with Translation and Commentary*, Cambridge: Cambridge University Press.

Keefer, Scott A. (2006), "Building the Palace of Peace. The Hague Conference of 1899 and Arms Control in the Progressive Era," *Journal of the History of International Law* 8 (1): 1–17.

Kempf, Beatrix (1973), *Woman for Peace: The Life of Bertha von Suttner*, Park Ridge: Noyes Press.

Kennedy, Thomas (1981), *The Hound of Conscience: A History of the No-Conscription Fellowship, 1914–1919*, Fayetteville: University of Arkansas Press.

Keynes, John M. (1920), *The Economic Consequences of the Peace*, London: Macmillan.

Kingsley-Kent, Susan (1990), *Sex and Suffrage in Britain 1860–1914*, London: Routledge.

Kinnebrock, Susanne (2005), *Anita Augspurg (1857–1943). Feministin und Pazifistin zwischen Journalismus und Politik*, Herbolzheim: Centaurus.

Knight, Linda (2010), *Jane Addams: Spirit in Action*, New York: W.W. Norton & Company.

Kojève, Alexandre (1999), *Athéisme*, Paris: Gallimard.

Koskenniemi, Martti (2009), *The Gentle Civilizer of Nations: The Rise and Fall of International Law, 1870–1960*, Cambridge: Cambridge University Press.

Koss, Stephen (1973), *The Pro-Boers*, Chicago: University of Chicago Press.

Kroll, Stefan (2015), "The Illiberality of Liberal International Law: Religion, Science, and the Peaceful Violence of Civilization," in Thomas Hippler and Miloš Vec (eds.), *Paradoxes of Peace in Nineteenth Century Europe*, 238–49, Oxford: Oxford University Press.

Kuehl, Warren F. (1969), *Seeking World Order: The United States and International Organization to 1920*, Nashville: Vanderbilt University Press.

Kuehl, Warren F. (1986), "Concepts of Internationalism in History," *Peace and Change* 11 (1): 1–10.

Kulka, Julius (1890), "Die Waffen nieder! Eine Lebensgeschichte von Bertha von Suttner (Dresden und Leipzig) von Julius Kulka (Wien)," in *Moderne Dichtung: Monatsschrift für Literatur*, IV: 264–5.

Lagerlöf, Selma (1911), *Home and State*, New York: Women's Suffrage Party.

Lammasch, Heinrich (1922), "Aus meinem Leben," in M. Lammasch and H. Sperl (eds.), *Heinrich Lammasch: Seine Aufzeichnungen, sein Wirken und seine Politik*, Vienna: Franz Deuticke.

Langer, William L. (1935), *The Diplomacy of Imperialism*, New York: n.p.

Langhorne, Richard (1981), *The Collapse of the Concert of Europe: International Politics 1890–1914*, New York: St. Martin's Press.

Laqua, Daniel (2014), "Alfred H. Fried and the Challenges for 'Scientific Pacifism' in the Belle Époque," in R. W. Boyd (ed.), *Information Beyond Borders: International Cultural and Intellectual Exchange in the Belle Époque*, London: Taylor & Francis.

Laurence, Richard R. (1978), "The Peace Movement in Austria, 1867–1914," in Solomon Wank (ed.), *Doves and Diplomats: Foreign Offices and Peace Movements in Europe and America in the Twentieth Century*, 21–41, Westport: Greenwood Press.

Laurence, Richard R. (1989), "Rudolf Grossman and Anarchist Anti-Militarism in Austria before World War 1," *Peace and Change* 14 (2): 155–75.

Lawrence, Thomas J. (1912), *The Third Hague Conference and Innocent Commerce in Time of War*, Westminster: National Peace Council.

Lebon, Gustave (1916), *The Psychology of the Great War*, New York: Macmillan. Harvard University digital online copy: https://archive.org/details/psychologygreat00andrgoog (accessed August 24, 2017).

Lee, A. Robert (1985), *Nineteenth-Century American Poetry*, London: Vision.

Lee, H.D.P., ed. (1936), *Zeno of Elea: A Text with Translation and Notes*, Cambridge: Cambridge University Press.

Leeuwin, Edward W. (2000), "The Arts of Peace: Thomas H. Mawson's Gardens at the Peace Palace, The Hague," *Garden History* 28 (2): 262–76.

Lerner, Paul (2008), *Hysterical Men: War, Psychiatry, and the Politics of Trauma in Germany, 1890–1930*, New York: Cornell University Press.

Lesaffer, Randall (2013), "The Temple of Peace: The Hague Peace Conferences, Andrew Carnegie and the building of the Peace Palace (1898–1913)," *Preadviezen. Mededelingen van de Koninklijke Nederlandse Vereniging voor Internationaal Recht*, 140: 1–38.

Lesaffer, Randall (2018), "The Congress of Vienna (1814–1815)," *Oxford Public International Law*, http://opil.ouplaw.com/page/congress-vienna-1814–1815 (accessed August 2, 2018).

Levine, Philippa (2010), "Anthropology, Colonialism, and Eugenics," in *The Oxford Handbook of the History of Eugenics*, 43–61, eds. Alison Bashford and Philippa Levine, Oxford: Oxford University Press.

Liddington, Jill (1989), *The Long Road to Greenham Common*, London: Virago.

Lieven, Dominic (2010), *Russia against Napoleon: The True Story of the Campaigns of* War and Peace, New York: Penguin.

Lischewski, Heike (1995), *Morgenröte einer besseren Zeit: Die Frauenfriedensbewegung von 1892 bis 1932*, Münster: DFG-VK Bildungswerk NRW e.V. agenda Verlag.

Low, Seth (1899), "The Hypocrisies of the Peace Conference," *Nineteenth Century* 45 (267, May): 689.

Lynch, John (1983), "Simón Bolívar and the Spanish Revolutions," *History Today* 33 (7): 5–10.

Macdonnell, John (1915), "Introduction," in Coleman Phillipson (ed.), *International Law and the Great War*, London: T. Fisher Unwin.

Machiavelli, Niccolò (1998), *The Prince*, Chicago: University of Chicago Press.

McKeough, Colm (2009), *Tolstoy's Pacifism*, Amherst: Cambria Press.

McMeekin, Sean (2013), *July 1914: Countdown to War*, New York: Basic Books.

MacMillan, Margaret (2001), *Peacemakers Six Months that Changed the World*, London: John Murray.

MacMillan, Margaret (2013a), *The War that Ended Peace: How Europe Abandoned Peace for the First World War*, London: Profile Books.

MacMillan, Margaret (2013b), *The War that Ended Peace: The Road to 1914*, New York: Random House.

McPeak, Rick and Donna Orwin, eds. (2012), *Tolstoy on War*, Ithaca: Cornell University Press.

Madigan, Edward (2013), "'Sticking to a Hateful Task': Resilience, Humour, and British Understandings of Combatant Courage, 1914–1918," *War in History* 20 (1): 76–98.

Mahan, Alfred Thayer (1890), *The Influence of Sea Power on History, 1660–1783*, Boston: Little Brown.

Maine, Henry (1888), "International Law: A Series of Lectures Delivered Before the University of Cambridge," London. Available online: https://archive.org/stream/internationallaw00mainiala#page/n21/mode/2up/search/peace (accessed January 4, 2017).

Manning, Clarence A. (1943), "Thoreau and Tolstoy", *The New England Quarterly* 16 (2): 234–43.

Marchand, C. Roland (1972), *The American Peace Movement and Social Reform, 1898–1918*, Princeton: Princeton University Press.

Marinetti, Filippo (February 5, 1909), "Futurist Manifesto," *Gazetta dell Emilia*, Bologna.

Marya-Chéliga (1900), "La femme et l'oeuvre de la paix universelle," in *Almanach Féministe 1900*, 76–88, Paris: Cornèly.

Marx, Karl and Friedrich Engels (1848), *Manifesto of the Communist Party* https://www.marxists.org/archive/marx/works/1848/communist-manifesto/ (accessed February 28, 2018).

Massie, Robert K. (2007), *Dreadnought: Britain, Germany and the Coming of the Great War*, London: Vintage.

Mayr, Josef Karl (1939), "Aufbau und Arbeitsweise des Wiener Kongresses," *Archivalische Zeitschrift* 45: 64–127.

Mazower, Mark (2013), *Governing the World. The History of an Idea, 1815 to the Present*, London: Penguin.

Mazzini, Giuseppe ([1849] 2009), "Toward a Holy Alliance of the Peoples," in *A Cosmopolitanism of Nations: Giuseppe Mazzini's Writings on Democracy, Nation Building, and International Relations*, eds. S. Recchia and N. Urbinati, Princeton: Princeton University Press.

Mead, Edwin D. (1905), "Introduction," in David Low Dodge (ed.), *War Inconsistent with the Religion of Jesus Christ*, Boston: International Union.

Mead, Lucia Ames ([1890] 1910), "Report of the Work of the NCW and ICW on Behalf of Peace and Arbitration".

Mélin, Jeanne Philomène (alias Thalès) (1957), *Memoirs*, dated 17 September 1957 in Archives départementales des Ardennes, Charleville-Mézièes Collection Jeanne Mélin: 1

Meron, Theodor (2000), "The Martens Clause, Principles of Humanity, and Dictates of Public Conscience," *American Journal of International Law* 94 (1): 78–89.

Meyer, Jessica (2009), *Men of War: Masculinity and the First World War in Britain*, Basingstoke: Palgrave Macmillan.

Miller, Robert J. (2005), "The Doctrine of Discovery in American Indian Law," *Idaho Law Review* 42 (1).

Monroe, James (1823), "Seventh Annual Message to Congress", December 2 ("Monroe Doctrine").

Moon, Michael D.H. (2013), "Civilization and International Legitimacy: The Hague Peace Conferences and Western Perceptions of the Far East," MA thesis, University of Auckland.

Mordell, Albert (1969), *Quaker Militant; John Greenleaf Whittier*, Port Washington, NY: Kennikat.

Morley, John (1903), *The Life of Richard Cobden*, London: T. Fisher Unwin.

Morrill, Dan L. (1974), "Nicholas II and the Call for the First Hague Conference," *Journal of Modern History* 46 (2): 296–313.

Morson, Gary Saul (1987), *Hidden in Plain View: Narrative and Creative Potentials in "War and Peace"*, Stanford: Stanford University Press.

Moses, John A. (2009), "The Theological Component of World Conflict: The Example of Anglo-German Antagonism 1914–18," *St Mark's Review* 209 (3): 39–55.

Mueller, John (1991), "Changing Attitudes towards War: The Impact of the First World War," *British Journal of Political Science* 21 (1): 1–28.

Munro, Thomas (2017), "The Hague as a Framework for British and American Newspapers' Public Presentations of the First World War," in Maartje Abbenhuis, Christopher Ernest Barber, and Annalise R. Higgins (eds.), *War, Peace and International Order? The Legacies of the Hague Conferences of 1899 and 1907*, New York: Routledge.
Munro, Thomas (forthcoming), "The Hague's War 1914–1918," draft PhD, University of Auckland.
National Peace Council (1911), *Year Book*.
Newcomb, Steve (1992), "Five Hundred Years of Injustice: The Legacy of Fifteenth Century Religious Prejudice", in *Shaman's Drum* Vol (no.): 18–20.
Newman, John Henry (1903), *An Essay in Aid of a Grammar of Assent, Part II*, London: Longmans Green.
Newton, Douglas J. (1985), *British Labour, European Socialism, and the Struggle for Peace 1889–1914*, Oxford: Oxford University Press.
Niboyet, Eugénie (February 15, 1844), in *La Paix des deux mondes*: 1–2
Niboyet, Eugénie (June 27, 1844), in *La Paix des deux mondes*: 1–2
Niboyet, Eugénie (July 4, 1844), in *La Paix des deux mondes*: 1
Nicolson, Harold (1933), *Peacemaking 1919: Being Reminiscences of the Paris Peace Conference*, Boston: Houghton Mifflin.
Nietzsche, Friedrich (2001), *The Gay Science*, Cambridge: Cambridge University Press.
Norgren, Jill (2007), *Belva Lockwood: The Woman Who Would be President*, New York: New York University Press.
Nye, R.A. (2007), "Western Maculinities in War and Peace," *The American Historical Review* 112 (2): 417–38.
Obkircher, Walther, ed. (1939), *General Erich von Gündell: Aus seinem Tagebüchen*, Hamburg: Hanseatische Verlagsanstalt.
Offen, Karen (1984), "Depopulation, Nationalism and Feminism in Fin-de-Siêcle France," in *The American Historical Review* 89 (3).
Olusoga, David (2014), *The World's War*, London: Head of Zeus.
Ossietzky, Carl von (1924), "Die Pazifisten," *Das Tage-Buch*, November 8, reprinted in Wolfgang Benz (ed.) (1988), *Pazifismus in Deutschland: Dokumente zur Friedensbewegung 1890–1939*, 13–14, Frankfurt: Fischer Taschenbuch Verlag.
Osterhammel, Jürgen (2014), *The Transformation of the World: A Global History of the Nineteenth Century*, Princeton: Princeton University Press.
"Österreichische Friedensgesellschaft" (1910), *Die Friedens-Warte*, 12.
Owen, Wilfred ([1917] 1983) "Anthem for Doomed Youth," in Wilfred Owen, *The Complete Poems and Fragments*, ed. Jon Stallworthy, I, p. 99, London: Chatto & Windus,
Pakenham, Thomas (1990), *The Scramble for Africa: The White Man's Conquest of the Dark Continent from 1876 to 1912*, New York: Random House.
Patterson, David S. (1976), *Toward a Warless World: The Travail of the American Peace Movemement 1887–1914*, Bloomington: Indiana University Press.
Patterson, David S. (2008), *The Search for a Negotiated Peace: Women's Activism and Diplomacy in World War 1*, New York: Routledge.
Patterson, David S. (2014), *Pacifism* in *1914–1918-Online: International Encyclopaedia of the First World War*, ed. Ute Daniel *et al.*, Freie Universität Berlin, 2014-10–18 DOI: 10.15463/ie1418.10125.
Peace Pledge Union (1938), *Peace News*, May 28.
Peace Society (1822), *Sixth Annual Report*.
Peace Society (1823), *Seventh Annual Report*.

Peace Society (1894), *Herald of Peace*, a. March 1; b. May 1; c. July 2.
Peace Society (1896), *Herald of Peace*, a. April 1; b. October 1.
Peace Society (1897), *Herald of Peace*, a. September 1; b. October 1.
Peace Society (1899), *Herald of Peace*, a. June 1; b. "Christmas Supplement".
Peace Society (1900), *Herald of Peace*, April 2.
Peace Society (1901), *Herald of Peace*, February 1.
Peace Society (1902), *Herald of Peace*, a. June 2; b. July 1; c. August 1.
Peace Society (1910), *Annual Report, 1909–10*.
Peace Society (1911), *Annual Report, 1910–11*.
Peace Society (1913), *Annual Report, 1912–13*.
Pearce, Cyril (2001), *Comrades in Conscience*, London: Francis Boutle.
Peet, Hubert W. ([1919] 1940), "The Men Sentenced to Death," in *Troublesome People*, London: Central Board for Conscientious Objectors.
Perkins, Gary (2016), *Bible Student Conscientious Objectors in World War I Britain*, Borwick, Lancashire: Hupomone Press.
Perris, George H. ([1911] n.d.), *A Short History of War and Peace*, London: William and Norgate.
Peterson, H.C. and Gilbert C. Fite (1957), *Opponents of War 1917–1918*, Madison: University of Wisconsin Press.
Petricioli, Marta, Donatella Cherubini, and Alessandra Anteghini, eds. (2004), *Les Etats-Unis d'Europe—The United States of Europe, Un Projet Pacifiste—A Pacifist Project*, Bern: Peter Lang.
Phelps, Christina (1930), *The Anglo-American Peace Movement in the Mid-Nineteenth Century*, New York: Columbia University Press.
Pick, Daniel (1989), *Faces of Degeneration: A European Disorder, c. 1848–c. 1918*, Cambridge: Cambridge University Press.
Piguet, Marie-France (1993), "L'Europe des Européens chez le comte de Saint-Simon," *Mots: Les languages du politique* 34 (1): 7–24.
Pirenne, Jacques-Henri (1946–9), *La Sainte-Alliance. Organisation européenne de la paix internationale*, 2 vols., Neuchâtel: Ed. de la Baconnière.
Pitts, Jennifer (2018), *Boundaries of International: Law and Empire*, Cambridge, MA: Harvard University Press.
Playne, Caroline Elisabeth (1936), *Bertha von Suttner and the Struggle to Avert the World War*, London: George Allen & Unwin.
Porter, Charles W. (1936), *The Career of Théophile Delcassé*, Philadelphia: University of Pennsylvania Press.
Potonié-Pierre, Eugénie (1895), letter to Elie Ducommun, in Bureau International de la Paix, V.A. 4, Correspondence.
Pyne, Thomas (Anon.) (1840), *An Address to all Nations by a Clergyman of the Church of England*, London.
Pypin, A.N. (2000), "Imperator Aleksandr i kvakery" [Emperor Alexander and the Quakers], in Pypin *Religioznye dviženija pri Aleksandre I* [Religious Movements under Alexander I], 398–416, Saint Petersburg: Akademičeskij Proekt.
Quataert, Jean (2014), "International Law and the Laws of War," *International Encyclopedia of the First World War, Online 1914–18*: https://encyclopedia.1914-1918-online.net/article/international_law_and_the_laws_of_war (accessed August 23, 2017).
Quidde, Ludwig (1939), "The Creation of the Inter-Parliamentary Union," in *The Inter-Parliamentary Union from 1889–1930. A Publication Issued by the Inter-Parliamentary Union Bureau to Commemorate the Fiftieth Anniversary of the Union*, Lausanne: Payot.

Rambaud, Renée (1901), "La Paix et le désarmement par les femmes," *La Fronde*, June 19.

Ravlo, Hilde, Nils Petter Gleditsch, and Han Dorussen (2003), "Colonial War and the Democratic Peace," *Journal of Conflict Resolution* 47 (4): 520–48.

Recchia, Stefano and Nadia Urbinati (2009), "Giuseppe Mazzini's International Political Thought," in *A Cosmopolitanism of Nations: Giuseppe Mazzini's Writings on Democracy, Nation Building, and International Relations*, ed. S. Recchia and N. Urbinati, 16–30, Princeton: Princeton University Press.

Riesenberger, Dieter (1999), "Katholische Militarismuskritik im Kaiserreich," in Wolfram Wette (ed.), *Militarismus in Deutschland 1871 bis 1945: Zeitgenössische Analysen und Kritik*, 97–114, Munich: Lit.

Robbins, Keith (1976), *The Abolition of War*, Cardiff: University of Wales Press.

Robinson, Ellen et al. (February 5, 1895), "Appel aux françaises," handwritten copy in Bureau International de la Paix, V A 4.6.

Robinson, James Harvey, ed. (1904–5), *Readings in European History*, 2 vols., Boston: Ginn and Co.

Robinson, Jo Ann (1973), "A. J. Muste and Ways to Peace," in Charles Chatfield (ed.), *Peace Movements in America*, 81–94, New York: Schocken Books.

Rogers, J. Guinness (1898), "The Tsar's Proposed Conference and our Foreign Affairs. II," *Nineteenth Century* 261 (November): 707.

Rogers, W.P. (1905), "War, Arbitration and Peace," *Michigan Law Review* 4 (2): 91–108, doi:10.2307/1272478.

Roper, Michael (2009), *The Secret Battle: Emotional Survival in the Great War*, Manchester: Manchester University Press.

Rosenne, Shabtai, ed. (2001), *The Hague Peace Conferences of 1899 and 1907 and International Arbitration. Reports and Documents*, The Hague: T.M.C. Asser Press.

Rossi, Marco (2014), *Gli ammutinati delle trincee: Dalla guerra di Libia al primo conflitto mondiale*, Pisa: BFS Edizioni.

Rousseau, Jean-Jacques (1795), *Extrait du projet de paix perpetulle de Monsieur l'Abbé de Saint-Pierre* (Amsterdam, 1761); Immanuel Kant, *Zum ewigen Frieden: Ein philosophischer Entwurf*, Königsberg.

Royden, Maude (1915), "The Nature of the Christian Obedience," in Joan M. Fry (ed.), *Christ and Peace*, 34–44, London: Headley.

Royer, Clémence (March 28, 1898), "Le Parti de la Guerre," *La Fronde*, 2–3.

Royer, Clémence (August 10, 1900), editorial, *La Fronde*, 1.

Ruddick, Sara (1989), *Maternal Thinking: Towards a Politics of Peace*, Boston: Beacon Press.

Rupp, Leila (1997), *Worlds of Women: The Making of an International Women's Movement*, Princeton: Princeton University Press.

Russell, Bertrand (1915), "The Ethics of War," *The International Journal of Ethics* (January), 127–42.

Rybachenok, I.S. (2005), *Rossiia i pervaia konferentsiia mira 1899 goda v Gaage*, Moscow, Russian Academy of Sciences.

Saint-Simon, Claude-Henri de (1807), *Introduction aux travaux scientifiques du XIXe siècle*, in *Oeuvres de Claude-Henri de Saint-Simon* (1966), vol. 6: 129.

Saint-Simon, Claude-Henri de and Auguste Thierry (1966), *De la réorganisation de la société européenne ou de la nécessité et des moyens* (1814), in *Oeuvres de Claude-Henri de Saint-Simon*, 6 vols., Paris: Anthropos, vol. I: 204.

Salter, Alfred ([1919] 1940), "The Religion of a C.O.," in *Troublesome People*, London, Central Board for Conscientious Objectors.

Sarkin, Jeremy (2007), "The Historical Origins, Convergence and Interrelationship of International Human Rights Law, International Humanitarian Law, International Criminal Law and Public International Law and their Application Since the Nineteenth Century," *Human Rights and International Legal Discourse* 125: 125–72.

Schelling, F.W.J. ([1809] 2006), *Philosophical Investigations into the Nature of Human Freedom (1809)*, Albany: State University of New York Press.

Schircks, Rhea (n.d.), *Die Martens'sche Klause. Rezeption und Rechtsqualität*, Baden-Baden: Nomos Verlagsgesellschaft.

Schott, Linda (1993), "Jane Addams and William James on Alternatives to War," *Journal of the History of Ideas* 54 (2): 241–54.

Schreiner, Olive (1911), *Woman and Labour*, London: T Fisher Unwin. Online digitised edition: https://archive.org/details/womanlabour00schrrich (accessed August 24, 2017).

Schulz, Matthias (2015), "Paradoxes of a Great Power Peace: The Case of the Concert of Europe," in Thomas Hippler and Miloš Vec (eds.), *Paradoxes of Peace in Nineteenth Century Europe*, 131–52, Oxford: Oxford University Press.

Schwimmer, Rosika (1913), "Twenty-five Years Peace Palace—August 28, 1913" (typed mansucript), Rosika Schwimmer Papers, New York Public Library, Folder 8.

Scott, James Brown (1908), "The Work of the Second Hague Peace Conference," *American Journal of International Law* January: 1–28.

Scott, James Brown (1909), *The Hague Peace Conferences of 1899 and 1907: A Series of Lectures Delivered Before the Johns Hopkins University in the Year 1908*, 2 vols., Baltimore: Johns Hopkins University Press.

Scott, James Brown (1916), *Resolutions of the Institute of International Law Dealing with the Law of Nations with an Historical Introduction and Explanatory Notes*, New York: Oxford University Press.

Scott, James Brown, ed. (1920), *Proceedings of the International Peace Conference. The Hague, May 18–July 29, 1899*, Washington, DC: Carnegie Endowment for International Peace.

Scott, Joan W. (1986), "Gender: A Useful Category of Historical Analysis," *The American Historical Review* 1/5 (December): 1053–75.

Scott Holland, Henry (1915), *A Bundle of Memories*, London: Wells Gardner.

Scriboni, Mirella (2008), *Abbasso la guerra! Voci di donne da Adua al Primo conflitto mondiale, 1896–1915*, Pisa: BS edizioni.

Sédouy, Jacques-Alain de (2009), *Le concert européen: Aux origines de l'Europe, 1814–1914*, Paris: Fayard.

Seigfried, Charlene Haddock (2013), "The Social Self in Jane Addams's Prefaces and Introductions," *Transactions of the Charles S Pierce Society* 49 (2): 127–56.

Selenka, Margarethe Leonore ([1899] 1994), "Women's International Demonstration for the Peace Conference, 1899," in Charles Chatfield and Rusanna Ilukhina (eds.), *An Anthology of Historic Alternatives to War*, Syracuse: Syracuse University Press.

Selenka, Margarethe Leonore (1900), *Die internationale Kundgebung der Frauen zur Friedens-Konferenz vom 15 mai 1899. La Manifestation Internationale des Femmes pour la Conférence de la Paix du 15 mai 1899. The International Demonstration of Women for the Peace Conference of 15 May 1899*, Munich: August Schripp.

Sewall, May Wright (1901), *Mémoire envoyé aux présodents de conseils nationaus des femmes*, Indiana.

Shand, James D. (1975), "Doves among the Eagles: German Pacifists and Their Government during World War I," *Journal of Contemporary History* 10 (1): 95–108.

Sharp, Ingrid (2013a), "Feminist Peace Activism 1915–2010: Are We Nearly There Yet?" *Peace and Change* 38 (2): 155–80.

Sharp, Ingrid (2013b), "'A foolish dream of sisterhood': Anti-Pacifist Debates in the German Women's Movement 1914–1919," in Christa Hämmerle, Oswald Überegger, and Brigitta Bader Zaar (eds.), *Gender and the First World War*, 195–213, Basingstoke: Palgrave Macmillan.

Sharp, Ingrid, Judit Acsady, and Nikolai Vukov (2017), "Internationalism, Pacifism, Transnationalism: Women's Movements and the Building of a Sustainable Peace in the Post-War World," in Ingrid Sharp and Matthew Stibbe (eds.), *Women Activists between War and Peace: Europe 1918–1923*, 77–122, London: Bloomsbury.

Shepela, Anja (2005), "Bertha von Suttner: Eine Frau steht ihren Mann," in Peter Pabisch (ed.), *Patentlösung oder Zankapfel? "German Studies" für den internationalen Bereich als Alternative zur Germanistik—Beispiele aus Amerika*, 227–50, Bern: Peter Lang.

Sheplar, Sherry R. and Anna A. Mattina (2012), "Paying the Price for Pacifism: The Press's Rhetorical Shift from Saint Jane to the Most Dangerous Woman in America," *Feminist Formations* 24 (1): 154–71.

Showalter, Elaine (2016), *The Civil Wars of Julia Ward Howe*, New York: Simon & Schuster.

Sklar, Kathryn Kish (2003), "'Some of Us who Deal with the Social Fabric': Jane Addams Blends Peace and Social Justice 1907–1919," *The Journal of the Gilded Age and Progressive Era* 2 (1): 80–96.

Sluga, Glenda (2013a), "The International Turn," in *Internationalism in the Age of Nationalism*, 11–44, Philadelphia: University of Pennsylvania Press.

Sluga, Glenda (2013b), *Internationalism in the Age of Nationalism*, Philadelphia: University of Pennsylvania Press.

Somsen, Geert (2012), "Holland's Calling: Dutch Scientists' Self-Fashioning as International Mediators," in Rebecka Letteval, Gert Somsen, and Sven Widmalm (eds.), *Neutrality in Twentieth-Century Europe*, New York: Routledge.

Somsen, Geert (2013), "Global Government through Science: Pieter Eijkman's Plans for a World Capital," in R.W. Boyd (ed.), *Information Beyond Borders: International Cultural and Intellectual Exchange in the Belle Époque*, London: Taylor & Francis.

Sorel, Albert (1904), *L'Europe et la Révolution française. 8, La coalition, les traités de 1815*, Paris: Plon.

Staël, Germaine de (1795), *Réflexions sur la paix, adressées à M. Pitt et aux Français*, Paris.

Stanton, H.E. (n.d.), *Will You March Too?*, unpublished manuscript diary, Leeds University, Liddle Collection WW1/CO/092.

Stead, William T. (1899), "Conversations with M. Bloch," reprinted in Gwyn Prins and Hylke Tromp (eds.), (2000), *The Future of War*, The Hague: 19–25.

Stengel, Karl von (1899), *Der ewige Friede*, Paris: H. le Soudier.

Stibbe, Matthew, Olga Shnyrova, and Veronika Helfert (2017), "Women and Socialist Revolution, 1917–1923," in Ingrid Sharp and Matthew Stibbe (eds.), *Women Activists between War and Peace: Europe 1918–1923*, 123–72, London: Bloomsbury.

Stöcker, Helene (2015), *Lebenserinnerungen Die unvollendete Autobiographie einer frauenbewegten Pazifistin*, eds. Reinhold Lütgemeier-Davin and Kirsten Wolff, Cologne: Böhlau.

Summers, Anne (2006), "Which Women? What Europe? Josephine Butler and the International Abolitionist Federation," *History Workshop Journal* 62 (1): 214–31.

Sun Yat-Sen (1941), *China and Japan: Natural Friends—Unnatural Enemies: A Guide for China's Foreign Policy*, Shanghai: China United Press.

Suttner, Bertha von [B. Oulot] (1877), "Schürze und Fächer," *Die Presse*, August 5: 1–2.
Suttner, Bertha von ([1888] 2000), "Brief an Irma von Troll-Borostyáni" (October), reprinted in Biedermann, Edelgard, "Eine Genossin des leibhaftigen Gottseibeiuns? Zu Bertha von Suttners Briefwechsel mit Irma von Troll-Borostyáni—1886–1890," in Kurt Bäckström *et al.* (eds.), *Österreichische Sprache, Literatur und Gesellschaft. Symposium zu Fragen des akademischen Sprachunterrichts*, 139–51, Münster: Nodus Publikation.
Suttner, Bertha von [Jemand] (1889a), *Das Machinenalter: Zukunftsvorlesungen über unsere Zeit*, Dresden: E. Pierson.
Suttner, Bertha von (1889b), *Die Waffen nieder! Ein Lebensgeschichte*, 2 vols., Dresden: E. Pierson.
Suttner, Bertha von (1891), "Der nächste Kongress in Rom", *Neue Freie Presse*, September 3: 1–2.
Suttner, Bertha von (1892), "Unsere Plattform," *Die Waffen nieder* (August): 48–58.
Suttner, Bertha von (1893), "Was wir wollen," *Die Waffen nieder* (January): 20–3.
Suttner, Bertha von (1898), "Schlusswort," *Die Waffen nieder*, (December), 119.
Suttner, Bertha von (1899), *Das Machinenzeitalter. Zukunftsvorlesungen über unsere Zeit*, Dresden: E. Pierson.
Suttner, Bertha von ([1900] n.d.), *Krieg und Frieden: Vortrag gehalten am 5.2.1900 im grossen Kaimsaale zu München*, Munich: A. Schupp.
Suttner, Bertha von (1900b), *Die Haager Friedensconferenz. Tagebuchblätter*, Dresden: E. Pierson.
Suttner, Bertha von (1901), *Die Haager Friedenskonferenz: Tagebuchblätter*, Dresden: E. Pierson's Verlag.
Suttner, Bertha von (1904), *Der Krieg und seine Bekämpfung*, Berlin: Continent.
Suttner, Bertha von (1906), "The Evolution of the Peace Movement," Nobel Peace Prize speech, April. Available online: http://www.nobelprize.org/nobel_prizes/peace/laureates/1905/suttner-lecture.html (accessed January 2, 2017).
Suttner, Bertha von (1909a), *Memoiren*, ed. Lieselotte von Reinken, Bremen: Carl Schünemann.
Suttner, Bertha von (1909b), "What Universal Peace Really Means," *Chicago Daily Tribune*, June 20: B5.
Suttner, Bertha von (1910), *Memoirs of Bertha von Suttner: The Records of Eventful Lives*, 2 vols., New York: Ginn.
Suttner, Bertha von (1912), "United Press Agency dispatch dated 20 April 1912," reprinted in *Advocate of Peace* 74/5 (May): 111.
Suttner, Bertha von (1914), "Letzter Brief an die deutschen Frauen," ed. Frauenbund der Deutschen Friedensgesellschaft, in Swarthmore College Peace Collection, Bertha von Suttner Collected Papers (CDG-B), Box 2.
Suttner, Bertha von (1917), *Der Kampf um die Vermeidung des Weltkriegs. Randglossen aus zwei Jahrzehnten zu den Zeitereignissen vor der Katastrophe (1892–1900 und 1907–1914)*, ed. Dr. Alfred H. Fried, Vol. I, Zurich.
Suttner, Bertha von [n.d.], *Die Waffen nieder. Roman*, with an Introduction by Friedrich Heer, Vienna: H. Javorsky.
Swartz, Marvin (1971), *The Union of Democratic Control in British Politics during the First World War*, Oxford: Clarendon Press.
Synge, Charles and Christopher Bowen (1868), *The "Alabama" Claims and Arbitration Considered from a Legal Point of View*, London: Longmans, Green and Co.
Tate, Merze (1942), *The Disarmament Illusion: The Movement for a Limitation of Armaments to 1907*, New York: Macmillan.

Taylor, A.J.P. (1957), *The Trouble Makers: Dissent over Foreign Policy, 1792–1939*, London: Hamish Hamilton.

Tirefort, Alain, ed. (2016), *Guerres et paix en Afrique noire et à Madagascar: XIXe et XXe siècles*, Rennes: Presses Universitaires de Rennes.

Tolstoy, L.N. ([1869] 2010), *War and Peace*, Oxford: Oxford University Press.

Tosh, John (2005), "Masculinities in an Industrialising Society: Britain, 1800–1914," *Journal of British Studies* 44 (2): 330–42.

Traz, Robert de (1936), *De l'Alliance des rois à la Ligue des peuples: Sainte-Alliance et SDN*, Paris: Grasset.

Treaty of Portsmouth (September 5, 1905), in Sydney Tyler, *The Japan–Russia War: An Illustrated History of the War in the Far East: The Greatest Conflict of Modern Times*, 564–8. Philadelphia: P.W. Ziegler.

"Tsar's rescript" (1909), reprinted in James Brown Scott (ed.), *The Hague Peace Conferences of 1899 and 1907: A Series of Lectures Delivered before the Johns Hopkins University in the Year 1908*, Vol. 2 Baltimore: Johns Hopkins University Press.

Tuchman, Barbara W. ([1966] 1996), *The Proud Tower: A Portrait of the World Before the War 1890–1914*, New York: Ballantine Books.

Tuider, Bernhard (2009), "Alfred Hermann Fried—ein 'Adlatus' oder 'Inspirator' von Bertha von Suttner? Neue Perspektiven auf die Beziehung zweier Leitfiguren der österreichischen Friedensbewegung," *Wiener Zeitschrift zur Geschichte der Neuzeit* 9/2: 134–62.

Tylee, Claire (1988), "'Maleness run riot'—The Great War and Women's Resistance to Militarism," *Women's Studies International Forum* 11 (3): 199–210.

Tyrell, Alex (1987), *Joseph Sturge and the Moral Radical Party in Early Victorian Britain*, London: Christopher Helm.

UNESCO (2017), "Culture of Peace and Nonviolence": http://en.unesco.org/cultureofpeace/ (accessed August 23, 2017).

Valone, Stephen J. (1988), "'There Must Be Some Misunderstanding': Sir Edward Grey's Diplomacy of August 1, 1914," *Journal of British Studies* 27, (4): 405–24.

van der Linden, W.H. (1987), *The International Peace Movement 1815–1874*, Amsterdam: Tilleul Publications.

van Reenan, Rykie, ed. (1984), *Emily Hobhouse, Boer War Letter*, Cape Town: Human and Rousseau.

Vellacott, Jo (1987), "Feminist Consciousness and the First World War," in R. Pierson (ed.), *Women and Peace: Theoretical, Historical and Practical Perspectives*, 114–36, London: Croom Helm.

Vellacott, Jo (2001), "Feminism As If All People Mattered: Working to Remove the Causes of War, 1919–1929," *Contemporary European History*, Theme Issue: Gender and War in Europe c. 1918–1949, 10 (3): 375–94.

Veseth, Frøydis Eleonora (2000), *Women and the Nobel Peace Prize Laureates and Nominees from 1901 to 1951*, unpublished MS, Hovedoppgae Vår.

Wagenknecht, Edward (1966), *Henry Wadsworth Longfellow*, Oxford: Oxford University Press.

Wallis, Jill (1991), *Valiant for Peace: A History of the Fellowship of Reconciliation 1914–1989*, London: Fellowship of Reconciliation.

Wank, Solomon (1988), "The Austrian Peace Movement and the Habsburg Ruling Elite, 1906–1914," in Charles Chatfield and Peter van den Dungen (eds.), *Peace Movements and Political Cultures*, Knoxville: University of Tennessee Press.

Ward, Adolpus W. and George P. Gooch (1923), *Cambridge History of British Foreign Policy 1783–1919. Volume III: 1866–1919*, Cambridge: Cambridge University Press.

Waszklewicz-van Schilfgaarde, Johanna, ed. (1900–2), *Vrede door Recht (Peace Through Law)*, Amsterdam.

Webster, Andrew (2017), "Reconsidering Disarmament at the Hague Peace Conference of 1899, and After," in Maartje Abbenhuis, Christopher Ernest Barber, and Annalise R. Higgins (eds.), *War, Peace and International Order? The Legacies of the Hague Conferences of 1899 and 1907*, New York: Routledge.

Wehberg, Hans (1939), "The Inter-Parliamentary Union and the Development of International Organization," in *The Inter-Parliamentary Union from 1889–1930. A Publication Issued by the Inter-Parliamentary Union Bureau to Commemorate the Fiftieth Anniversary of the Union*, Lausanne: Payot.

Weisser, Henry (1975), *British Working-Class Movements and Europe 1815–48*, Manchester: Manchester University Press.

Wernitznig, Dagmar (2015), "'No Documents, No History': A Political Biography of Rosika Schwimmer (1877–1948)," DPhil diss., Oxford University.

Wette, Wolfram (2017), *Ernstfall Frieden: Lehren aus der deutschen Geschichte seit 1914*, Bremen: Donat.

White, Andrew Dickson (1905), *Autobiography*, vol. 2, New York: The Century.

White, Andrew (1912), *The First Hague Conference. Reprinted from Dr White's Autobiography*, Boston: World Peace Foundation.

Wickert, Christl (1991), *Helene Stöcker 1869–1943 Frauenrechtlerin, Sexualreformerin und Pazifistin. Eine Biographie*, Bonn: Dietz.

Wilkinson, Alan ([1986] 2010), *Dissent or Conform? War, Peace and the English Churches, 1900–1945*, Cambridge: Lutterworth Press.

Wilkinson, Alan ([1978] 2014), *The Church of England and the First World War*, Cambridge: Lutterworth Press.

Wilmers, Annika (2008), *Pazifismus in der internationalen Frauenbewegung 1914–1920*, Klartext: Essen.

WILPF (1919), "2nd Congress Resolutions, Zurich, Switzerland": http://wilpf.org/resolutions-from-wilpfs-triennial-congresses/ (accessed August 28, 2017).

Wiltsher, Anne (1985), *Most Dangerous Women: Feminist Peace Campaigners of the Great War*, London: Pandora Press.

Winkler, Henry (1952), *The League of Nations Movement in Great Britain, 1914–1919*, New Brunswick: Rutgers University Press.

Winter, Jay M. (1980), "Military Fitness and Civilian Health in Britain during the First World War," *Journal of Contemporary History* 15 (2): 211–44: http://www.jstor.org/stable/260511 (accessed August 23, 2017).

Winter, Jay (2006), *Dreams of Peace and Freedom: Utopian Moments in the Twentieth Century*, New Haven: Yale University Press.

Wohlstand für Alle (Vienna) (1914), July 8–29: 6.

Workmen's Peace Association (1895), *Arbitrator*, January.

World Alliance (1915), *Goodwill* 1 (1).

Wylie, Neville (2017), "Muddied Waters: The Influence of the First Hague Peace Conference on the Evolution of the Geneva Conventions of 1864 and 1906," in Maartje Abbenhuis, Christopher Ernest Barber, and Annalise R. Higgins (eds.), *War, Peace and International Order? The Legacies of the Hague Conferences of 1899 and 1907*, New York: Routledge.

Zeiger, Susan (2002), "Teaching Peace: Lessons from a Peace Studies Curriculum," *Peace and Change* 25 (1): 52–69.

Ziegler, Valerie H. (1992), *The Advocates of Peace in Antebellum America*, Bloomington: Indiana University Press.

Zimmermann, Susan (2015), "The Politics of Exclusionary Inclusion: Peace Activism and the Struggle on International and Domestic Political Order in the International Council of Women, 1899–1914," in Thomas Hippler and Miloš Vec (eds.), *Paradoxes of Peace in Nineteenth Century Europe*, 189–218, Oxford: Oxford University Press.

Zweig, Stefan (1918), "Berta v. Suttner: Eine Ansprache anläßlich der Eröffnung des Internationalen Kongresses für Völkerverständigung in Bern," *Neue Freie Presse*, June 21: 1–4.

Zweig, Stefan ([1943] 1964), *The World of Yesterday: An Autobiography*, Lincoln: University of Nebraska Press.

CONTRIBUTORS

Dr Maartje Abbenhuis is Associate Professor in Modern History at the University of Auckland, New Zealand. She works on the history of war, peace, neutrality, and internationalism, with a particular focus on Europe in the period 1815–1919. She is the author of three monographs: *The Art of Staying Neutral: The Netherlands in the First World War, 1914–1918* (Amsterdam University Press, 2006); *An Age of Neutrals: Great Power Politics 1815–1914* (Cambridge University Press, 2014); and *The Hague Conferences in International Politics 1898–1915* (Bloomsbury, 2018). She is about to start a new research project with the working title "Dum-dum: the global history of a bullet."

Clive Barrett is Chair of Trustees of the Peace Museum, Bradford, and active in the International Network of Museums for Peace. An Anglican priest and Visiting Fellow in Theology and Religious Studies at the University of Leeds, he has published on peace movement history, ecumenism, and international peace museums. He is the author of *Subversive Peacemakers: War-Resistance 1914–1918, an Anglican Perspective* (Lutterworth Press, 2014).

Martin Ceadel is Emeritus Fellow of New College and Professor of Politics at the University of Oxford where he taught from 1979 to 2015. The most recent of his five single-authored books with Oxford University Press is *Living the Great Illusion: Sir Norman Angell, 1872–1967* (2009). He is currently working on a comparison between the peace movement and other progressive campaigns in modern Britain and on a study of how the UK acquired the political system it did.

Sandi E. Cooper is Professor Emerita in Modern European History at the College of Staten Island and The Graduate School—City University of New York. She is the former Chair of the Coordinating Committee on Women in History and The Berkshire Conference of Women Historians, University Faculty Senate—CUNY. She has written widely on peace movements, women and peace, and higher education in the United States peace history, including *Patriotic Pacifism: Waging War on War in Europe, 1815–1914* (Oxford University Press, 1991) and "French Feminists and Pacifists, 1889–1914: The Evolution of New Visions," *Peace and Change* 36.1 (Jan. 2011) 5–33.

Laurie R. Cohen is currently a high school history teacher in Lübeck, Germany. After completing her Dr. phil. in East European History (University of Vienna), authoring a monograph on everyday life in Smolensk under Nazi German occupation and co-authoring another on the long nineteenth century with a focus on neighboring Austrian–Russian border towns (currently in Ukraine), she moved her focus to peace studies. Since 2009 she has taught history and gender studies at the University of Innsbruck. Relevant to this publication is her edited volume *"Gerade weil Sie eine Frau sind . . ." Erkundungen über Bertha von Suttner, die unbekannte Friedensnobelpreisträgerin* (Braumüller, 2005).

Stella Ghervas is Professor of Russian History at Newcastle University and Associate of the Department of History at Harvard University. Her main interests are in the intellectual and international history of modern Europe, with special reference to the history of peace and peace-making, and in Russia's intellectual and maritime history. She is the author of *Réinventer la Tradition: Alexandre Stourdza et l'Europe de la Sainte-Alliance* (Honoré Champion, 2008) and *Conquering Peace: From the Enlightenment to the European Union* (Harvard University Press, forthcoming 2019), and the co-editor of *Lieux d'Europe: Mythes et limites* (Maison des Sciences de l'Homme, 2008) and *A Cultural History of Peace in the Age of Enlightenment 1648–1815* (Bloomsbury, 2019).

Jeff Love is Research Professor of German and Russian at Clemson University. He has published two books on Tolstoy, *The Overcoming of History in "War and Peace"* (Rodopi, 2004) and *Tolstoy: A Guide for the Perplexed* (Continuum, 2008). He is also the co-translator of *Schelling's Philosophical Investigations into the Essence of Human Freedom* (SUNY Press, 2006), co-editor of *Nietzsche and Dostoevsky: Philosophy, Morality, Tragedy* (Northwestern University Press, 2016), and editor of *Heidegger in Russian and Eastern Europe* (Rowman & Littlefield, 2017). His most recent book is *The Black Circle: A Life of Alexandre Kojève* (Columbia University Press, 2018).

Ingrid Sharp is Professor of German Cultural and Gender History in the School of Languages, Cultures and Societies at the University of Leeds. She is currently researching cultures of resistance in Germany during and after World War I and leading a project on women's role in the German Revolution of November 1918. Recent publications include two volumes co-edited with Matthew Stibbe, *Women Activists between War and Peace: Europe 1918–1923* (Bloomsbury, 2017) and *Women's International Activism during the Inter-War Period, 1919–1939* (Routledge, 2018).

INDEX

Page numbers in **bold** refer to figures.

Abbenhuis, Maartje, 7
abolitionist movement, 15
absolute monarchs, 24
Abyssinia, 30
Académie française, 24
Addams, Jane, 14, 16, 45, **45**, 49–55, **54**, **55**, 69, 125
Adolf, Antony, 20
aggression, innate, 13–14
Aix-la-Chapelle, Congress of, 27
Alabama (privateer), 36, 122
Aleramo, Sibilla, 68
Alexander I, Tsar, 24, 26, 27, 27–8, **27**
Algeria, 32, 58, 61
Allegret, Jean, 118–19
alma dolens, 67–8
American Civil War, 36, 59, 114
American Journal of International Law, The, 107
American Peace Society, 57, 113–14, 120, 122
Amerindian populations, 32
anarchists, 93
Angell, Norman, 10, 44, 54, 71, 125
arbitration, 36, 62, 82–3, 84, 93
arms race, 37
Arnaud, Émile, 34, 87, 92, 119, 126
Association de la paix par le droit, 118
Association Internationale des Femmes, 60
Augspurg, Anita, 47–8, 62–3, **63**, 127, **127**
Austria, peace societies, 10
Austrian Peace Society, 93, 99–100, 101, 103, 119

Bakunin, Mikhail, 11
Baricelli, Camilla, 67
Barker, Canon William, 84–5
Barnett, Canon Samuel Augustus, 85
Basel, International Socialist Congress, 1912, 12–13
Becker, Lydia, 60
Belloc, Hilaire, 30–1

Benham, William, 82
Bentham, Jeremy, 112
Berlin, Isaiah, 146, 147
Bibbings, Lois, 48–9
Biedermann, Edelgard, 103
Birmingham Peace Association, 116
Bloch, Jan Gottlieb, 103
Bloch, Jean (Ivan) de, 10, 82
Bodin, Marguerite, 68
Boer War, 14, 17, 37–8, 43–4, 46, 55, 65–6, 84–5, 123, 138
Bolivar, Simon, 32
Boston School Peace League, 68
Boxer Rebellion, 64, 137, 138
Bremer, Fredrika, **58**, 59
Bright, John, 81, 92
British Peace Society, 57
  Ladies Auxiliary, 60
Brockway, Fenner, 87
Brockway, Lilla, 87
Bryce, Viscount, 124–5
Burritt, Elihu, 77–8, **78**, 80, 114, 116
Buss, Septimus, 82–3
Butler, Josephine, 15, 60

Cabet, Étienne, 10
Carlier, Madeleine, 68
Carnegie, Andrew, 86, 103, 121–2, **121**, 141
Carnegie Endowment for International Peace, 121–2
Ceadel, Martin, 8, 74, 132
censorship, 21
Central Organization for a Durable Peace, 126
change, elimination of, 145
Chartist movement, 11, **11**, 116
Cheney, Thomas, 7
Chickering, Roger, 120, 131
China, 30, 33, 64, 117
Christian pacifism, 120
Christian peace, 26
Christian traditions, 24–5

Church of England, 74
civilians, 65
civilizing mission, 31–2, 33–4
Clarkson, John, 79
Clarkson, Thomas, 78, 79
Cobden, Richard, 80, 81, 116
Cohen, Laurie, 10
colonialism, 31–2, **31**
concentration camps, 14
Concert of Europe, 3, 5, 37
conflict resolution, 36
confusion effect, the, 157
Congress System, 25–6, 27–8, 41
Conrad, Joseph, 156
conscientious objectors, 53, 88, 91–2, **91**, 119, 124, 126
    imprisonment, 88–90, **89**
conscription, 8, 19, 46, 124
Constant, Benjamin, 24, 39
Continental System, 24
"Convention for the Amelioration of the Conditions of the Wounded in Armies in the Field", 6, **6**
Cooper, Sandi, 5, 15–16, 104, 119, 129, 131–2
Cosmopolitan Clubs, 121, 125
Court of International Arbitration, 82
Cremer, Randal, 122
Crimean War, 4, 6, 6–7, 10, 37, 39, 59, 80–2, 117, 122, 123
Crook, Paul, 13
Crystal Palace, 1851 Exhibition, 2, **2**, **117**
Czartoryski, Count, 28–9

Darby, William Evans, 38, 123, 135
d'Arcis, Clara Guthrie, 72
Darwin, Charles, 9, 13, 43, 44, 106
declarations, 130
Deegan, Mary Jo, 50, 51
defencism, 112, 112–13, 117
definition, 22, 23–41, 111
    Académie française, 24
    Christian peace, 26
    colonial context, 31–2
    dark side, 28–9
    Eurocentrism, 29
    geographic scope, 29–34, **31**
    as law and order, 28–9
    as legal process, 35–8
    non-political, 24–5
    pacification, 33–4
    post-Napoleonic era, 25–9, **26**, **27**
    through law, 34–5

Delcassé, Théophile, 135
democracy, growth of, 8
Despard, Charlotte, 17
deterrence, 37–8, 111–12
Die Waffen nieder, 93, 100–2, 106
difference, and conflict, 149–50
directorial system, 28–9
disarmament, 140
Dodge, David Low, 78, 113
Dostoevsky, Fyodor, 144
Doyle, Michael W., 13
Dudink, Stephan, 43, 46
Dunant, Henry, 6, 165n8
duration, 28
Dutch Anti-War Council, 126

Eckstein, Anna, 71
Edinburgh Missionary Conference, 79
education, 9
Eiffel Tower, Paris, 2
Empire, Age of, 1–4, 23, 39
engineering metaphor, 38, 39, 40
Enlightenment, Age of, 23
equality, 22, 33
equilibrium, principle of, 28
Eurocentrism, 29
European system, 38
Evans, Alfred Bowen, 81–2
Evans, Richard, 14
evolutionary biology, 44, 52
evolutionary peace biology, 13–14, 49–55

Fabian Society, 11
Fawcett, Millicent Garrett, 65, **66**
Fellowship of Reconciliation, 19, 87, 124, 125
Ferry, Jules, 33
Fischer, Marilyn, 51
Flammarion, Sylvie, 66–7
foreign policy, 24
Fourier, Charles, 10
France, 8, **31**, 37, 39, 117–18
    annexation of Algeria, 32
    peace movements, 117, 118–19, 126–7
    women's activism, 64, 66–7, 68, 68–9, 69–70
François I, Emperor, 24
Franco-Prussian War, 60
Franz Ferdinand, Archduke, 39
freedom
    and conflict, 154
    and life, 158, 159
    overcoming, 156–8

and self-assertion, 152–4
and self-preservation, 154–6
French Empire, 23–4
French language, 28
French Revolution, 23–4, 27, 33, 41
French Revolutionary wars, 1, 4, 23
Freud, Sigmund, 50, **51**, 53, 55
Fried, Alfred Hermann, 100, 101, 119–20, **119**, 127, 139
Friend of India & Statesman, 133–4
Friends of Peace, 80

Gandhi, Mohandas, 15
Garrison, William Lloyd, 114, 120
Gaudie, Norman, 91
gender justice, 52
General German Workers' Association, 11
General Peace Convention, 1843, 115, 118
Geneva Convention, 1864, 6, **6**
genocide, 14
Gentz, Friedrich von, 28
geographic scope, 23, 29–34, **31**
German East Africa, 14
German Peace Society, 119–20, 127
Germany, 37, 44, 46, 47–8
  New Fatherland League, 18
  peace movements, 127–8
  peace societies, 10
  Social Democratic Party, 2–3
  unification of, 8
Ghervas, Stella, 22
Ginn, Edwin, 121
Gladstone, William, 122, 123
Glasgow Peace Congress, 1901, 87
global ecumenical movement, 79
God
  Kingdom of, 87–8
  law of, 34–5
  responsibility to, 76
Goegg, Marie, 59–60
Gooch, G. P., 141
good offices, 36
Gore, Charles, 85
Gouges, Olympe de, 15
Great Britain, 8
  Boer War, 37–8, 43–4, 55, 65–6, 84–5, 123
  Chartist movement, 11, **11**
  inability to ratify the Declaration of London, 140
  invasion threat, 113
  No Conscription Fellowship, 19
  peace movements, 114–17, 122–3, 124–5

Great Exhibition, London, 1851, 2, **2**, **117**
Griess-Traut, Virginie, 61
Grossman, Rudolf, 120

Haeckel, Ernst, 13, 14
Hagemann, Karen, 46
Hague conferences, 128, 129–42
  1899, 4, 6, 7, 37, 55, 62–3, 103–5, 129, 130, **131**, 132–9, **133**, **135**, **136**, 139
  1907, 4, 6, 7, 38, 55, 129, 139–41
  achievements, 130–1, 135–6, 140, 141
  declarations, 130
  importance of, 129–30, 131–2
  legacies, 141–2
  messages, 138
  newspaper coverage, 136–7, 138
  relevance, 132
  support, 134
  third, 141
Hallowes, Frances, 71
Hardie, Keir, 12, 17, **18**
Harvey, Edmund, 88
Heraclitus, 148, 158
Herren-Oesch, Madeleine, 130
Herzl, Theodor, 105
Heymann, Lida Gustava, 47–8, 127, **127**
Hippel, Theodor von, 15
history, Tolstoy and, 143–51, 156–8
Hobhouse, Emily, 65–6, 85
Hodgkin, Henry, 86
Holland, Henry Scott, 85
Holy Alliance, the, 4, 26–7, 41
Holy Roman Empire, 26
Howe, Julia Ward, 60–1
Hughan, Jessie Wallace, 125
Hugo, Victor, **9**, 10, 34, **35**, 118
human nature, 43–56, 55
  Addams's view of, 49–55, 56
  gendered view of, 43–4, 45–55
  as immutable, 43
  separate sphere ideology, 45–6
human rights, 22, 53, 130
humanitarianism, 130, 132

Illuminism, 27
imperialism, 14–15
India, British rule, 14
Indian mutiny, 14
indigenous peoples, 30, 32
Industrial Revolution, 37
industrialization, 1
influenza pandemic, 71

Institut de droit international, 136
institutionalization, 111, 111–13
International Arbitration and Peace
 Association, 83, 122
International Arbitration and Peace Society,
 99, 101
International Arbitration Associations, 82–3
International Arbitration League, 122
International Committee of Women for
 Permanent Peace, 16
International Council of Women, 15, 45,
 64–5, 71, 104, 134, 138–9
International Court of Arbitration, 4
International Labour Organization, 20
International Law, 38
International Museum of War and Peace,
 Lucerne, 82, 103
International Peace Bureau, 9, 44, 61, 61–2, 118
International Peace Congresses, 9–10, **9**
International Peace Crusade, 134
international relations, 5, 7
International Socialist Congress, Basel, 1912,
 12–13
International Suffrage Association, 69
International Suffrage Congress, 69
International Women's Conference, 1915, 16,
 16
International Women's Congress, 56
International Women's Peace Union, 62
International Women's Suffrage Alliance, 15, **66**
internationalism, 9–10, **9**, 18, 74, 80–2, **81**,
 92, 113, 129–30, 132
Inter-Parliamentary Union, 61, 100, 118,
 135–6, 138, 139
interventionism, 32
Irish potato famine, 2
Italy, 67–8, 120, 163n20

Jacobins, 28
Jacobs, Dr. Aletta, 16, 69, **70**, 72
James, William, 14, 49, 52, **53**
Japan, 30, 34
Jaurès, Jean, 12, 18
Jones, Edgar, 48
Jordan, David Starr, 125
juripacifisme, 126–7
jurisprudence, 36
just war theory, 73–4

Kant, Immanuel, 8, 23, 34, 39
Keynes, John Maynard, 19, 20
King, Martin Luther, Jr., 73, 76

Kingsley, Charles, *The Water Babies*, 3
Kitchin, G. W., 85
Knab, Cornelia, 130
Kropotkin, Petr, 49
Kuehl, Warren, 130

labor movements, 11–13, **11**
Ladd, William, 113–14
Laddey, Clara, 107
Lagerlôf, Selma, 69
Laguerre, Odette, 68
L'Alliance universelle des femmes pour la paix
 par l'education, 63–4
Lambeth Conference, 1908, 83
Lansbury, George, 87
Lassalle, Ferdinand, 11
law, 5, 28
Lawrence, T. J., 140
Lawson, Ernest, 90
League for Peace and Liberty, 9
League of Nations, 20, 22, 53
 aims, 41
 Covenant, 40, 128
 foundation, 1, 6, 19, 111
League of Nations Society, 124–5
League of Universal Brotherhood, 77–8, 116
League to Enforce Peace, 125
legal process, peace as, 35–8
Lemonnier, Charles, 118
Lenin, Vladimir Ilyich, 11, 128
Lerner, Paul, 48
liberal internationalists, 129
Liebknecht, Karl, 18, 127–8, **128**
Liebknecht, Wilhelm, 105
Ligue des femmes pour le désarmement
 international, 63–4
Ligue international de la paix et de la liberté,
 59, 60, 62, 118, 119
Lochner, Louis P., 125
London, Crystal Palace, 1851 Exhibition, 2, **2**,
 117
London, Declaration of, 140
London Peace Society, 115–17, 122–3, 124
Love, Alfred H., 120
Love, Jeff, 10
Lowell, James Russell, 74–7, **75**, 84, 90–1, 92
Lucerne, International Museum of War and
 Peace, 82, 103
Luxemburg, Rosa, 11

Machiavelli, Niccolò, 156
MacMillan, Margaret, 20, 21

Madigan, Edward, 48
Marinetti, Filippo, 68
Marx, Karl, 9, 11–12
masculinity, 14, 43–4
   military, 46
   and war, 46–7, 48–9
   and World War I, 48–9
Massachusetts Peace Society, 113
Mazzini, Giuseppe, 34–5
Mead, Edwin, 68
Mead, Lucia Ames, 68
mediation, 36
medical knowledge, 3
Mélin, Jeanne, 68–9
Metternich, Count Klemens von, 57
Mexico, 38
Meyer, Jessica, 46, 48
Middle Ages, 30
militarism, 8, 13, 67
military spending, 67–8
Mill, John Stuart, 15
Moneta, Ernesto, 120, 163n20
Monroe, James, 32
moral radicals, 116
Morson, Gary Saul, 147

Napoleon, 23–4, 143, 148, **149**, 152, 154–5, 157
Napoleon III, Emperor, 39, 117, 118
Napoleonic Wars, 1, 4, 30, 167n3
National Peace Congresses, 118–19
New England Non-Resistance Society, 114
New Fatherland League, Germany, 18
new pacifism, 86–8
New York Peace Society, 78, 113
New York Times, 52
Niboyet, Eugénie, 58–9
Nicholas II, Tsar, 7, 37, 131, 132, 140
Nicolson, Harold, 20
Nietzsche, Friedrich, 158
Nightingale, Florence, 7, **7**
Nikolai, Georg Friedrich, 14
Nobel, Alfred, 4, 10, 96, 102–3
No-Conscription Fellowship, 87, 88, 124
Nonconformist Churches, 74
non-cooperation, 15
non-violent resistance, 15
novels, socially critical, 3, 10
Nye, Robert, 46

Olive Leaf Circles, 78, 116
Olusoga, David, 14–15

Opium Wars, 14–15
Ossietzky, Carl von, 107
Ottoman Empire, 30, 37, 39
Owen, Richard, 10
Owen, Wilfred, 40

pacification, 14, 32, 33–4, 41
pacificism, 122, 123, 123–4
   failure of, 74
   scientific, 120
   socialist, 128
pacifism, 8, 10, 35, 86, 92, 106, 112, 113–14
   Addams, 51
   Christian, 120
   new, 86–8
   patriotic, 119, 120–2
   stagnation, 122
   Tolstoy's, 159–60
Paris, Eiffel Tower, 2
Paris commune, suppression of, 2
Paris Peace Congress, 1849, 9–10, **9**, 34, **35**
passivity, 143
Passy, Frédéric, 118
patriotic pacifism, 119, 120
Patterson, David S., 8
Pax Napoleonica, 24
peace activism, World War I, 19, 21
peace conferences, 3–4
Peace Congress Committee, 80, 116
peace movements, 9, 44, 111–28
   absolutist, 112, 114, 116
   Anglo-American-led, 111, 113–18
   European-led, 111, 118–23
   first, 112
   institutionalization, 111, 111–13
   leadership, 44
   reformist, 112, 115–16
   and World War I, 123–8
Peace of Nations Society, 116
Peace Palace, The Hague, 38, **38**, 103, 141
peace societies, 3–4, 8, 57
Peace Society, 78–9, 80, 82, 83, 84–5, 115
Peace Sunday, 82, 83
peace through law, 129
peace treaties, World War I, 19–20
peaceful violence, 33–4
People's Council for Democracy, 126
Percival, John, Bishop of Hereford, 83
Permanent Court of Arbitration, 6, 130, 137
Permanent Court of International Justice, 20
philanthropists, 102–3
Philipps, Sir Richard, 115

Pirquet, Peter Baron, 100
Poland, 28–9
Portsmouth, Treaty of, 34
positive peace, 53
Potonié-Pierre, Eugénie, 62
power, balance of, 30, 38
Pratt, Hodgson, 99
press, the, role of, 7
Prussia, 8, 11, 44, 118
public hygiene, 3
Pyne, Thomas, 77

Quadruple Alliance, the, 25, 27
Quakers, 28, 36, 57, 74, 77–8, 79, 80–1, 82, 88, 113, 122
Quidde, Ludwig, 137

Rankin, Jeanette, 72, **72**
Realpolitik, 37
Red Crescent, 6
Red Cross, 6, 102
Richard, Henry, 80, 116, 122, 123
Richmond Castle, 88–90, **89**
rights-based discourse, 22
Roberts, Richard, 87
Robinson, Ellen, 61–2
Rochefoucauld-Liancourt, Duc de, 58
Rogers, J. Guinness, 132–3
Rolland, Romain, 127
Roosevelt, Theodore, 34, 139
Roper, Michael, 48
Rousseau, Jean-Jacques, 23, 34, 39
Roussel, Nelly, 69–70
Royden, Maude, 87
Royer, Clémence, 64, 67
Russell, Bertrand, 108
Russell, Howard, 7
Russia, 33, 34, 128
Russian revolutions, 1917, 18, 21–2, 40
Russian–Turkish war, 96
Russo-Japanese War, 34, 138, 139–40
Ruyssen, Theodore, 126

Saint-Pierre, Abbé de, 23, 27, 28, 37
Saint-Simon, Comte de, 10, 29
Salter, Alfred, 88
Schelling, Friedrich, 158
Schiff, Paolina, 67
Schott, Linda, 52–3
Schreiner, Olive, 47, 65
Schwimmer, Rosika, 126
scientific pacifism, 120

Scodnick, Irma Melany, 67
Scott, J., 79
Scott, James Brown, 141
Scouting, 46
Second International, 12, 83, 93, 120
security, 28, 112–13
segregation, 33
Selenka, Margarethe Leonore, 62–3, 134
self-assertion, and freedom, 152–4
self-interest, extinguishment of, 143
self-preservation, and freedom, 154–6
Sellon, Count Jean-Jacques de, 58, 118
Sellon, Valentine de, 58
separate sphere ideology, 45–6
Séverine, 64
Sewell, May Wright, 65
shared vision, 22
Sharp, Ingrid, 13
Siegmund-Schültze, Friedrich, 86
Sklar, Katherine, 49, 50
slavery and the slave trade, 3, 59, 76, 80, 114
social attitudes, 22
social Darwinism, 4, 13
Social Democratic Party, Germany, 2–3
social justice, 3, 55, 59
social movements, 22
social order, 1
social problems, 2–3
social progress, 52
socialism, 10–13
socialist pacifism, 128
Société de la morale chrétienne, peace movements, 118
Société de la paix de Genève, 118
Société d'Education Pacifique, 68
Société française pour l'arbitrage entre nations, 118
Society for Abolishing War, 115
Society for the Promotion of Permanent and Universal Peace, 57
Society of Friends, *see* Quakers
Solferino, Battle of, 6, 165n8
Sorel, Albert, 27
South Africa Conciliation Committee, 85
Spanish–American war, 33
Spencer, Herbert, 13
Stead, William T., 103, 134
Stephens, William, 85
Stöcker, Helene, 45, 48
Stowe, Harriet Beecher, *Uncle Tom's Cabin*, 3, 10, 105
Sturge, Joseph, 116

suffrage, extension of, 22
Suttner, Bertha von, 4, 15, 22, 71, 93–109, **94, 96, 106, 109,** 119, 165n8
  achievement, 94–5, 106–7
  caricatures, 104
  Das Maschinenalter, 99
  death, 71
  Die Waffen nieder (journal), 93–4, 100–2, 106
  Die Waffen nieder! (Lay Down Your Arms), 3, 10, 44, 61, 62, 93, 97–9, 105
  education, 95
  feminist advocacy, 99
  Hague Peace Congress, 1899, 103–5
  Lay Down Your Arms,
  legacy, 105–9, **106**
  marriage, 96
  Nobel Peace Prize, 93–4, 102, 107
  and pacifism, 106
  peace work, 99–105
  and philanthropists, 102–3
  political vision, 108
  speeches, 102, 106
  status, 93–4, 104
  travels, 102
  unconventional approach, 93
  and women's rights, 101
  writing career, 97, 97–9
  youth and formative years, 95–7
Swain, John, **81**
Switzerland, 18
system of war, 37

Taylor, A. J. P., 112
Taylor, Jeremy, 82
Temple, William, 87
Thomas, Norman, 125
Thoreau, Henry David, 75
Tolstoy, Leo, 22, 105, 120, 143–60, **144, 145, 160**
  Anna Karenina, 143
  approach to history, 143–51, 156–8
  calculus, 143–6, 146–8, 149, 150
  and freedom, 152–8, 159
  The Kingdom of God Is Within You, 143
  pacifism, 159–60
  Resurrection, 143
  status, 143
  War and Peace, 10, 143, **144**, 145–6, 146–8, 151, **151**, 152–8, **153**, 156–8, 159, 160
Tosh, John, 46

trade fairs, 2, **2**
Trades Union Congress, 11
transport, development of, 1
Treitschke, Heinrich von, 55
Trueblood, Benjamin H., 120
Tuchman, Barbara, 130, 136
Tyneside International Arbitrational and Peace Association, 85

UNESCO, 53
Union internationale des femmes pour la paix, 62
Union of Democratic Control, 86, 124
United Nations, 22
United States of America, 29, 32, 59, 102
  conscientious objectors, 126
  interventionism, 32
  invasion threat, 113
  pacifism, 113–14
  peace movements, 113–14, 120–2, **121**, 125–6, 132
  women's activism, 60–1, 68, 69, 71, 71–2, **72**, *see also* Addams, Jane
Universal Declaration of Human Rights, 33
Universal Peace Congresses, 9, 52, 61, 83
Universal Peace Union, 120
urbanization, 1
Utrecht, Peace of, 23, 24, 26–7

Versailles, Treaty of, 17, 19–20, 40, 41
Victoria, Queen, 32
Vienna, 99–100
Vienna, Congress of, 1, 3, 4–5, 5, 6, 22, 23, 25, **26**, 28, 37, 38, 57
virtù, 156
volunteerism, 8

Waldron, Arthur John, 83–4
war
  approaches to abolition, 112
  benefits of, 13–14, 54
  evolutionary benefit, 44
  folly of, 3
  Freud on, 50
  justifications, 98
  and masculinity, 46–7, 48–9
War of 1812, 113–18
War Resisters International, 19
Ward, A. W., 141
Washington, Treaty of, 36
Waszklewicz-van Schilfgaarde, Johanna, 64
water supplies, 3

Webb, Beatrice and Sydney, 49
Webster, Noah, 28
Westcott, Basil Brooke Foss, 83
Westphalia, Peace of, 26–7
White, Andrew Dickson, 105
Wilhelm II, Kaiser, 137
William I, Kaiser, 39
William III, Frederick, King of Prussia, 24
Wilson, Woodrow, 20, **21**, 40
   "Fourteen Points", 16, 49
Winter, Jay, 48
Wiszniewska, Princess Marie-Gabrielle Hortense Hugo, 63–4
Wollstonecraft, Mary, 15
women
   control of bodies, 69–70
   discrimination, 15
   letters, 9
   role of, 57–72, 78, 126
   suffrage, 22
   view of peace, 45
Women's International Congress, 1915, 49
Women's International Congress, Zurich, 1919, **17**, 19
Women's International League for Peace and Freedom, 16, 17, 49, 53, 86, 87, 93–4
Women's Local Peace Association (Wisbech), 61–2
women's movement, 15–17, **16**, **17**
Women's Peace Party, 49

women's rights, 15, 55, 68, 101
Worcester, Noah, 79, 113
Workers International Association, 12
Workmen's Peace Association, 122
World Alliance for Promoting International Friendship through the Churches, 35, 85–6
World Council of Churches, 85
World Petition to Prevent War Between Nations, 71
World War I, 1, 10, 14, 17–19, 39, 55, 99, 107, 141
   aftermath, 22
   colonial subjects, 14–15
   conscientious objectors, 88, 88–92, **89**, **91**
   and masculinity, 48–9
   murderousness, 40
   mutinies, 40
   new pacifism, 86–8
   origins of, 132
   peace activism, 17–18, **18**, 19, 21, 123–8
   peace treaties, 19–20
Wylie, Neville, 132

Yat-sen, Sun, 34

Zeno, 147
Zetkin, Clara, 12, 72
Zietz, Luise, 12
Zweig, Stefan, 97, 108